Small enterprise development:
policies and programmes

Small enterprise development: policies and programmes

Management Development
Series No. 14

Edited by Philip A. Neck

International Labour Office   Geneva

ISBN 92-2-101851-2

First published 1977
Second impression 1979

ILO publications can be obtained through major booksellers or ILO iocal offices in many countries, or direct from ILO Publications, International Labour Office, CH-1211 Geneva 22, Switzerland. A catalogue or list of new publications will be sent free of charge from the above address.

Printed by Imprimerie du Journal de Genève, Geneva, Switzerland

CONTENTS

APPENDIX

INTRODUCTION

Two reasons prompted us to publish this work.

There is, firstly, the acknowledged economic and social importance of the small enterprise sector. It is now being recognised that development cannot be achieved solely by establishing and promoting large organisations in the industrial and other sectors. For various reasons small enterprises will have to play a major development role in the forthcoming decades.

Secondly, following a period of relative inactivity, some might even say benign neglect, many interesting developments have recently taken place in industrialised and developing countries. In many cases these represent new approaches to old problems facing the sector. It appears, therefore, to be useful and timely to review recent experiences and their underlying rationale, with a view to identifying approaches producing beneficial results as well as examining those that have been disappointing.

Since little has been done to describe and analyse integrated development approaches, we have attempted to collect and make known information on current policies and programmes from both the developing and the more industrialised countries. To this end we asked authors, with wide-ranging experiences and country backgrounds, to collaborate in providing an opportunity to compare and contrast different development strategies. We do not feel, however, that any single approach to effective small enterprise development should be expected to accommodate all socio-economic, cultural or political systems. We leave it, therefore, to readers to choose, or adapt, such information as may suit their purpose.

The International Labour Organisation has been actively involved in small enterprise development for more than twenty years through its technical co-operation, research, information and other activities. In most cases this action has taken the form of technical co-operation projects in individual countries working with small business or small enterprise development centres and institutes, or with national productivity or management development institutions. This publication draws on the expertise accumulated over this period. Our experience in implementing programmes in cooperation with governments and various national agencies is thus made available to readers, together with the views and experiences of the individual experts who kindly agreed to contribute to this book.

Target audience

The book is intended for all persons likely to be involved in developing the sector such as:

- small enterprise managers and owners,
- counsellors and management consultants,
- management teachers, trainers and research workers,
- officials in government, public or private organisations providing finance, technical services or developmental assistance to small enterprises,
- national planners and policy makers interested in long-term policies and programmes for developing the sector.

Layout of the book

The book is divided into 20 chapters grouped in 5 parts. These are followed by an appendix.

Part I (Chapters 1-4) presents an overview of the socio-economic role of small enterprises and discusses such issues as policies, types of structures and programming implications.

Part II (Chapter 5) proposes a conceptual approach to small enterprise development and outlines a diagnostic and remedial model.

Part III (Chapters 6-10) deals with new initiatives in developing small enterprises. Examples of policy-making, training, financing and developmental schemes are provided.

Part IV (Chapters 11-18) reviews approaches of a sample of countries promoting small enterprises.

Part V (Chapters 19-20) provides two regional scenarios of some developing and more industrialised countries.

The appendix provides information supplementing the main text of the book.

Authors and acknowledgments

This book is a collective effort. The main authors are referred to in their respective chapters. In addition, contributions of colleagues in the Management Development Branch, field projects and other units of the ILO are also acknowledged with thanks.

The book was edited by Philip Neck and typed for offset reproduction by Marianne Guertchakoff.

PART I

SMALL ENTERPRISE DEVELOPMENT IN PERSPECTIVE

ROLE AND IMPORTANCE OF SMALL ENTERPRISES

Philip A. Neck[1]

1

Small enterprises have a history as long as that of enterprise itself. However, it is only recently that attention has focussed on the wider social goals to which they can contribute.

1.1 DEVELOPMENT TRENDS

In terms of time scale we can point to the small enterprise as the first link in the long chain of social and economic progress when, in the very beginnings of civilisation, trading was a major component of the communication process among primitive people.[2] Studies and theories concerning socio-economic factors affecting small enterprises arose during the industrial revolution, with notions of entrepreneurial importance gaining favour early in the twentieth century.[3] During the 1960s the behaviour of the individual first emerged as a possible major factor contributing to entrepreneurship and small-enterprise development.[4]

However, for the most part, it has been only during the past two decades that fully comprehensive programmes, designed to promote small-enterprise development as part of national development plans, have taken shape. While the problems of small-enterprise development undoubtedly receive most attention in countries with market economies, this concern for the sector is also shared by countries where economic development is centrally planned. Furthermore, concern for the sector is expressed by countries at all levels of industrial development albeit the support for the sector is often based on quite dissimilar grounds.

---

[1] *Management Development Branch, International Labour Office, Geneva.*

[2] *G.C. Moon: Society influences on motivation and the effects of social evaluation. (Proceedings of Rencontres de St. Gall, Swiss Research Institute of Small Business, 1976).*

[3] *J.A. Schumpeter: Economic theory and entrepreneurial history, in Change and the Entrepreneur (Cambridge, Harvard University Press, 1949), p. 64.*

[4] *D.C. McClelland: The achieving society (Princeton, New York, D. van Nostrand Co.,) 1961).*

On the one hand, the basis for support may be the perceived need to stem the decline of the sector as noticed in Western Europe. On the other hand, such support may be to promote economic and social development, particularly in developing countries.

References to the decline in relative numbers of small enterprises are made, for example, by Watkins[1] who points to the reduction in numbers of small enterprises in Western Europe in general and the United Kingdom in particular. Koblenski, Administrator of the US Small Business Administration (1976), addressing Rencontres de St. Gall in Merlingen in 1976, referred to small enterprises as an "endangered species" in the United States, and Leihner (see Figure 1.1) provides a generalised forecast of the retail trade in Germany in which nominal and retail turnovers are shown to be constantly increasing whereas the number of retail outlets are correspondingly decreasing.

FIGURE 1.1: GENERALISED RETAIL TRADE TRENDS IN GERMANY
(after Leihner)

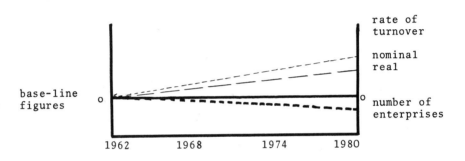

Leihner, at Rencontres de St. Gall, 1976 discussed Figure 1.1 which was calculated using 1962 as a base year, assuming a real rate of turnover increase of 2 per cent per year with inflation calculated at 4 per cent per year. The generalised figure illustrates the decline in the number of enterprises in spite of a continual increase in sales figures. Leihner estimates that the number of companies in the retail trade in 1980 will be only two-thirds as many as in 1962.

---

[1] *D.S. Watkins: Toward an empirical basis for public policy on business initiation and agrandissement (Proceedings of Rencontres de St. Gall, Swiss Research Institute of Small Business, 1976).*

From another point of view, agencies dealing with developing countries consider small enterprise development to be an important component of industrialisation[1] and employment creation.[2] Such programmes tend to promote new enterprise development, rather than viewing assistance to the sector as, primarily, a stabilisation and maintenance undertaking for the sector. In Malaysia and the Philippines small enterprise development programmes are part of a deliberate strategy for introducing nationals into the economic sector of the country's activities.

Regardless of the reasons adopted for supporting development of small enterprises we face something of a paradox. In a world where the largest number of established enterprises can be labelled "small", where they absorb a significant percentage of the labour force and contribute in large part to a nation's well-being in economic and social terms, compared to other economic sectors, they receive in many cases, only the barest minimum of legislative, financial, technical and other forms of assistance.

Interesting theories might possibly be advanced to explain neglect of the sector in the past. What appears important, however, is the need to develop and implement programmes designed to ensure healthy growth of small enterprises to solve pressing and ever-increasing economic, social and political problems.

Providing assistance to the small enterprise sector can no longer remain a personal, local or regional problem. It is a concern possessing national and international dimensions where, if the problems are not faced, defined, interpreted and tackled with the resources and skill they demand, unwarranted economic and social waste may result.

As might be expected, the more industrialised countries usually have better assistance programmes than most developing countries. Although there are common features between industrialised and developing countries' assistance programmes, there are also distinct differences in the policies, structures and types of programmes employed. When transferring approaches between, and within, industrialised and developing countries, we need to consider many influencing factors if optimal results are to be obtained.

Unfortunately, not all assistance programmes work to assist the sector. For example, Peterson[3] notes that the financing and managing of social programmes can fall heavily on economic units of the productive sector having the least market power, namely the small enterprise. Such activities often divert attention and effort from manpower training and national programmes of apprenticeship training, leaving the sector with only marginally skilled workers because

[1] UNIDO: Second general conference of UNIDO, (United Nations Industrial Development Organisation, 1975).

[2] ILO: Employment, incomes and equality: a strategy for increasing productive employment in Kenya (Geneva, ILO, 1972).

[3] R. Peterson: Progress towards a small firms policy for Canada (Proceedings of Rencontres de St. Gall, Swiss Research Institute of Small Business, 1976).

of competition in the market place. Consequently, sector development is retarded. Additionally, there appears to be a tendency, in times of economic and social pressures, to demand action on grand (i.e. large-scale solutions) schemes. This may lead to an expansion of large organisations, leaving small industrial and other units to stagnate.

Most developing regions possess unique characteristics. Consequently, assistance programmes may require innovation and local orientation to accommodate their special events and conditions. Furthermore, based on the results obtained by Harper[1] and others, it seems likely that evolutionary and adaptive phases may have to be considered rather than the straightforward selection and implementation of standard approaches.

1.2 A FEW WORDS ABOUT DEFINITIONS

There can be little doubt that small enterprises exist in most economic environments. However, there is probably some truth in the allegation that it is often difficult to locate a small enterprise "community" because little communication seems to take place between individual enterprises making up that sector. This may be a major factor explaining why it is that development programmes have relatively little impact in assisting small enterprises.

That being said, discussion as to what may constitute an acceptable common definition of a small enterprise may prove more interesting than useful. Most definitions appear to be governed by the interests of the perceiver, the purpose of the definition, and the stage of development of the particular environment in which the definition is to be employed. For instance, one study of small enterprises identified more than 50 different definitions in 75 countries.[2]

It can be safely assumed that there is no lower limit to the size of a small enterprise, which can be taken to include the formal and informal sectors represented by the self-employed, family businesses, sole-owners, partnerships, companies and co-operatives. A problem does arise, however, when attempting to establish an acceptable upper limit for the definition. Although the small enterprise is not considered to be dominant in its field of operations, specific issues usually arise:

financiers often talk in terms of upper levels of fixed assets, or net worth;

labour officers may refer to the total number of persons employed;

---

[1] M.H. Harper: *A prototype experiment to test the possibility of an effective extension service for small-scale general retailers: Discussion paper No. 193 (Institute for Development Studies, University of Nairobi, 1974), p. 22.*

[2] *An international compilation of small-scale industry definitions, (Industrial Development Division, Engineering Experiment Station, Georgia Institute of Technology, Atlanta, Georgia, USA, 1975).*

traders could point to a ceiling limit in sales volume;

services personnel may use the total numbers of customers;

manufacturers may prefer to use maximum levels of energy required for production;

different criteria may be combined in attempting to state the point at which the enterprise ceases to be "small".

From a managerial point of view, it may be useful to describe the small enterprise in qualitative terms as one in which the operational and administrative management lie in the hands of one or two people who are also responsible for the major decisions. In many respects it is this characteristic which explains the particular behaviour of the small enterprise. In this connection Galbraith[1] provides the following definition: "... no agreed level of sales or assets divides the millions of small firms making up half of the economy /Canada/ from giant corporations which are the other half. But /there are/ sharp conceptual differences between enterprises fully under control of individuals and those not entirely excluding influence of individuals which could not exist without their organisation".

The following suggested classification covers the major categories of enterprises, urban and rural (non-farm), likely to benefit from co-ordinated small enterprises assistance schemes:

commerce includes wholesale and retail trade, with particular emphasis on decentralisation of distribution centres;

services includes activities such as restaurants and laundries;

maintenance and repair includes such activities as mechanical, textiles and electrical;

transportation includes truck, bus and taxi enterprises;

construction includes indigenous contractors and subcontractors;

manufacturing includes the modern, traditional and home or cottage industries;

excavation includes mining and allied undertakings.

The informal sector, identified[2] as enterprises characterised by: "ease of entry; reliance on indigenous resources; family ownership; small-scale operation; labour-intensive and adapted technology; skills acquired mainly outside the formal system of education and training; and unregulated and competitive markets" should also be considered part of the small enterprise sector, although requiring specialised treatment.

Recent writers have focussed considerable attention on the informal sector, identified as contributing significantly to rural

---

1
    J.K. Galbraith: *Economics and the public purpose* (Scarborough, Canada, The New American Library of Canada, 1975), p. 43.

2
    Employment, incomes and equality: a strategy for increasing productive employment in Kenya (Geneva, ILO, 1976), p. 6.

and urban employment. The need to use non-formal instructional techniques and new approaches in providing technical and financial assistance is constantly emphasised. Unfortunately, much remains to be learned about the scope, size and type of enterprises in the informal sector, as well as how they start, grow and develop before coordinated assistance programmes can be used to best effect.

1.3 THE IMPORTANCE OF THE SECTOR

To deny the economic and social importance of the small enterprise sector is to ignore the facts, lose excellent development opportunities and create frustration, despair and hardship in many quarters. Many arguments can be presented to support assistance for the sector.

Economic significance

The small enterprise sector is only one of several contributors to the economic strength of a nation. However, it requires consideration in terms of its direct output of goods and services, as well as its role in supplying requisite inputs to large-scale enterprise and government efforts. Industry and commerce often grow progressively from the small to the large enterprise sector where shifts towards capital intensity may become a key feature of the enlargement process.

In most economies the numerical majority of a country's manufacturing enterprises (usually from 60 to 80 per cent in industrialised countries, and up to or more than 90 per cent in developing countries) are classified as small. They may account for more than one-half of total employment, with the added possibility of being able to employ even more.

In addition to serving their own specialised markets, small enterprises are often called upon to produce components, or intermediate goods, for large-scale manufacturers unable to meet their own demands. The Confederation of British Industry (CBI)[1] argues that if small firms closed down tomorrow, "most of the large firms would grind quickly and painfully to a halt". A large proportion of such service industries, maintenance and repair, entertainment, transport, lodging, and restaurants, are provided specifically by the small enterprise sector.

Other benefits which support the case for assisting small enterprises, particularly when they reach the medium-scale range, include:

-   the development of a pool of skilled and semi-skilled
    workers as a basis for future industrial expansion;

-   improvement of forward and backward linkages between
    economically, socially and geographically diverse sectors
    of the economy;

-   non-requirement of some of the sophisticated managerial
    and technological techniques normally required by larger
    enterprises;

---

[1] *CBI: Britain's small firms: their vital role in the economy (London, Confederation of British Industry, 1970), p. 3.*

- opportunities for developing and adapting appropriate technological and managerial approaches;
- increases in savings and investment by local personnel and more effective use of scarce capital;
- increased mobility for the improved development of scarce capital;
- increased mobility for the improved development of natural resources;
- the promotion of special subcontracting arrangements.

It is difficult to make clear-cut decisions in favour of the economic advantages of small- rather than large-scale enterprises, or vice-versa, because of the difficulty in interpreting the mass of data as evidenced in the Bolton Committee report.[1] For instance, a good deal of present-day "bigness" in business has not necessarily been the result of economies of scale but, on the contrary, stems simply from reorganising small and medium enterprises under common ownership.[2] In any event, it should not be a case of large versus small but, rather, how best they might complement each other so that existing small enterprises might, in turn, become medium and large in scale.

Apart from the planned outputs there are often unscheduled ripple effects from small enterprise development schemes which bene-fit other sectors such as in rural development. The small enter-prise sector is also well placed to overcome the problem of capital scarcity, by perhaps using capital better or employing readily avai-lable labour as its major factor of production. Other advantages include adaptability, close personal relationships between customers and suppliers and, usually, sound knowledge of regional market strengths and weaknesses. A key characteristic of the small enter-prise is its closeness to risks; markets; people such as workers, suppliers and customers; technology; and its long distance from readily available finance.

Social arguments

If small enterprise development programmes were to require a single objective, it could well be expressed as "improvement in the quality of life". In this respect, the strongest arguments have social orientations.

Because neither public nor private large-scale enterprises in developing countries appear likely to be easily able to absorb the existing unemployed, let alone future additions to the labour force, it behoves the small enterprise sector to assist in tackling this critically important social problem. Small, rather than large, en-terprises may be able to undertake this task under certain conditions since they often require less capital in the form of fixed assets for the creation of each new job. World Bank reports assess the capital requirement for each job in small enterprises as only one-

---

[1] *Bolton Committee: Small firms - Reports of the Committee of Inquiry on Small Firms (London, HMSO, 1971).*

[2] *R. Peterson - see footnote 3 on p. 7.*

third of that in large-scale enterprises. Furthermore, small enterprises may be better suited for the unskilled and marginally skilled workers who can be employed, efficiently, using labour-intensive techniques. However, a close watch needs to be kept to ensure that productivity is maintained at an acceptable level.

Increasing public awareness of the sociological problems such as the strain placed on existing infrastructure by excessive on-site energy and labour demands, mass production techniques and environmental pollution has been created by writers such as Schumacher.[1] This, together with the support for new forms of work organisation, amongst which one could possibly include the promotion and creation of small enterprises as an alternate to existing large-scale corporations,[2] also supports the idea of promoting small enterprise development.

Improvements in personal skill and propensity for effective contribution to community use are likely to be more encouraged in the small enterprise, where learning by doing can take place in a "total" situation, than in the relatively compartmentalised and isolated unit of a large-scale enterprise. Additionally, where necessary, the smaller firm is in a position to provide a more flexible transition from a traditional to an industrial life-style, while ensuring the stability of community groups and by welding them more tightly by increasing their material well-being.[3] There is also some support for the idea that new industries can be established more effectively when built on local skills and culture.[4] Small rather than larger enterprises may be better placed to exploit this opportunity. By contrast, Bahen and Peterson[5] report that technical innovation is uncommon in large firms under foreign ownership, not because of capital shortages, but because of the inherent make-up and attitudes of most professional managers.

Labour and human relations play a very special role within the small enterprise. Because they can be relatively harmonious in the small enterprise, due to enhanced opportunities for direct manager-worker contacts and consequent improved communications, possibilities exist for workers to obtain greater meaning from their efforts which in turn, provide incentives for improved productivity and increased incomes.

---

[1] E.F. Schumacher: Small is beautiful (London, Blond and Briggs, 1973).

[2] M. Hanan: Venturing corporations - think small to stay strong (Harvard Business Review, May-June, 1976), p. 139.

[3] F.J. Moore: Some aspects of industrialisation and co-operative development in underdeveloped areas (Indian Economic Review, Vol. 1, No. 4, 1953), pp. 1-21.

[4] R.W. Stopford: Some problems involved in the development of industries in West Africa (Africa, London, Vol. 14, No. 4, 1943), pp. 165-69.

[5] S. Bahen and R. Peterson: A general report to the Ministry of Industry and Tourism of the Province of Ontario (Division of Research, Faculty of Administrative Studies, York University, Canada, 1973).

However, the absence of safeguards for the workers may also lead to paternalistic behaviour, or even exploitation, by management. Examples include:

(i) exploitation factors such as the non-payment of wages to family members and so-called apprentices who reimburse employers for the privilege of being trained for a job;

(ii) absence of welfare and social benefits including annual and sick leave, pensions, enforceable safety regulations and health insurance.

Small enterprise development schemes may also provide a means of introducing equity of income distribution to members of the workforce excluded from participating in the monetary system of the country.

However, as well as providing gainful employment, development schemes should allow freedom of spirit and should stress the value of human dignity. In addition, development schemes can also create an awareness of industrialisation and productivity improvement amongst cultural groups whose upbringing and beliefs have prevented them from enjoying the benefits of development schemes in the past. It is important to guard against personal and family hardships caused by the all-too-frequent collapse of the enterprise, resulting in the loss of collateral securities and anticipated income.

While it is granted that "bigness" is necessary in particular instances, such as in petrochemical installations, there are many opportunities to use small enterprises for effectively developing and transferring appropriate and adaptive technology from more advanced to less developed regions. Therefore, small enterprises can assume this transfer and development role, working in association with assisting institutions, agencies and enterprises.

Perhaps the most telling argument of all is that *for the greater part of the poverty group the small enterprise is the only activity in which they can usefully hope to be engaged, particularly in the immediate future.*

POLICY ISSUES

Philip A. Neck[1]

2

Before adopting sector policies they should first be thoroughly examined to see whether or not they are required. If they are needed, consideration can then be given to areas likely to benefit, problems to be faced and steps to be taken.

2.1 POLICY IMPLICATIONS

The small enterprise sector should harmonise with large enterprise and other economic sectors to make up the total economic effort. Unfortunately, the small enterprise sector, and outsiders, are often inclined to view the sector as something apart, at times granting it only second-class status.

Although governments may feel that they give due consideration to the needs of the small as well as the large enterprise sector, it is almost impossible for them to be neutral. For the most part, existing legislation, educational and training policies, financial incentives and the like indisputably favour big rather than small business. As a result some efforts are being made to promote the notion of countervailing power so that small enterprises can present their views more strongly. However, this approach is not likely to succeed if, as is usually the case, small enterprises commence from disadvantaged starting positions.

Apart from obvious inequalities, such as access to finance, existing between small and large enterprise, small enterprise also needs to be more adequately represented in the science of business. This means involving small enterprise management in such institutions as management development and productivity centres, institutes of technology, universities, vocational training institutions and primary and secondary schools.

Policy issues can be expected to vary considerably, but it remains to be said that the small enterprise sector should generally aim at selective rather than total growth and development.

---

[1] *Management Development Branch, International Labour Office, Geneva.*

2.2 POLICIES - YES OR NO !

The question is, simply: *How necessary is it to have national or regional policies for small enterprise development?* Some arguments levelled against formulating policies are self-defeating. For instance, the argument that there is a lack of data on which to build sound policies only highlights the need to have such critical data in times of high demand and scarce resources. Other contra-arguments point to relatively successful development in the apparent absence of set policies; that there are enough small enterprises to look after their own interests without recourse to outside help; and that the cost of supporting special policies for the sector is too high for the community to carry. Such arguments are not really convincing.

In some countries, examples being the United Kingdom and Switzerland, individual small business owners often resent (state) intervention in the form of policy measures, and a "leave us alone" attitude may prevail. On the other hand, the Canadian small enterprise sector represents a different school of thought. It is concerned that existing socio-economic models do not appear to be working properly since such warning signs as high inflation, unemployment, energy shortages, growing regional disparities, labour unrest, decreasing international competitiveness and capital scarcity - thought to be caused by an overdependence on foreign capital inflows cheap energy and utilisation of non-renewable resources, are clearly evident. Consequently, the small enterprise sector is keen to see that appropriate policies are established.

To put the matter in proper perspective we should perhaps return to fundamental objectives and assess, case-by-case, whether we need development policies at all. If they are not required, the whole issue is settled and nothing further needs to be done. On the other hand, if they are, or might possibly be required we should provide for the small enterprise sector within over-all economic and social development policies.

2.3 AREAS LIKELY TO BENEFIT FROM POLICIES

Every aspect of the small enterprise scene seems to require appropriate policies. Readily noticeable key areas include:

Finance

Sources of seed money, venture capital, equity and fixed and working capital are often given top priority in development plans for the sector. This field can be extended to cover related areas such as tariff protection; differential taxation; credit facilities; discounting services; fixed interest rates; and moratorium on loans.

Training

Management and technical training are clear examples of existing practices favouring large-scale enterprise and government. Educational and social reforms are required to establish the facilities, resources and curricula needed to serve the sector.

Markets

Small enterprises are typically frozen into traditional markets where their growth is limited by outdated distribution networks. A solution lies in improving communications and distribution where sound policies can contribute to low-cost growth particularly in rural areas. Other useful devices include preferential government purchasing schemes and reserving certain fields for small enterprises. The use of subcontracting also bears on this point, although particular conditions are required to ensure the success of such schemes.[1]

Access to raw materials

Blocked access to scarce raw materials, often ear-marked for privileged and protected enterprises, has put paid to many potentially successful small enterprises. Licensing regulations, and practices, may allot resources to ineffective organisations while preventing possible high growth enterprises from developing. Innovative changes may be needed.

Manpower

Developing appropriate management skills for small enterprises should go hand in hand with preparing an adequate labour force. Activities might begin with manpower planning schemes, subsequently extended to develop appropriate educational, labour and related policies.

Technology

Small enterprises appear to be particularly suited to the transfer and development of appropriate technology. Policies to protect and enhance the sector's interest in this potentially rewarding field are required. For the moment, the sector seems to have little defending its interests, and even less success in obtaining anything approaching adequate research and development inputs. This is particularly so when the sector's resources are compared to the endowments lavished on sectors such as defence, agriculture, large-scale industry and health. Policies are required to encourage local capacity to undertake original research and technological innovation.

Assistance

The sector allegedly suffers from a high death-rate when failures are compared with successes. Prescriptions are needed to maintain the health of small enterprises once they are set up. One possible remedy is to organise strong sectoral associations, as in Sweden, where government assistance can be focussed.

1

S. Watanabe: Reflections on current policies for promoting small enterprises and subcontracting, in International Labour Review, Vol. 110, No. 5, 1974.

Community relations

Policies of community relations are needed to draw attention to the sector's career possibilities, its role as a consumer and producer of goods and services, its importance as an employment agent and its role in servicing large-scale enterprises.

2.4 PROBLEMS TO BE FACED

Policies need to be based on sound analysis, to proclaim commitment to action and to ensure that adequate and established means of support are available.

Because national, regional and sectoral data are often lacking it is difficult to provide the means necessary for research-based development policies. For instance, in the United Kingdom, Watkins[1] claims that it is virtually impossible to assemble representative data for small enterprises. The ILO's studies in several developing countries fully support this finding. In many, if not most, cases governments are neither organised to collect information nor to report on the performance of the sector. Without such data, established policies may not necessarily reflect the real needs of the sector.

It is also often difficult to identify an agency with the responsibility and authority to commit the resources necessary to implement policy. Additionally, small enterprise associations are seldom able to create the social and political pressures to ensure that policies are established and converted into action.

Policies established without due regard to the small enterprise sector usually discriminate against it. Examples are educational systems and vocational guidance practices.[2] These often jeopardise the supply of personnel to the small enterprise sector because they place emphasis on grooming people for large-scale enterprise or government service.

Overall economic controls with corresponding money currency, and credit policies are not without dangers to the sector because such burdens as income tax, death duties, VAT, turnover and payroll tax are disproportionately heavy for the small enterprise sector. Even such tasks as preparing documents for the government are often a heavier burden to small than to large-scale enterprise management.

Labour legislation and social programmes applied indiscriminately can also impose unduly on the small enterprise sector. The sector sees itself reaping few of the rewards of these measures, but obliged to contribute fully to their support.

---

[1] *D.S. Watkins: Regional variations in the industrial ecology for new, growth-oriented business in the UK (Proceedings of Project ISEED, the Center for Venture Management, Milwaukee, 1975),pp.459-463.*

[2] *M.J.K. Stanworth and J. Curran: Growth and the small firm — an alternative view (The Journal of Management Studies, Vol. 13, No. 2., May 1976), pp. 95-110.*

In some cases, it is quite possible that the small enterprise sector has behaved in such a way that it deserves many of the constraints apparently placed on it. However, a case can be made for reconsidering several policy issues inhibiting sector growth and development

Small enterprise development is definitely not a simple issue which can be illustrated by a straight-line growth path. It needs to be integrated with large-scale industrial development and comprehensive national manpower plans. Developing sector policies in this context is difficult and time-consuming and not likely to be given priority treatment by government planning ministries.

In spite of the many problems to be overcome, one cannot help feeling that if there is to be a dramatic breakthrough in small enterprise development, it will stem from appropriate policy development.

2.5 STEPS TO BE TAKEN

The purposeful relationship which ought to exist between research and formulating policies is often overlooked. Social and real life distances between research institutions, government planners, cabinet decision-makers, institutions providing assistance and the small enterprise sector are immense. A first step towards lessening these distances is to collect and monitor relevant data.

With access to pertinent data, policies might be established to introduce, for instance, multi-tiered legislation with special provisions for small and medium enterprises. A further bonus could be that the sector, if provided with relevant economic information, might be less prone to undertake risky fly-by-night schemes and more likely to invest in sounder long-term projects.

Unfortunately, researchers and policy-makers appear to put themselves on something of a collision course. Many researchers feel either that policy proposals, which should emerge almost as a matter of course from analysis and interpretation of their data, never seem to do so; or, alternatively, their political masters force them to investigate non-relevant subject areas. Conversely, policy makers may argue that most non-directed research is irrelevant to existing conditions.

Research to improve policy-making includes:

evaluating financial, technological, managerial and developmental institutions by analysing the internal and external forces shaping events;

examining the formal relationships between personnel providing assistance and small enterprise management, paying attention to the formal processes as laid down and the actual relationships which take place under varying external pressures and circumstances;

studying the increasing international interdependence of this sector since many national and regional problems have transnational implications;

upgrading existing data, establishing relevant new sources and developing more appropriate measuring instruments;

examining the possibilities of relating management training directly to the sectoral nature of the small enterprise, rather than the generalised approach commonly used; and to include managerial practices in all levels of vocational and educational training.

Gordon's comments[1] that (applied) researchers should interest themselves in "relevance with as much rigour as possible" and not "rigour regardless of relevance" are very applicable.

2.6 POLICIES AND OBJECTIVES

If policies are adopted for the small enterprise sector it should be useful to relate them to the following objectives:

"To increase the absolute and relative rate of new enterprise formation, the number of persons employed and the amount of GNP produced by the sector."

In this way quantifiable goals can be set, measured and corrective action taken where necessary.

Valid sector policies need to be based on certain basic assumptions which are set out in Chart 2.1.

---

[1] *R.A. Gordon: Rigour and relevance in a changing institutional setting, in The American Economic Review (March 1976), pp. 1-14.*

CHART 2.1: BASIC ASSUMPTIONS UNDERLYING SMALL ENTERPRISE DEVELOPMENT POLICIES (after Peterson[1])

Positive features	Problem areas
• *Existing and future economic development will require viable large and small enterprises.*	• *Lack of managerial talent accounts for the failure of many small enterprises and is a serious handicap to development particularly in developing countries.*
• *Large enterprises need viable small enterprises to serve their sector.*	• *Small enterprise development has been retarded by inappropriate training, limited access to capital and raw materials, conservative distribution systems, relatively competitive markets, inadequate technical assistance and a poorly trained labour force.*
• *Small enterprises can be economically efficient and effective in specific instances.*	
• *Small enterprises can be a major source of innovation and entrepreneurial activity.*	• *The small enterprise manager is often unaware of the services offered by professional sources, associations, institutions and agencies.*
• *Small enterprises have a propensity for labour intensity and job creation at relatively low capital cost.*	• *In many areas minority groups establish a disproportionately high number of small enterprises.*
• *Small enterprises have an important role to play in social development, particularly in providing stability and viability to communities in rural areas.*	
• *Most regions and countries have people with small enterprise managerial interest and talent.*	

[1] *R. Peterson: Progress towards a small firms policy for Canada (Proceedings of Rencontres de St. Gall, Swiss Research Institute of Small Business, 1976).*

STRUCTURAL CONSIDERATIONS

Philip A. Neck[1]

3

Structures assisting small enterprises may operate as institutions, associations, agencies, corporations, companies, professional associations, firms and practitioners, distributors or individuals.

They may deal with any or all of the following functions:

financial

technological

managerial

developmental

Such structures may operate under the auspices of central or local government, public corporations, private enterprise, voluntary institutions, individuals or any combination of these bodies. They share one aspect in common in that they are usually service-type structures seldom exercising managerial or majority ownership control over the small enterprise.

3.1 TYPES OF STRUCTURES

Financial structures may assume different forms of ownership, management and operations. They exist, essentially, to provide fixed capital, long-term finance, working capital, equity, hire purchase, leasing and factoring facilities.

Services include pre-investment studies; selection of prospective enterprises and managers; project development and implementation; purchasing schemes; infrastructural development; management and technological services and subcontracting arrangements.

Difficulties mentioned most often include shortages of sound projects and suitable managers; inadequate market research; and unreliable supply of raw materials.

---

[1] *Management Development Branch, International Labour Office, Geneva.*

Further details of forms, objectives, types of assistance and problems are provided in Appendix 1.

3.2 OPERATIONAL ISSUES

Operational activities are largely governed by two major considerations:

Ownership

The ownership of a particular structure be it a development finance company, machinery distributor, trade association or industrial estate will shape its method of operations. In spite of structures sharing a common target audience, namely small enterprises and their constituent personnel, types of ownership and of operation vary tremendously.

On the one hand, some structures operate on a "top-down" basis. Examples include state controlled or directed institutions where, by virtue of its "ownership" role, the state sets objectives and organises formal institutional arrangements. In these cases the recipient small enterprises are subject to specific constraints and controls. On the other hand, structures may operate on a "bottom-upwards" basis, as in trade associations where individual owner-members set their own objectives and methods of operation. Thus, the method of operation may differ according to ownership, which, in turn, usually depends on the particular political and economic environment.

Objectives

Particular objectives of structures also influence operational methods. Examples are provided by the "here and now" project evaluation and appraisal adopted by, say, merchant banks, compared with the social investment outlook and operations of a vocational training institution.

Problems of co-ordination

The small enterprise manager is responsible for bringing together the available financial, technological, managerial and developmental assistance. However, extension service advisers familiar with the sector can often help.

Many advisers, skilled in one field such as managerial or technological expertise, may have only limited knowledge of the existence and need for other forms of assistance. Consequently, training programmes for advisers need to ensure that advisers:

have thorough subject knowledge of all forms of available assistance;

know how the structures operate;

make small enterprises aware of these assistance structures and how to use them effectively.

The make-up of a small enterprise adviser needs to combine several factors[1]:

(i)   a broad knowledge of the general setting in which the small enterprise sector is located (*environment*);

(ii)   in-depth knowledge of the structures providing assistance (*agent*);

(iii)   an acceptable profile as adviser to the management of small enterprises (*host*).

Advisers may operate from any structure but need to know how to relate their efforts to those of other developmental structures.

---

[1] *ILO: Management consulting: a guide to the profession (Geneva 1976), p. 229-231.*

PROGRAMMING IMPLICATIONS

Philip A. Neck[1]

4

Sectoral assistance programmes consist of a series of events where successive inputs are provided to help small enterprises. Such programmes need to be formulated, implemented and evaluated.

4.1 PROGRAMME PHASES

Sequential programme phases involve:

Formulation

This phase should prescribe sector policies based on needs and opportunities analyses. In this way strategies for the structures providing assistance can be operationally defined. In particular, small enterprise programmes should deal with specific sectors, regions and product groups.

Implementation

The most important factor needed to carry out worthwhile development programmes is the quality of the people responsible for getting the job done. Other factors become relatively unimportant.

Evaluation

Programmes can only be evaluated properly if evaluating procedures are taken into account when the programme is being drawn up. Unfortunately, many programmes exist which do not even possess a statement of objectives let alone a means of measuring them.

Constraints, unforeseen when the project was being prepared, may come into play jeopardising the validity of the evaluation under its original mandate and necessitating a rewrite of the terms of reference.

Management Development Branch, International Labour Office, Geneva.

4.2   PROGRAMME TIMING

In tracing the life cycle of a small enterprise it is soon evident that appropriate help is useful at all stages:

Pre-project stage

Owner-managers of small enterprises are usually more receptive to external assistance at the pre-project stage than at any subsequent period. This finding is reflected in the relevant 233 research reports conducted by the US Small Business Administration. Consequently, the US Economic Opportunity Act 1964/65 specifies that the borrower may need to seek technical assistance before the loan is approved.

Appreciation of assistance by the borrower usually stems from such practical considerations as the need to present detailed financial and operating plans before receiving approval for funds from financial sources. Since a change process is usually encountered, psychological considerations may also come into play, where feelings of "cognitive dissonance" (doubting the wisdom of the new approach and a desire to return to the old) often arise, support is often solicited and accepted.

Furthermore, at this stage, the would-be manager is usually prepared to invest time, money and effort in attending management development programmes; an event not likely to reoccur easily once the day-to-day pressures of maintaining the enterprise are encountered.

Start-up stage

While the enterprise is being launched, the most effective form of assistance is generally supplied by extension services from managerial and developmental agencies. For obvious reasons the manager finds it difficult to leave the premises during working hours - the very time when help is most needed. Productive in-house discussions with extension agents at this stage help develop a more permanent assistance-seeking mentality on the part of the manager, which should enhance the viability and longevity of the enterprise.

Sustaining enterprises after formation

The successful start-up of a venture depends greatly on the manager's efforts. However, the enterprise's growth and development often needs additional outside support.

It is at this stage that assistance schemes can help in forming associations of small enterprises to act as a focal point for inputs. Many resource institutions can be called on whose effectiveness is increased when directed towards collected groups.

Formal and non-formal assistance efforts, ranging from vocational training programmes for workers, to action-learning and self-help programmes for managers, are equally applicable.

When organising this type of assistance, Meredith[1] highlights the need for government and private enterprise to co-operate at all levels, to use multiplier agencies, to upgrade services provided by professional advisers, to establish referral centres, to train venture manager advisers and to monitor performance through comparison schemes. He also stresses the need to establish national policies for implementation at regional levels.

Organisational problems are likely to occur during the growth phase of the small enterprise. Therefore, programmes are needed to warn management of such possible problems and to suggest ways of dealing with them.

One such development programme reported success[2] when combining motivation development and management-skills training based on principles of behaviour change involving goal setting exercises.

Smyth[3] obtained similar results in another study in three different cultural settings where participants experienced increased profits and sales, improved self-confidence and job satisfaction, and a benefit to cost ratio of 4:1 in the first year of the programme.

These results are supported by the ILO's findings when evaluating a series of combined management-skills and achievement-motivation programmes in a developing country[4].

Such programmes have progressed a long way from the ABC (accounting-book-keeping-cash collection) approach which now include sophisticated financial, technological, managerial and developmental, techniques. Buchele[5] defines three major areas requiring attention:

(i)   help in formulating and reformulating competitive strategy;

(ii)   assistance in maintaining a high level of motivation (supported by the emphasis placed on behavioural science inputs);

(iii)   help in anticipating, recognising and coping with key internal crises which account for high failure in the first year of existence as well as significant failure rates at a number of stages of later growth.

[1] G.G. Meredith: *Sustaining ventures after formation* (Proceedings of Project ISEED, the Center for Venture Management, Milwaukee, 1975), p. 516-519.

[2] R. Handy and G.F. Smyth: *Evaluation of a management development programme for small firms* (Irish Management Institute, 1975).

[3] G.F. Smyth: *Management development for owner-managers* (Proceedings of Project ISEED, the Center for Venture Management, Milwaukee, 1975), p. 503-508.

[4] P.A. Neck: *Report on achievement motivation programmes conducted in Uganda, 1969-70* (Geneva, internal report, International Labour Organisation).

[5] R.R. Buchele: *Business policy in growing firms* (Scranton, Pennsylvania, Chandler Division, International Textbook Company, 1967).

Buchele maintains that programmes should be directed towards developing managerial experience, alleviating undercapitalisation and introducing data systems to prevent early collapse of the enterprise. At a later stage, cashflow planning techniques become critical to ensure continued planned growth.

Further programmes should aim at overcoming crises involving delegation and leadership when building a management team. Other problems likely to occur are caused principally by: financial shortages preventing expansion, the prosperity crises of complacency, or too rapid growth.

A final crisis area is management succession created by the "flaw of the individual" reported by Finney[1] and Kilby[2]. The demise of the founder is, unfortunately, too often the prelude to the collapse of the enterprise. Programmes should prepare successors well in advance of their being required.

A description of the types and forms of assistance particularly applicable to the small enterprise sector are set out in a recent ILO publication.[3]

4.3 MEANS OF ACTION

It is the responsibility of each country to establish its own development programme, to decide priority sectors and to allocate resources for attaining goals. No outside agency or institution should do more than provide assistance when called on to do so. Development programmes must take into account historical perspectives, economic and social issues, cultural patterns and political realities.

If this can be agreed, it remains to be noted that most countries adopt programmes designed to lead them to self-reliance and self-sustaining growth. At the same time, there is an awareness of the need for some outside assistance which, happily, has been provided in some instances. Nevertheless, true development is self-development, and a major strategic weapon in this battle can be seen to be the development of nationally owned small enterprises.

A review of the development programmes for most developing countries shows that priorities are usually directed towards (i) agriculture; (ii) infrastructure; and (iii) industrial development, in that order. The common link between all sectors can be supplied by small enterprises, which also contribute to the pivotal area of rural development. As a means of action for improving the performances of developing countries, the small enterprise sector has a lot to offer if dealt with properly.

---

[1] B.R. Finney: Big men and business, entrepreneurship and economic growth in the New Guinea Highlands (Honolulu, University Press of Hawaii, 1973).

[2] P. Kilby (Ed.): Entrepreneurship and Economic Development (New York, The Free Press, 1971).

[3] See chapter 22 of ILO: Management consulting: a guide to the profession (Geneva, 1977), third edition.

Planning

Within a country's economic and social development plans the
roles of the various sectors require to be clearly spelt out. This
is just as valid for the small enterprise sector as it is for foreign
investment if a workable plan is to be drawn up.

However, realistic plans require to be based on valid data which,
frequently, are unavailable. Consequently, monitoring and appraising
the small enterprise sector's needs and opportunities should be
carried out, with the findings being translated into manpower planning,
managerial and technical training schemes.

If special assistance is to be provided the sector needs to be
defined. Alternatively, large-scale enterprise and government sectors could be confined to specified areas, with certain priorities
and privileges allocated to the remaining small and medium-sized
undertakings.

Directing and operating

Research and planning functions call for expertise. Where such
national expertise is missing priority should be given to filling
this void. Personnel capable of preparing plans, building development systems, conducting required studies, devising patterns of institutional support, and related activities are basic to any development programme.

Operational measures seem to be required as a package where
financial assistance is co-ordinated with relevant technological,
managerial and developmental inputs. Such co-ordination calls for
special institutions. Therefore, a strong case can be made for
establishing small enterprise development corporations or institutions where comprehensive programmes can be directed to the sector.
Such corporations should be seen to co-ordinate rather than directly
control measures of assistance.

Ideally, the corporation should be able to introduce prime-mover
industries such as the mini-hydral generators in Nepal able to provide
the basis for a whole line of development including manufacture,
repair and maintenance, installation and spin-off industries using
the power generated. Such corporations could instigate development
schemes to prevent them becoming "cathedrals in the desert" removed
from the main-stream of development. They should organise financial
institutions so that recognisable access to credit is available to
the sector. Developing and adapting appropriate technology needs to
be catered for, as well as ensuring that quality control facilities
act not only in a disciplinary manner, but also serve to educate and
assist manufacturers in improving their products.

These corporations should be responsible for expanding existing
and creating new markets for recognised sectoral groups, examples
include handicrafts for exports or, alternatively, sold for utilita-
rian domestic use. Major subcontracting activities could be channel-
led through such corporations as well as setting up group procurement
schemes for raw materials and equipment.

A small enterprise development corporation should ensure that managerial training is directly related to, and if possible concurrent with, vocational and technical training. The sector's needs should be recognised and catered for within the whole educational system and the corporation should act as a watchdog in this respect. The corporation should also represent the sector in vital matters of legislation, communications and in developing the appropriate infrastructure which it has been denied so much in the past.

Such corporations could contain representatives from ministries and bodies related to productive sectors such as transport, agriculture, industry, commerce and finance. The corporation should ideally be multidisciplinary and might report, through its Governing Board, to a ministry responsible for economic and social development. In this way it would be able to link efforts of the sector with those of the large-scale and other sectors.

The more visible activities of such a corporation would include project identification and preparation services. Extension services could assist sectoral associations in managerial and technological matters, as well as relating these efforts to financial and other forms of assistance.

Perhaps the most important activity of such a corporation would be to bring together the varied forms of available assistance to consolidate development efforts which, in the absence of a co-ordinating mechanism, can easily be wasted.

PART II

CONCEPTUAL APPROACHES TO DEVELOPMENT

A MODEL FOR SMALL ENTERPRISE DEVELOPMENT PROGRAMMES

5

Philip A. Neck[1]

Programmes of national and international assistance for small enterprises have been fashionable for more than 25 years. Most adopted a single-factor orientation, such as providing a financial input, without relating it to other factors such as training. In spite of a warning more than a decade ago by Staley and Morse[2] that such an approach "is likely to be ineffective and wasteful" a good deal of such effort has been expended and found wanting[3].

Recent evaluations[4] indicate that the "integrated programme" strategies proposed by Staley and Morse are proving worthwhile. Such approaches are supported by financial and technical assistance agencies who propose co-ordinated policies, structures and programmes for developing the sector.

In this chapter a model is used initially to provide a diagnostic framework for analysing problems of small enterprises. Secondly, the model can be used to identify the inputs, or contributory factors, thought to be required in a co-ordinated approach for development of small enterprises.

This type of model is often used to provide a basis for tackling identified social problem areas. The prime factors are labelled as "host", taken to be the recipient human element; "agent", or intermediary responsible for delivering the causal elements; and "environment", or immediate surroundings contributing to the conditions which develop. Examples include road safety campaigns where the host is the driver, the agent is the vehicle and the environment is the road conditions.

---

[1] *Management Development Branch, International Labour Office, Geneva.*

[2] E. *Staley and R. Morse: Modern Small Industries for developing countries (New York, McGraw-Hill, 1965), Chapter 13.*

[3] *P. Kilby: Entrepreneurship and economic development (New York, The Free Press, 1971), p. 384.*

[4] *Entrepreneurship and enterprise development: a world-wide perspective (Proceedings of Project ISEED, the Center for Venture Management, Milwaukee, 1975).*

The model enables specific diagnostic and remedial action to be undertaken. Another example is a malaria eradication programme where, in the diagnostic phase, the following factors of host as patient, agent as mosquito, and environment as lakes, swamps and water supplies, can be identified. Remedial action can then be taken to deal with the individual factors as part of a co-ordinated programme where the host can be treated medically with suppressants, the agent destroyed by insecticide spray and the environment improved by drainage.

The model provides a framework for developing small enterprises by improving managerial practices (*host*) in skill, knowledge and attitudes, assisted by structures (*agent*) such as financial, technological, managerial and developmental institutions operating in a supportive climate (*environment*) including such elements as appropriate legislation, workers, materials and markets.

The key feature of the model lies in linking remedial activities to provide a co-ordinated development effort, rather than emphasising the contributions of individual inputs. Used in this way the model attempts to capitalise on benefits of the synergic phenomenon whereby the correct combination of several inputs produces a net result in excess of that obtained from the same inputs contributed separately, or in the wrong combinations.

A further possible advantage of the model is that it can accommodate local to national level programmes and may be further expanded as a multi-dimensional matrix to incorporate spatial, functional and subsectoral areas. The model's components are illustrated in Chart 5.1.

CHART 5.1:   THE TWO-STEP MODEL FOR SMALL ENTERPRISE DEVELOPMENT

	Prime Factors	Step 1 Diagnostic phase (*analysis of*)	Step 2 Remedial activity (*development of*)
I	Host	Training needs of managers and workers	Programmes to provide the appropriate - skill - knowledge - attitudes
II	Agent	Activities and relationship of structures providing assistance	Suitable institutions to provide assistance in matters - financial - technological - managerial - developmental
III	Environment	Appropriateness of existing elements such as infrastructure, legislation, access to raw materials, information, markets, labour and sources of finance	Appropriate policies and support

PART III

NEW INITIATIVES FOR PROMOTING SMALL ENTERPRISES

STRATEGIES FOR ACCELERATING REGIONAL SMALL INDUSTRY DEVELOPMENT

6

Joseph E. Stepanek[1]

Underlying strategies for accelerating regional development is the need to identify the basic problems preventing growth. This can usually be arrived at by studying relevant documentation supported by study visits to selected areas.

The prescribed "new approach" draws on fresh governmental approaches, available managerial skills, current knowledge on entrepreneurship, and incorporates recent initiatives by financial institutions. The conclusion is drawn that small industry development strategies introduced during the mid-1950s, termed the Mark I strategy, should be replaced by a modern Mark II strategy.

Appropriate strategies should relate to national industrial policies, and activities and capacities of supporting institutions and organisations.

6.1 THE SETTING FOR REGIONAL DEVELOPMENT

Organised programmes need to accommodate current issues affecting development. These include:

(i)   that many industrialisation trends are oriented towards a welfare approach, without the necessary base for the viable and rapid industrialisation essential to reduce dangerously high and rapidly growing levels of underemployment;

(ii)   realising that small-scale industry cannot play the only role in district development. A multi-level mix combining large, artisan and small-scale industry is essential to maximise employment and production;

(iii)   the need to establish industrial development regions composed of clusters of up to four areas, which include an

[1] *Director, Appropriate Technology International,*
Washington D.C., USA. The author submitted these ideas in a report
to the International Labour Office entitled: An entrepreneurial
approach to accelerated small industry development in selected Indian
districts, April 1976. This condensed version of the report is felt
to apply to many developing countries.

industrial centre with potential for rapid growth to stimulate growth in that region. This strategy is based on the thesis that reinforcing present trends is more likely to be successful than attempts to establish new ones;

(iv) that regional industrialisation is more likely to be determined by the motivations, attitudes and skills of key development officials and entrepreneurs, than by the level of physical resources;

(v) that unskilled and semi-skilled labour is not only less costly but likely to be more reliable in less developed than urban areas;

(vi) with improved entrepreneurial, managerial and technical skills the range of products suitable for regional manufacture can be widened. Certain products can be mass produced by linking output from several small factories or artisan shops;

(vii) insufficient attention is usually given to mobilising capital already available in the region.

6.2 PROBLEMS OF REGIONAL INDUSTRIALISATION

In reviewing rural development Haque et al[1], summarise the problems of industrialisation as .....

"The industrialisation model employed by most Asian countries had the following characteristics:

(a) Central planning, control and co-ordination of the economy as a top-down process.

(b) Industrialisation and expansion of the modern sector as a mean of rapid economic growth and take-off.

(c) Assistance from developed countries to bridge the savings or foreign exchange gap whichever was dominant, and transfer of international technology.".....

..... "In practice the model failed for two basic reasons:

(1) External aid, both in terms of resources and of adequate transfer of technology failed to materialise at the necessary rate; on the contrary the 'gap' kept on widening, leading to increasing dependence on foreign sources and the inevitable loss of autonomy.

(2) Internal resources for development had to come mainly from rural areas where, having alienated and exploited the peasants, the possibility of transferring surplus labour into realised savings was greatly diminished. On the other hand, the regimes were unable to use coercive methods of capital accumulation which countries with stronger administrative systems and commitment have successfully employed even while agricultural production has stagnated." .....

---

[1] *W. Haque, N. Mehta, A. Rahman and S. Wignaraja: Towards a theory of rural development (United Nations Asian Development Institute, Bangkok, 1975).*

..... Whereas "Of all the new values to be created, self-reliance is the single most important" .....

..... Therefore, "In essence, the development philosophy and objectives we have enunciated centre around five core concepts which stand inseparably together:

1. Man as the end of development - which is therefore to be judged by what it does to him;

2. De-alienation of man in the sense that he feels at home with the process of development in which he becomes the subject and not the object;

3. Development of collective personality of man in which he finds his richest expression;

4. Participation as the true form of democracy; and

5. Self-reliance as the expression of man's faith in his own abilities." .....

6.3 CONCLUSIONS

Experience gained from past studies and evaluations of on-going programmes suggest the following:

Multi-industry approach

Present practice tends to promote the small factory as the dominant force in regional development, particularly in new growth centres, whereas artisan industry accounts for village-level development programmes. Unfortunately, relatively little attention has been paid to the role of medium and large-scale industry in district development. A better approach would be to promote all types of industry - large, artisan and small-scale - in a mix designed to maximise employment and production.

Welfare approach

Attempting to provide employment in regions with low potential for long-term viability may prove to be better social welfare than industrialisation. Special industrialisation efforts are justified only in regions having potential for rapid growth and an industry mix with potential for viability.

Operational programmes

The lack of success of the large number of pilot village and regional industrialisation projects in the past suggests a departure from the pilot project approach and a move towards broad programmes of phased regional industrialisation.

"Pull" from the district

If bottom-up planning is to be initiated, the first step is to encourage local officials and leaders to establish mechanisms for "pulling" resources into the district as a counter-balance to the long tradition of "pushing" resources in from the top. Once strong, educated, and practical "demands" emanate from the region, it will go a long way towards successful development, self-reliance and economic power.

Growth centres

In each regional cluster, hierarchies of potential growth centres should be identified where consultant skills, amenities and other scarce resources can be concentrated. Such major growth centres need relatively large population potentials.

6.4   JUSTIFICATION AND OBJECTIVES OF PROPOSED NEW STRATEGIES

Over the past thirty years experienced and capable officials have planned and directed regional industrialisation schemes. In spite of the talent and resources brought to bear, most informed persons agree that results have not been satisfactory.

What, then, might be done to bring about satisfactory development? Fortunately, recent developments are making it possible to accelerate industrialisation in less developed regions; these include:

(i)   rapid increase in the number of highly skilled individuals able to make entrepreneurial decisions;

(ii)   development of new behavioural technologies permitting the identification of potential entrepreneurs and enhancement of their skills;

(iii)   decisions of commercial and developmental banks to provide development loans to regional industry on a modern, businesslike basis;

(iv)   administrators becoming motivated to use more innovative, even risky, approaches because of an increased awareness of the explosive potential of underemployment in less developed regions;

(v)   political support providing a framework and justification for new approaches.

The Mark II approach

The approach outlined here might be called the Mark II approach. It contrasts with the common approach of the last twenty years which was essentially Mark I.

Certain characteristics of Mark I and II are noted in Chart 6.1.

CHART 6.1: SOME CHARACTERISTICS OF PRESENT AND INNOVATIONAL
SMALL INDUSTRY DEVELOPMENT STRATEGIES

Factor	Mark I strategy	Mark II strategy
1. Definition of a small enterprise	*Size limited by amount of fixed capital.*	*Supplement fixed capital definition by one based on a high output to capital ratio (would vary with the industry) to encourage high employment regardless of the amount of fixed capital required in a single enterprise.*
2. Objectives	*Increase employment and production. Range of 20-40% of industrial value. added*	*Increase range to 30-50% of industrial value added.*
3. Central planning	*Some attention given by central planning authorities.*	*Major attention given by central planning authorities.*
4. Basic strategy	*Financial assistance plus some advisory services.*	*Policies and policy instruments to encourage growth. Intensive entrepreneurial training to maximise response to inducements. Advisory services. Financial assistance.*
5. Inducements	*Subsidise scarce resources, finance electric power, etc. High dependence on financial incentives.*	*Subsidise abundant resources - unskilled labour, etc. Low dependence on financial incentives.*
6. Advisory service mechanism	*Primary dependence on government civil servants.*	*Dependence on a wide variety of mechanisms including banks, private consultants, etc.*
7. Financial institutions	*Primary dependence on special small industry institutions.*	*Dependence on a wide variety of development and commercial banks.*
8. Training	*Training considered important.*	*Training considered essential - especially for entrepreneurs.*
9. Self-help measures	*Some encouragement.*	*Strong encouragement - e.g. to associations, co-operatives, etc.*
10. Industrial estates	*Over emphasis on industrial estates as an inducement for small industries, in establishing common facilities, etc.*	*Emphasis on sound industrial land planning and provision of land with utilities, etc. Expect self-help to provide most common facilities.*
11. Sector interactions	*Tendency to link small industry with handicrafts.*	*Encourage strong link between small and large industry.*

6.5 IMPLEMENTING NEW STRATEGIES

Innovative legislation and administrative mechanisms for establishing modern small industries have been largely successful in
larger cities. The time has come to apply the lessons learned to
the less developed regions.

One important component in implementing programmes is to decentralise decision-making by government officials. Other important
inputs include establishing practical regional development objectives by means of planning strategies which can be periodically up-
dated rather than adhering to a fixed five-year plan. Important
elements of the planning strategy include the availability of human
resources to achieve employment targets.

Signals need to be designed to indicate how the strategy is
working, together with evaluation schemes to provide appropriate
corrective action, if required.

The following procedural steps need to be followed when implementing new strategies:

Selecting regions

Industrialisation may be accelerated where development regions
can be made up of several clusters of districts, or smaller areas.
The region must include one major growth centre with existing industry and potential for rapid growth and stimulating expansion in
neighbouring districts. Inducements should be provided for entrepreneurs to set up in industrial development regions.

Raising the entrepreneurial level

The industrial atmosphere can be significantly improved by using
new techniques for identifying potential entrepreneurs and subsequently enhancing their entrepreneurship and management skills.

Maintaining the entrepreneurial level

Entrepreneurial spirit must be constantly reinforced by highly
skilled persons who organise the package of essential services
required by entrepreneurs.

Mobilising development executives

Highly skilled administrators and consultants need to be selected and recruited who are capable and willing to promote regional
development.

Technical consultants

Support to entrepreneurs is also essential from technical consultants located in the major growth centre of each region. The
consultants could form a pool to be used jointly by financing institutions, industrialists and government officials.

Equity loans

Equity loan systems could be established with the consultant consortium appended as a technical department. New institutions may be required or new functions added to existing institutions.

Infrastructure

A minimum infrastructure, including amenities for promoting considerable increase in the rate of industrial growth, is essential. At the outset new industries would have to be selected to fit the available infrastructure.

Chart 6.2 illustrates the organisational elements required to implement this new strategy for regional development.

CHART 6.2: GENERALISED ILLUSTRATIVE ORGANISATION FOR REGIONAL DEVELOPMENT

AREA LEVEL

- Entrepreneurs	- Entrepreneurs	- Entrepreneurs
- Development officials	- Development officials	- Development officials
- Commercial bankers	- Commercial bankers	- Commercial bankers
- Others	- Others	- Others

REGIONAL LEVEL

C O N S U L T A N T   C O N S O R T I U M

E Q U I T Y   F I N A N C E   S Y S T E M

STATE LEVEL

- *Industrial development co-ordination committees*
- *State financial corporations*
- *Managerial and technological extension service units*

CENTRAL GOVERNMENT

- *Ministerial representatives of industry*
- *Headquarters of financial institutions*
- *National training and research institutions*
- *Equity finance support system*

ENTREPRENEURIAL INITIATIVES AND COMMUNITY NEED FULFILMENT

7

Richard Morse[1]

The woman or man who starts a new enterprise is the host, the active organism, in the host-agent-environment framework provided by Philip Neck in Chapter 5. The entrepreneur conceives the project, nurtures it through hazy information about the future, mobilises sufficient resources for the start-up, and on the basis of a still incomplete vision takes the decision to create a new venture. This Chapter 7 plans to explore interactions between the entrepreneur and his or her community in identifying needs in the local environment as the basis for new ventures. In addition steps to strengthen the capacity of extension agents to pinpoint and generate relevant technical information and R & D support, assisting local innovators to meet basic needs, are briefly described.

7.1 MOTIVATIONS FOR CHANGE

Change occurs partly from dissatisfaction with present and past conditions and social relationships. As change becomes reality it shapes the future. Shaping the future calls for personal and collective qualities of intuiting, estimating, creating. What sources of foresight and creativity are personified in the entrepreneur?

Creativity and social change have long been enigmas for development theorists and practitioners. Dissatisfaction with results of economic planning in the United States and Burma in the 1950s led Everett Hagen to psychology and sociology as guides to motivation and change. David McClelland, from studies in motivation at about the same time, formulated theories relating economic progress to "need for achievement," or Nach. With support from organisational entrepreneurs including R.N. Jai, Joseph Stepanek and Jaime Cortes, training programmes centering on achievement motivation moved from pilot to professional stages in the 1960s. It should be noted that the appeal of these programmes was not confined to industrial change agents. Community development and agricultural extension agents had been sorely puzzled by the weakness of motivation to change in rural societies in spite of - or because of - the physical deprivation

---

[1] *Research Associate, Technology and Development Institute, East-West Centre, Honolulu, Hawaii, USA.*

which these societies endure. Perceptions of personal, community and technology change were brought together in the inter-personal and inter-disciplinary tensions of institutions that pioneered in motivation development.

In light of current strategies for meeting basic needs in poor communities, it is timely to search for connections between motivation factors and the origin of successful projects. What can theories of motivation tell us about originality, creativity and the capacity to perceive needs of the community? Is the entrepreneur motivated to start a new enterprise primarily by a need for achievement or power? Or is it a vision of creating something new, filling a need in the environment, that captures his energies and daily activities?

These questions are practical and pertinent. If the individual's need for achievement and his process of identifying community needs are only randomly linked, new enterprise creation will achieve much less than we expect in terms of economic and social development, and success rates of new firms will fall below acceptable levels in the use and allocation of resources.

Women's role as entrepreneurs adds important new dimensions to these questions. Jaime Cortes reports that of new enterprises established in Swaziland in the past three years, more than half were founded by women. Ruth S. Finney advances the hypothesis that women's "need for affiliation," leading to awareness and feeling for the needs of others, stimulates perception of market and technological opportunities. These observations suggest that women's potential contribution as innovators in defining and meeting community needs has been seriously neglected in past development efforts.

7.2 CREATIVITY AND COMMUNITY

Societies close to nature provide insights that may help us in the search for unifying sources of motivation, creativity and awareness of the needs of others.

"Autonomous motivation" is such a concept[1]. This is the phrase coined and elaborated by Dorothy Demetracopoulou Lee to explain the "exertions" and "exuberance" of traditional cultures that are beyond limits she could explain as motivated by needs or drives. "What explains the running, the skipping, the bounding?... I ... came to see man as moving rather than motivated, as thrusting forward, striving, aspiring ... I hope to show that where there is full engagement of the individual in his life, he is invited to act, rather than motivated to act."

The discovery of tennis by Dorothy Lee's son reinforced her understanding. "Tennis had an inviting horizon, a horizon which could never stop him because it retreated as he moved... He played far into exhaustion ... He chose for himself partners who were bound to defeat him... who would draw from him the full exercise of

---

[1] *D. Lee, Valuing the self (Prentice-Hall, Inc., 1976).*

all that was in him ... who would evoke him ... invited him to actu-
alise all his capacities... engage his whole being to full commitment." This quality of "striving to be fully human," she found akin
to Gordon Allport's propriate striving," or "own striving."

Entrepreneurial traits are brought to mind in these words. A
recent multi-country workshop on entrepreneurial education, for
example, identified personality characteristics of entrepreneurs
such as: persistent; self-starter; constantly under stress; hard-
working on things he wants to do; non-structured; dynamic - identified with creating and changing. The concept of "autonomous motivation," indeed, reinforces Christopher J. Kalangi's emphasis on
"need for independence" as a source of entrepreneurial initiatives.

Dorothy Lee's observations take us further in our search for
ties between entrepreneurial motivation and community need fulfillment. In cultures observed by Lee, "Man was viewed as a colla-
borator with the rest of nature or the universe in building the world
of experience ... It is human striving in response to evocation,
which takes the form of a call to create one's world in collaboration." Her son pointed out to her that he did not play a game of
tennis "against" a competitor: "The two partners collaborated to
create the game." "The individual is impulseful ... The impulse
to activity is directed outward from the individual toward the objective he wishes to achieve or the object he wishes to affect."[1] We
hear resonance between aspiring and creating in these words.

The relation of the individual to his community in these cultures offers further insights. "Interpenetration of the experience
of the self and others" is expressed in the very structure of the
language of the Wintu Indians of the Dakota nation, as recorded by
Lee. To the verb: "I am ill," the father simply adds a suffix which
changes the meaning to: "I am ill my son." Later: "I am recovered
my son." The father's self is differentiated from his son's, but
each is open to participating in the experience of the other. We
usually term this empathy. In Dorothy Lee's phrase, "Autonomy and
Community" build each other. She concludes: "In the beginning I said
I was not speaking of autonomous motivation. I have tried to show
that I speak of striving and thrust instead, and that an individual,
if he is to strive with all his capacity, is not completely autonomous; he needs to see himself as collaborating."

7.3 THE ENTREPRENEUR AS MAKER

Personality traits of entrepreneurs fit these processes of movement and collaboration. The workshop I have mentioned identified
these further entrepreneurial characteristics: sensitive and percep-
tive of people and environment; good communication with people;
opportunity seeker; ability to exploit situation; imaginative;
realistic; desires feedback and learns from experience, recognizing
errors; failure as step toward success; future-oriented. The workshop's discussions evoked this definition of an entrepreneur: "The
entrepreneur is a maker. He or she is a maker of something new. If
effective, he creates a new good, service or organization that satisfies a need of a significant number of people. Thus he is a maker
of value."

[1] *F.C. Gruber, ed., Anthropology and Education (University of
Pennsylvania Press, 1961).*

A successful entrepreneur of Hawaiian-Norwegian ancestry, George Henrickson, launching the multi-country programme described below, cited Henry Kaiser's definition of an entrepreneur: "An individual who is prepared to find the needs of the community and then service those needs." Extending this statement to Dorothy Lee's view of individual and community we could say that the community's partly formed projections or perceptions of needs are crystalised through the entrepreneur, as through a prism, into the act of creation of the new good or technology. Value arises from meeting needs. Value basically arises from the community. It takes specific shape through the organising power of the entrepreneur, the maker.

The maker imperfectly reflects the community's needs. Yet the newness of his creation makes an impact. It gains acceptance if it has utility or beauty, or both. The measure of acceptance of the innovation, the value placed on it in the marketplace, measures the tension of interplay among needs and desires on the part of different members of the community. This is part of the tension between the present and future: being and becoming. Entrepreneurs face the future, and have an uncommon role as makers of the future. In their role as job-makers, they further contribute to the creation of value.

7.4 CONFIDENCE INTERVALS AND ORGANISATIONAL BARRIERS

When gaps exist between the perceptions, motivations and resources of the entrepreneur and the community, as my colleague Gene R. Ward has pointed out, development may be skewed or aborted. The potential entrepreneur may lack confidence in his relations to the community. He may fear rejection, failure. "Let someone else do it." "I could never be a businessman." In poor communities, in turn, basic needs are obscured by lack of purchasing power. Needs as expressed in effective demand may not enable the new enterprise to break even, to generate a positive cash flow, or become profitable in the short-run pay-back period that is relevant to the entrepreneur in comparison with alternative uses of his resources.

Action research in which we have been engaged at the East-West Technology and Development Institute in partnership with 30 institutions in Asia, the Pacific and the United States is aimed, essentially, at helping bridge this gap between entrepreneurial initiatives and community needs, including the need for productive new employment and local technologies, to generate self-sustaining growth in low-income communities.

7.5 MULTI-COUNTRY ACTION STRATEGIES

These partnership institutions represent a broad cross-section of the kinds of specialised resources which the framework paper describes as necessary to facilitate small enterprise development. They include industrial extension and training agencies, development banks, agricultural and urban development agencies, entrepreneurial training institutes, management institutes, technology R & D centres, industry associations, departments of education and secondary and vocational schools. In each country, the configuration of institutes that have joined in this programme differs somewhat from that in other countries. Such institutional groupings reflect, to a degree, the principle of selectivity: the need in each country, at different periods, for particular priority elements and combinations of support facilities for small and medium enterprise development. Research, field experiments and educational programmes are proceeding, in this multi-country effort, on six interacting dimensions of entrepreneurial development and expansion toward increased employment opportunities:

The entrepreneur: his identification, selection, and development

General education for entrepreneurship

The development and testing of training programmes in business management for the small scale entrepreneur

Fostering local innovators and technological change agents

Cross-national evaluation of entrepreneurship development programmes

Entrepreneurial expansion with increased job opportunities

The principal objectives of these separate but integrally connected projects are:

The entrepreneur (Project I)

To ascertain the principal entrepreneurial traits, characteristics and behaviour of entrepreneurs among the focal groups in the participating countries and to develop practicable selection procedures for entrepreneurial development programmes.

General education (Project II)

To make general education of children and adults, in schools, and in nonformal education, more effective in preparing for self-employment and for employment-creating entrepreneurship.

Training programmes (Project III)

To strengthen training programmes and methods for entrepreneurial development, with specific emphasis on four areas or modules, as follows:

(i)   Psychological training

(ii)   Training in enterprise-building skills

(iii)   Training in managerial skills

(iv)   Special training for trainers and project leaders

Technological change (Project IV)

To promote innovativeness and technological diffusion by multi-disciplinary community experiments with three main objectives:

(i)   Fostering successful local innovators and project initiation by better local definition of needs and communication of appropriate technologies;

(ii)   Strengthening capabilities of field personnel and development agencies for assisting local entrepreneurs and communities in:

- obtaining relevant technical information and ideas
- local and regional market assesment
- testing and modifying product or process concepts and prototypes
- pre-feasibility and feasibility analysis
- project implementation

   (iii) Accelerating development and use of relevant information on selected industry sectors through procedures that will facilitate the strengthening of national and international centres for lateral exchange of information on alternative technologies and on factors influencing their use and adaptation.

Evaluation (Project V)

To document and evaluate existing entrepreneurial development programmes in the various cooperating countries, assess and exchange lessons and results of these evaluations, and develop feasible methods of continuing self-evaluation of these programmes.

Entrepreneurial expansion (Project VI)

To facilitate effective entrepreneurial expansion with increased job opportunities through:

   (i)   Entrepreneur-Manager course

   (ii)   Specialised functional courses on work organisation, finance and marketing

   (iii)   Training and orientation programmes for loan officers of financial institutions

   (iv)   Case writers' training

   (v)   Intercountry workshop on assessment of programme effectiveness and its specificity or universality with respect to culture, country and industry

   (vi)   Trainer guides and trainer development

7.6   FOSTERING LOCAL INNOVATION TO MEET BASIC NEEDS

New linkages between the small farm sector and small industry, needed for increased output and employment, are emphasised in Project IV. The project takes off from the fact that many indigenous production and distribution activities, as well as recent adaptations of these activities, serve as good starting points for defining and meeting new rural needs. As pointed out by Zenaida Toquero of the International Rice Research Institute, successive generations of craftsmen, farmers, small industrialists and traders in rural areas have accumulated an immense stock of knowledge and know-how pertinent to economic development in their specific local conditions. It is often possible and desirable to build on these local technology traditions as a basis for further innovations.

Project IV attempts to integrate several factors needed if local innovation is to occur:

(i)   End-user assessment and projection of needed technologies. Judgments of small farm producers, workers, housewives, teachers, health assistants, transport operators, food processors, and rural traders must be tapped to define and set design criteria for relevant technologies

(ii)   Specific information, trial equipment, and organising methods needed to fill technology gaps and to quicken and stimulate ideas for new forms of services, products and production techniques

(iii) Access by entrepreneurs to such end-use specifications and information

(iv)   Commissioning of R, D & E by local entrepreneurs, farmers' groups and other rural end-users to guide science and technology centres in research priorities and design parameters

In the first phase of the project, an international team representing six to eight participating institutions will intensively study local instances of successful innovation in three countries, with the object of distilling generalisable lessons on how the above factors combine, or may be fostered, in generating need-based innovation. The international team will combine capabilities in industrial and agricultural engineering, managerial economics and marketing, small farm cropping systems, home economics and rural entrepreneurial development. This interdisciplinary group will of course face the fact that innovations in each sector and geocultural area are quite particularised, in response to specific, varied conditioning factors. Keeping the chief focus on small farm linkages, the choices of locations for field observations will enable the team to see alternative current examples of innovation - or adaptation - in sectors basic to the progress of poor communities, such as:

equipment for small farm use, ground water location and conservation, crop processing and storage, animal care and upgrading, algae fixation of nitrogen, food processing, and related inputs for increasing small farm productivity;

sources of safe drinking water, sanitation, renewable sources of energy for cooking, heating, and lighting, and other household consumption needs. Women's potential role as innovators in defining community needs and designing appropriate local technology will be stressed in field inquiries;

communication and transportation;

building materials, housing, and community structures.

Based on this series of micro-observations, the international team will prepare a Field Manual for End-User Assessment and Project Initiation, containing practical, flexible yet rigorous procedures for putting together mixes of factors needed for local innovation. The team will conduct in-country training of technological change agents, and contribute to the planning of area experiments and demonstrations that will constitute phase two of the local innovators project.

In short, this multi-country effort seeks to create active face-to-face relationships and information exchange among:

- rural end-users of technology
- local and regional entrepreneurs
- industrial, farm and home extension agents, and
- research, development and engineering institutes.

The project also seeks to develop new capabilities on the part of rural producers and householders in defining what their priority needs are; to present visible choices among different technological options, through prototype use, experimentation, and assessment; and through these means to quicken the ability of local entrepreneurs to identify and initiate incremental or quantum changes in existing technologies and services.

7.7 THE STRUCTURE AND POETRY OF CREATION

All technology springs from work, and is a transformation of work. The ergs of work a man puts in on the soil or the workbench, or the woman at the hearth or marketplace, bring invisible nerve responses that, over time, form signals and signs for creation of greater usefulness, harmony, and social meaning in the work process.

Man as innovator is a mover, a sign-reader, a maker. Many of the signs guiding his creations in the modern era are discovered and structured by science into systems of knowledge. In transforming man's technologies, both the old signs and the structured new signs must be guides.

As technological change and extension agents, we may come to see ourselves as collaborators in an evolving participatory process: working with local producers and users of technology to evoke and define needed improvements, to quicken the interpenetration of entrepreneurs and communities in making physical and social advances, and to find notes and chords of information which communities, entrepreneurs and technologists can orchestrate into new structures and rhythms. "Men work together, I told him from the heart, whether they work together or apart."[1] The community of work, transformed by innovators, is open to our contributions as agents of knowledge and change. So we get closer to the mysteries of collaborating with nature and each other: the mystery of folk, work and place, keeping our hold on the planet.

"Maker", in old English, was the word for a poet. Poets are makers of word magic. The word magic sings the interpenetration of the self and nature, the self and others. To develop entrepreneurs, perhaps one should say a good deal of poetry. Be poets, and you will be makers of people, who themselves are makers.

---

[1] R. Frost: "The Tuft of Flowers", in Collected Poems (Holt, Rinehart and Winston).

EDUCATION AND ENTREPRENEURIAL INITIATIVES

8

Robert E. Nelson[1]

"Today, as in the past, our relationship to work activity is a fundamental determinant of the way we live."[2]

8.1 ENTREPRENEURIAL INITIATIVES

Entrepreneurship education is an essential factor both (i) as a means of employment generation and (ii) as a means of encouraging economic growth. It is important for a nation to realize that their most valuable resource is their people. Every society is composed of key individuals who have the potential to spark and sustain business and economic growth. These persons may be defined as entrepreneurs. Abraham Maslow, a psychologist known for his theories regarding human needs, indicated that "the most valuable 100 people to bring into a deteriorating society would not be economists, or politicians, or engineers, but rather 100 entrepreneurs."[3]

The importance assigned to any job is determined (i) by society and (ii) by the attitude of the individual engaged in the work. Much of the literature pertaining to career education in the United States relates to the identification of occupational clusters, job families and career ladders. Other career education materials identify specific concepts which may be helpful to potential employees in obtaining and maintaining an occupation. Many of the career education materials and curriculum guides for secondary and post secondary vocational educational programs emphasize the role of the schools in developing the talents and abilities of students for the "world of work". In the final analysis, it may be concluded that most career education programmes in the United States, and elsewhere, focus on the development of job seekers (employees).

[1] *Chairman, Division of Business Education, University of Illinois, Urbana, USA.*

[2] *F. Best: The Future of Work (Prentice-Hall, Inc., Englewood Cliffs, N.J., 1973), p. 1.*

[3] *A. Maslow: Readings in the Economics of Education (United Nations: UNESCO, 1968), p. 623.*

8.2 BUSINESS OWNERSHIP

The identification and teaching of career opportunities in the area of small business ownership and management has been a neglected part of the total career education concept. However, small, independently owned and operated businesses have always played a vital role in the American economy.

Small business, after all, is a national resource of enormous proportions, providing the livelihood for 100 million Americans and comprising 97 percent of all business, which creates 43 percent of the Gross National Product.[1]

Based on Internal Revenue Service statistics for the latest year computed, 1973, there are approximately 13.6 million businesses in the U.S. including 3.3 million farms[2]. Small independent businesses represent a vital and significant force in the American economy.

Career opportunities exist for small business ownership in most sectors of our economy. There are over ten million small businesses throughout the United States which provide fifty-eight percent of our business employment[3]. Given these statistics, it can be projected that approximately four students in the typical high school classrooms will become business owners, and perhaps another three to five students have the potential to do so.

Traditionally, the largest number of small business firms in the United States have existed in retail trade. However, the number of service firms is now a very important sector of small business[4]. In the United States today, 64 out of every 100 workers are engaged in providing services; by 1980 about 70 out of every 100 will be employed in the service industries[5]. Clearly, the nature of work is changing.

In addition, the population of small business owners is likely to be broadened to include more women and members of minority groups as these individuals become more aware of opportunities for owning and operating their own businesses. A pilot study of women who have started their own businesses was recently conducted in Milwaukee, Wisconsin. The study was undertaken to: (i) provide data on the personality traits of female entrepreneurs; (ii) reveal the extent

---

[1] *Statement by A. Vernon Weaver, Administrator-Designate of the U.S. Small Business Administration. Before the Senate Small Business Committee, Thursday, March 31, 1977.*

[2] *U.S. Small Business Administration 1976 Annual Report, Superintendent of Documents, (U.S. Government Printing Office, Washington D.C., 20402), p. 14-15.*

[3] *Presidential documents, Proclamation 4429, Small Business Week, 1976, April 13, 1976.*

[4] *R. Holland: Global challenges of free competitive enterprise, (keynote address at the International Symposium on Small Business, Tokyo, Japan, November 18, 1975).*

[5] *D. Bell: The clock watchers: Americans at work, (Time, September 8, 1975), p. 55-57.*

of entrepreneurial activity among women; and (iii) provide a basis for the encouragement of women who are interested in starting their own businesses[1].

In the area of minority group involvement, a government Task Force on Education and Training for Minority Business Enterprise recently prepared a report to assist in developing a national policy and programme for providing needed business management skills to existing and potential minority entrepreneurs. The report was also intended to "mold a system for introducing minority youth to the potentialities of business ownership as a career."[2] The study concluded that there is an important relationship between education and training in management and technical skills, and the success and survival of all small business enterprises.

8.3 EDUCATION FOR ENTREPRENEURSHIP[3]

In the past, programmes at all educational levels have not considered entrepreneurship and business ownership as an essential part of the curriculum. Most business programmes at the college level teach students how to be managers or to become employees within large business organizations. Recently, educators have been giving serious thoughts to increasing the number of courses and programmes relating to entrepreneurship and small business enterprise development.

For instance, the University of Northern Colorado at Greeley recently announced the formation of a new programme in Small Business Management. The programme leads to a Bachelor of Science in Business Administration with a specialization in Small Business Management. After taking the business core courses required of all Business Administration majors, persons in this programme will take courses from all of the disciplines that have been developed with the small business person in mind. There will also be a series of three courses that are solely for small business problems. These courses deal with the creation of a small business, operation of the business and a small business capstone course.

This new degree will be among the few in the United States that is offered solely for the benefit of small businesspersons. Some of the other schools that offer such a programme are the University of Southern California, Southern Methodist University, Texas A & M, and Wharton.

However, offering such programmes only at the collegiate level may not be the best possible alternative. In a recent report, H.K. Charlesworth, former Dean of a graduate entrepreneurship programme in Malaysia, indicated that "Although it is not probable that entrepreneurs can emerge in the short run, over a longer period of time,

---

[1] J. Schreier: The female entrepreneur: A pilot study (Center for Venture Management, Milwaukee, Wisconsin, March, 1975), p. 1.

[2] Report of the Task Force on Education and Training for Minority Business Enterprise, U.S. Department of Health, Education, and Welfare, January, 1974, p. XV.

[3] See also Chapter 18, United States, Part 18.2.

increased educational opportunities and cultural changes together with
government support can effect an increase in the number of entrepreneur."[1] Entrepreneurship programmes may initially be started at the
collegiate level, but to be really effective, entrepreneurship concepts must eventually be integrated into vocational programmes at all
educational levels. If specific personal characteristics are essential to business success, then "the education of the potential entrepreneur must not wait until he has grown up, by which time he has
acquired non-entrepreneurial habits".[2]

Education for entrepreneurship should start during the student's
formative years in primary and secondary school and also should be
extended to activities in the home and in the community. Entrepreneurial motivation involves a developmental process which must be
integrated throughout one's formal and informal education and training. Young men and women must be encouraged to develop their entrepreneurial talents. Only in this way can a society use its "human
resources" in an effective manner.

Entrepreneurship is most commonly used in terms of business.
However, entrepreneurship may be related to all dimensions of life.
In the broadest sense of the term, entrepreneurship can be the means
to stimulate the creativity and innovation necessary to create a
better community, a better nation and a better world. This aspect
of entrepreneurship has been grossly neglected in the United States.

There appears to be some agreement that most people in the
United States do possess entrepreneurial qualities to some extent
and in some combination. Everyone may be thought of as having a
certain degree of drive, ambition, capacity to take risks, and to
innovate. Alleged shortages of entrepreneurs in many countries is
probably due, not so much to any difference in the inherent capacities of the population, but to cultural and institutional factors.[3]

8.4 IMPLICATIONS FOR VOCATIONAL EDUCATION

Most individuals start work as employees, and a significant
proportion of those who do so eventually start their own businesses
after they have accumulated experience, knowledge, and capital.
Service as an employee is viewed as necessary experience for those
individuals planning to become entrepreneurs. Those who have gained
the necessary experience are likely to be more successful than those
who work for a time as employees and then suddenly decide to open
their own businesses - not because they are prepared for this step,
but because they are bored and frustrated by working for others.

Many of the vocationally oriented programmes at the high school
and post-secondary levels emphasize the training and skill development

---

[1] *K.K. Charlesworth: An unpublished research report submitted
to the MARA Institute of Technology, Shah Alam, Selangor, Malaysia,
p. 5.*

[2] *Y.B. Poh: Entrepreneurs in economic development, (Malaysian
Business, February 1976), p. 44.*

[3] *L. Reynolds: Economics: a general introduction (4th edition,
Richard D. Irwin, Homewood, 1973), p. 521.*

of students for occupations that are available in business. Many of these skills are taught, however, with the expectation that students will become employees working *for* some other person or business.

Occupational education materials are needed for concepts related to small business ownership and management as a career option. As more and more of these materials become available, it is hoped that they can be integrated into the curriculum at various levels.

Awareness of self-employment opportunities could be included in courses at the secondary level. At the post-secondary level, programmes could be developed consisting of two or three sequential courses in small business management. Related courses such as small business marketing and small business accounting could be included in the programme and thus allow students to major in small business ownership and management. These post-secondary programmes would serve to expose students to skills, personal characteristics, and knowledge necessary for success in owning and managing small businesses.

THE WORLD BANK
AND SMALL ENTERPRISE DEVELOPMENT

9

Philippe Nouvel[1]

Most developing countries are characterized by a rapidly growing population and labour force. While agriculture will continue to absorb a large part of the increase in the labour force, it is clear that an increasing amount of labour will have to be employed in non-farm occupations, either in villages or small towns, or in the larger towns and cities.

Thus, balanced growth and cross sectoral job creation demands major efforts to expand non-farm employment in urban areas, together with intensification of agriculture, which would help to reduce the emigration of rural population and increase their ability to buy urban products.

In this context, development of industry - in the wide sense including both services and productive enterprises - in urban areas, appears to be a major preoccupation and challenge for most developing countries. At the same time, given the scarcity of capital in most LDCs, emphasis has to be put on utilizing capital as wisely and efficiently as possible in order to create the greatest possible demand for labour.

Employment generation

The IBRD's lending to industry has traditionally been done through development finance companies (DFCs) for mostly medium-scale industry, and directly for large industrial projects. Lending to DFCs has been increasing sharply in the last decade. According to recent studies, it is estimated that the average fixed investment per direct job generated through these DFC loans/credits is about $16.000 for industrial projects assisted during 1976 and that at least half of the projects have a fixed cost/job ratio below $8.000. (The overall employment effect of these industrial projects including

---

[1] *Division Chief, Eastern Africa, Industrial Development and Finance Division, International Bank for Reconstruction and Development (IBRD) - also known as the World Bank. The views expressed in this Chapter are those of Mr. Nouvel and do not necessarily reflect the official policy of the IBRD.*

indirect employment is hard to assess, but it can be roughly estimated that over the longer term each job created in industry results
in three or more jobs created indirectly mainly in services.)

The above mentioned studies have also tended to demonstrate that
small-scale enterprises - SSE - (using as a definition enterprises
with no more than $250.000 in fixed assets in 1976 prices) are gene-
rally more labour-intensive compared to larger firms. (These SSEs
are meant to include modern manufacturing industry, organized non-
manufacturing activities such as construction, transportation and
trading, and traditional or "informal" activities.) The following
table clearly indicates such a conclusion, although the figures have
to be used with caution. In particular, asset values would be sub-
stantially higher in 1976 prices and it is likely that SSEs would now
show an average fixed assets/direct employment ratio of between
$1.000 and $3.000.

Fixed assets/direct employment in selected countries

Size of enterprise	India[1] (1965/1973)	Colombia[2] (1974)	Mexico[3] (1970)	Philippines[4] (1970)
	$	$	$	$
Small	278	3.000	3.700	1.020
Medium	557		4.500	2.850
Large	2.450 (5.000)	13.400	14.500	8.000

Such studies also tend to demonstrate that, although generally more
labour-intensive than larger enterprises, SSE projects create jobs
which have lower ratios of value added/employee and of capital/out-
put.

Responding to Governments' preoccupations, the IBRD has recently
been putting more emphasis on employment creation in urban areas,
through assistance to small-scale relatively labour-intensive modern
and informal sector enterprises. This means enlarging the spectrum
of end-users of IBRD assistance, and also enlarging the spectrum of
intermediaries used for such assistance. Most DFCs channelling
funds to industry until now have tended to cater to the needs of
modern medium and large-scale manufacturing enterprises and have been
built-up and developed to support such enterprises. They are not on
the whole equipped at present to service SSEs.

---

[1] *Data from Annual Survey of Industries, 1965, and (in parenthe-
sis) ICICI publication Financial performance of companies, 1973/74,
p. 23.*

[2] *Banco de la República, El mercado de capitales en Colombia,
Bogota, 1974. Other estimates of the cost/job in Colombian medium/
large enterprises, quoted in the Bank's 1972 OED report on Colombia,
range as high as 115.000 - 22,000.*

[3] *Data from 1970 Industrial Census.*

[4] *ILO: Sharing in development, (Geneva, 1974).*

This new mission is indeed not an easy one for financial intermediaries; also in the SSE sector, major differences exist between
modern SSEs in industry and services, and the SSEs in the informal
sector. Given the socio-economic features of these two types of
enterprises different approaches will be necessary, as well as different mechanisms for delivery of assistance. However, some rather
simplistic observations can be made.

9.1 POLICIES AND GOVERNMENT COMMITMENT

Development of SSEs in general cannot be achieved if the general
policy context in a country is not supportive. Investment codes in
many African countries tend to favor capital-intensive investment in
modern medium and large-scale industrial enterprises. A prerequisite
to effective development of the SSE sector appears to be the sensi-
tization and commitment of the Government to such an objective, and
the setting up of an adequate policy framework or at least the reduction of the policy biases against SSE development.

9.2 INTEGRATED ASSISTANCE PACKAGES

Assistance to SSEs has to combine various degrees and forms of
technical and financial assistance, under some sort of integrated
delivery package. Needs for technical assistance are varied: vocational training, accounting, and management are often quoted. An
important element of technical assistance is marketing (locally or
abroad) which can take various forms such as exploring and finding
markets, subcontracting, enforcing quality standards, etc... Assistance in new product development and selecting, installing and operating equipment is also needed. This external technical assistance
may have to be obtained from external sources in some countries.
However, the costs are high. For complete coverage local extension
services are the only viable long term solution. Success of local
extension services is limited to date and this problem is perhaps the
most important constraint to SSE development in many countries.

Financial and technical assistance can be delivered jointly or
separately. In the latter case close coordination between the two
delivery mechanisms has to be ensured. Regarding financial assistance, traditional DFCs (development banks) can effectively channel
funds to modern SSEs through establishment of a separate department
or regional agencies, in order to have broader geographical coverage.
Also, use of other intermediaries, such as commercial banks, leasing
companies, hire purchase institutions could be encouraged. In some
cases a single institution specializing in SSE assistance will prove
useful. Careful examination of the financial network in a country is
needed before selecting the intermediary(ies) to deal with financial
assistance to SSEs. For the informal sector, it is conceivable that
typical financial institutions won't be able or will not be willing
to provide assistance. Other channels (such as workers' banks, community development funds, cooperatives), may be available or possible
to establish. In any case mechanisms for delivering packages for
technical/financial assistance have to be adapted to the country's
needs and existing institutional set-up. In many cases innovative
and imaginative approaches will have to be looked at.

9.3 LENDING PROCEDURES, CRITERIA AND ADMINISTRATION

Lending to SSEs cannot apply under the same sophisticated and orthodox criteria and procedures as for medium and large-scale enterprises. Appraisals of SSE projects will necessarily rely on the quality of the manager/entrepreneur much more than on an in-depth study of the projects technical/financial/economic aspects. This leads to more subjective judgement on the viability of an SSE project, and also to simplified project implementation (including loan documentation) and supervision procedures. It means also for external lenders that less attention should be put on determining and financing the foreign exchange component: the local cost of fixed assets in SSE projects is likely to be higher than for larger projects, and thus external aid agencies should be ready to finance a proportion of local costs, under some simplified disbursement mechanism.

Lending to SSEs is usually - but not automatically - more risky than for larger projects. The experience tends to demonstrate that rates of defaults and failures (the mortality rate) for SSE are high. With an efficient combination of technical and financial assistance, this risk may be reduced. However, financial institutions have generally considered SSE lending as a risky and time consuming operation.

SSE development is rather costly - not only in terms of administrative expenses for the intermediary concerned but more generally, given the input of technical assistance to be provided, and the various subsidies often granted. Including the estimated cost of technical assistance in SSE projects, in a recent case, resulted in increasing by about 60 percent the estimated investment cost/job and decreasing internal rates of return from about 25-30 percent to 12-15 percent. Technical assistance is often provided under the form of grant from international or bilateral agencies. However, such aids are temporary by nature; local counterparts have to be trained and the bill for their employment has finally to be paid by the local economy. Whereas it is generally accepted that technical assistance should be provided without charge to SSEs, at least in the beginning, consideration should be given to its ultimate cost, and ways and means should be explored to have the recipient progressively bear a part of the bill.

9.4 PROBLEMS AND ISSUES

Apart from the usual problems of selecting entrepreneurs and how best to coordinate the flow of technical/financial assistance, there are a few general questions that need to be addressed in the SSE field. They are: what degree of subsidisation for SSE development is acceptable. Linked to this issue is the much debated problem of the interest rate to be charged to SSE borrower. The problem of collateral requirements by financial institution is also a major problem, in particular for loans to meet working capital needs of SSEs. Finally, I will touch upon the issue of the difficulties met by the entrepreneurs who "transfer" from the informal sector to the modern one.

Subsidies

The whole question of subsidisation or protection of industrial development as a whole is a subject of much debate. Leaving it aside

however, and assuming some degree of subsidisation is necessary to
help develop infant industry in LDCs, the question of subsidisation
of the SSE sector specifically needs to be addressed. Subsidisation
may take various forms: provisions of land or buildings at no or low
cost, provision of free technical assistance, low cost tariffs for
utilities, support of activities through preference for local industries, low interest rates... Leaving aside the latter for the time
being, it would seem that three general principles could be agreed
upon: (i) assuming subsidisation of SSEs is necessary to support
its development, the costs should be evaluated to permit the authorities to monitor the programmes in terms of tentative cost benefit
analysis; (ii) recipients of such subsidised assistance should be
made aware of the subsidy involved so that they recognize that they
are not performing in normal "market" conditions, and (iii) subsidisation should progressively be eliminated, or SSE recipients should
progressively bear the full cost of the assistance rendered.

Interest rates

The interest rate for lending to SSEs (including in this the
rental costs for land, buildings and equipment) has been much
debated. The IBRD has sometimes been criticized for saying that
project beneficiaries should normally be charged, insofar as possible,
the full costs of facilities and services furnished to them. Specifically, the policy that interest rates to ultimate borrowers should
be "significantly positive in real terms" often results in rates
somewhat higher than those specified by Governments. This attitude
is not an expression of capitalistic bias or creditor's self interest,
but aims at encouraging financial intermediation in the country
through developing savings collection and mobilization for investment
purposes. Unduly low interest rates may not only reduce incentives
to save but can also lead to higher capital-intensive investments,
and possibly encourage investments with low return. This leads to
misallocation of resources. Turning back to SSE lending, two additional points may be made:

> (i) the main problem for SSEs, most often, is not the cost
> of credit, but access to it, for both investment capital
> and also for working capital requirements. Sometimes they
> must look for credit, if any, to the local money lender,
> whose charges are substantially higher than the commercial
> development bank rates. When institutional interest rates
> are kept artificially low, both mobilisation and allocation
> of savings are hindered and credit has to be rationed; in
> the process the smaller enterprises generally get pushed to
> the end of the queue and their opportunities for growth are
> often stifled;

> (ii) there is need for higher spreads for SSE lending;
> not only are the administrative costs higher but since these
> operations are usually more risky, financial institutions
> need a higher spread to cover the risk element. One could
> calculate that to cover a 10 percent estimated default rate
> for loans averaging 7.5 years duration including 2.5 years
> grace period, the spread element needed is 2.8 percent. If
> one adds to this risk element the administrative costs and
> the profit element necessary to keep the equity of the
> financial institution stable in real terms, it can be said

that the spreads for institutions lending to SSEs should
be a minimum of 4-5 percent excluding technical assistance
costs. Finally, people tend to be psychologically more
sensitive to the interest rate problem than to the other
terms of financing offered. As an example, the payments
needed for servicing - on an equal capital + interest,
installment basis - a 6 years loan at 6 percent are equal
to the cost of servicing a loan of the same amount at
13 percent over about 8 years.

Collateral

An important point is the question of the collateral usually
required by financial institutions, who have sometimes tended to rely
more on the guarantees offered than on the viability of the project
and the qualities of the entrepreneurs. To overcome that difficulty, solutions have been used or can be explored in the areas of
leasing of buildings and equipments (or hire-purchase schemes or
pooling of equipment). For working capital requirements, an often
neglected area of concern for SSE development, subcontracting by
large firms of Government orders - provided there are no delays for
payment - can be another partial solution. Also, many countries
have used guarantee schemes, with various degrees of efficiency and
successes. Here again there is no simple adequate solution, but this
problem needs to be carefully looked into when establishing SSE
development schemes.

Attitudes to borrowing

Another issue that could be mentioned related to the attitudes
of the entrepreneur, particularly in the informal sector, vis-a-vis a
programme of assistance that would result in putting him in the
modern "normal" market world. Growing into the modern industrial
sector puts the entrepreneur in a new environment he is not familiar
with, including labor laws, minimum wage legislation, income tax
administration, etc... thus possibly creating some reluctance on his
part. Lending from a bank may be a sign of economic maturity, but
is probably looked with some reluctance by the small entrepreneur
who may be afraid of borrowing on the official market rather than
from the money lender, if he sees himself in danger of losing the
control of his enterprise. The above point is made just to mention
that programmes of SSE development should probably be designed carefully so as to be psychologically understood and accepted by the
persons assisted.

9.5   EXAMPLES OF WORLD BANK ASSISTANCE

A few recent projects assisted by IBRD in Africa are specifically geared towards SSE and are conceptually different from previous
ones. (Note: In many countries DFCs associated with the WBG have
traditionally been assisting SSEs as part of their normal operations,
and that some DFCs have already done much in this field.)

Ivory Coast

A project was developed in association with the Government,
Crédit de la Côte d'Ivoire (CCI) and the Office de Promotion de l'Entreprise Ivoirienne (OPEI). It has as central concept the development of "model" or prototype projects in pre-identified subsectors,

which can be used for repetitive operation, thus reducing risk of failure, capital cost and administrative overhead. The CCI, which provides financial assistance (except for working capital to be made available by commercial banks), and the OPEI, which provides technical assistance, are closely associated in the project to provide combined financial/technical assistance on agreed terms.

Kenya

A project recently appraised in Kenya aims at developing institution - the Kenya Industrial Estates - as the single channel for both technical and financial assistance to SSIs and outside industrial estates. The approach is thus different from the previous project. It raises the interesting question of how to build an institution that can both perform financial and technical assistance roles and at the same time develop into an autonomous institution self-supporting and capable of borrowing by itself in the long run.

Upper Volta

The Bank recently appraised a project of assistance to informal sector artisans and medium-scale and small-scale industries. A prime objective of the intervention is to integrate modern sector lending by the financial intermediary, BND, with project promotion and follow-up by the technical assistance agency, OPEV. In addition, in response to an urgent need for management training in Upper Volta we plan to help OPEV establish the basis for a management training centre, using students in the centre in a work-study role to supplement technical assistance to existing entrepreneurs. Finally, to reach informal sector artisans, we propose to broaden a system of credit-in-kind and marketing assistance, which relies not on a formal sector financial intermediary, but a mobile technical team which can dispense credit-in-kind, market artisanal output and provide technical assistance.

INNOVATIONS IN PROMOTING AND DEVELOPING NEW ENTERPRISES

10

Vihari G. Patel[1]

Three innovative schemes in finance, entrepreneurship and infrastructure introduced by Gujarat State industrial agencies have broken new ground for small enterprise development in India.

Financial constraints facing new entrepreneurs have been removed due to 100 percent financing of project costs being met by a specially set up investment company. Potential entrepreneurs are identified and developed by means of a comprehensive training programme providing project counselling, motivation development, managerial guidance and work experience. A specialised infrastructure agency also provides ready sheds for immediate project implementation. This innovative package of assistance has diversified sources of industrial entrepreneurship and accelerated small enterprise development.

Problem areas

Ability to save and invest has often been identified as a critical issue limiting economic development in developing countries.[2] In industrial development these scarcities have meant (i) inadequate funds to set up ventures (financial constraints on entrepreneurs), and (ii) lack of entrepreneurship in perceiving opportunities, organising resources and setting up and running industrial ventures. Where entrepreneurs with ability to invest exist, fund shortages are likely to hinder entreprise formation. Where there are funds, entrepreneurs are not coming forward. Alternatively, latent entrepreneurship may exist but is not finding outlets.

Industrial credit does not flow into the hands of entrepreneurs due to rigidities in the policies and procedures of conventional lending institutions. Potential entrepreneurship is not cultivated

---

[1] *Chief Economic Adviser, Gujarat Industrial Development Corporation, Ahmedabad, Gujarat, India.*

[2] *A.O. Hirschman: The strategy of economic development (Yale University Press, New Haven, 1958), p. 35. Also B. Chenery and A.M. Strout: Foreign assistance and economic development, AID, Discussion paper No. 7 (Revised) Dept. of State, (Washington, D.C., June 1965), p. 7.*

and nurtured. Enterprising persons lack the self-confidence necessary to take initiative and risk. Only limited industrial growth
takes place because only a few established industrial groups and
families perpetuate an unequal distribution of industrial ownership.

However, it is feasible to alleviate these scarcities and accelerate the process of industrial development using imaginative measures, backed up by sound institutional arrangements. This has been
successful in the State of Gujarat, India, by setting up several specialised state supported industrial finance and entrepreneurship
development agencies, with their innovative measures for small-scale
industries development. These have been well-tested over the years
and are now models for small enterprise development in India. With
modifications to suit local conditions, one expects they could be
adopted elsewhere.

10.1   INNOVATIONS IN INDUSTRIAL FINANCE

Until 1968-69, commercial banks were the only source of industrial finance for new entrepreneurs. Conservative, commercial and
cautious in their approach, their policies restricted new enterprise
formation in several ways.

Primarily, banks preferred financing short rather than long
term. Accordingly, 80 percent of loans were limited to commercial
(commodity) rather than industrial loans, while 70 percent of selected industrial loans were for short-term working funds rather than
long-term fixed asset financing. This assured quicker turnover,
higher return and less risk (because of hypothecation of goods).

Secondly, when industrial loans gradually expanded with the
pressure of industrial development in the country, 60 percent of
loans were provided to established industrialists for expansion or
diversification, since success was assured by entrepreneurs who were
well-known. New loans were provided to merchants and traders having
adequate financial resources to contribute 40 percent or 50 percent
margins, plus deposits of securities in personal properties.

Thirdly, the debt-equity ratio was kept close to 1:1 so that
the entrepreneur's own stake was fairly high, reducing the Banker's
risk correspondingly. Margins ranged from 40 to 60 percent. As a
result only well established, less competitive projects were financed
which had high returns and short pay-back periods of 3-4 years.

Such a policy meant that industrial finance was mainly available
only to those who already had sufficient resources of their own. A
competent, enterprising person with a viable project could not secure
finance unless he also happened to be financially sound. Industrial
entrepreneurship remained concentrated in the hands of few. Sources
of industrial entrepreneurship were limited to traders, merchants
about 40 percent, and established industrialists about 50 percent.

A state industrial investment company

It would have been futile to try persuading bankers to change
their commercial, conservative policies since they were in the business of sophisticated money lending and not industrial development.
The State Government of Gujarat decided to fill the gap by providing

finance for new entrepreneurs in setting up a separate state institution called the Gujarat Industrial Investment Corporation (GIIC).

This was a public limited company with a share capital of
Rs 50 million subscribed by the State[1]. Its objectives were to promote new entrepreneurs in small and medium-scale industry[2], to develop non-traditional new industries, and to undertaken those functions
which existing institutions could or would not. As an autonomous
Corporation, governed by its own Board of enlightened industrialists
and senior government officials, it could form its own policies and
develop its own norms for industrial finance.

It operated as a development bank which could afford the low
returns and high risks required for diversifying entrepreneurship,
and promoting innovations and backward area development. It would
undertake the pre-investment functions of industrial surveys, identifying opportunities, and preparing project reports. Its viability
was to be determined not strictly in terms of dividends paid, and
profits earned, but by the number of new entrepreneurs financed,
diversified industries set up and regional balance achieved.

The technicians' scheme

In 1969, the unconventional technicians' scheme was introduced
by GIIC. Any technically qualified or experienced person with a
sound project and ability to set up and run an industrial enterprise
would be financed 100 percent of the value of fixed assets, plus
working capital margin[3] and preliminary and pre-operative expenses.
The project size should be limited to Rs.200, 000 for a single entrepreneur and Rs.300, 000 for a partnership. However, the limit could
be extended up to Rs.500,000 on techno-economic viability grounds.
The loan would be repaid under the following attractive terms:

> (i)   no repayment for the first 3 years, followed by
> annual instalments spread over 7 years;

> (ii)   interest to be paid at 4½ percent (50 percent subsidy)
> for the first 3 years, and at 9 percent subsequently;

> (iii) no collateral or third party guarantees would be
> required;

> (iv)   assets created by the loan to be hypothecated
> to the Corporation.

Rational and assumptions of the technicians' scheme

The scheme possessed a definite philosophy of new entrepreneurship formation and its terms of assistance a well-thought-out
rationale.

---

[1] *$5.5 million (US) at the rate of Rupees (Rs).9/- = $1.00*

[2] *Small scale in India was defined as a project where investment
in plant and machinery did not exceed Rs.750,000*

[3] *Commercial banks would normally finance 60 percent of the
working funds needs. The balance of 40 percent would be the margin
to be loaned by GIIC to the entrepreneur.*

Why technicians?: A large number of technicians have the manufacturing experience and production skills to identify production
opportunities. They often develop a desire to be self-employed
after long service as employees frustrated in subordinate or unchan-
ging roles. Usually they cannot set up their own small enterprises
since the 50 percent or 60 percent finance from banks, rarely available to such unknown persons, would not be enough since their
meagre savings would not meet the margins required, nor would they
be able to offer tangible securities against the assumed higher risk
of financing them.

There are also young engineers and technical graduates with
enterprising and innovative ideas. Many are unable to find jobs.
Some of them have the potential to be self-employed in small industrial ventures but cannot do so unless need-based finance is available to them (see Table 10.1).

Why 100 percent?: These were potential entrepreneurs from
unconvential sources possessing scarce production skills, enterprise
and competence, unable to contribute preliminary expenses of
Rs.10,000, let alone working capital funds. 100 percent finance was
the only answer if their enterprise, industrial skills and project
ideas were to be converted into actual industrial enterprises.

Moratorium: In addition, moratorium on repayment was essential
to help them settle down and start earning before loan repayment
began. It normally took 18 to 24 months from the date of loan sanc-
tion to reach break-even. The small projects would generate only
small surplus for income and repayment. Therefore, a long repayment
period was essential to reduce the monthly instalment's size.

Entrepreneur's stake: Although having only a limited financial
stake in the venture, their real stake is the decision to leave a
secure job, take the risk of uncertainty of income, the prospects
of losing social prestige in case of failure and loss of any future
economic opportunities if they failed. That stake was high enough
for "low-income" and "middle-class" technician employees to emerge
from traditionally non-business communities. Such persons, having
the rare opportunity to become owners of small industrial units
would be dedicated, sincere and trustworthy and would not fail the
Corporation; - this was the ultimate assumption that the integrity,
motivation and competence of the entrepreneurs would be the key
"securities".

Project viability and appraisal

The entire scheme depended on the competence of the entrepreneur and the viability of the project. Other conventional norms
were dropped. To identify the entrepreneurial and managerial competence of the individual, and the viability of the project, a professional organisation was set up within GIIC.

Experienced industrial experts with management backgrounds were
appointed to assess the adequacy and relevance of the entrepreneur's
experience, enterprise and competence for the project, and the
techno-economic viability of the proposal. Market researchers ensured the adequacy of demand for the product, the nature of the competition and to develop project ideas for new entrepreneurs.

Comprehensive technical, financial and entrepreneurial appraisal was to be prepared by technical experts before a loan was recommended.

Thus, liberal finance was provided, on the basis of a careful selection of entrepreneurs and projects. Industrial experience and understanding of the proposed business were given high weight in assessment. Commitment to the project, motivation and alternate plans were also important.

Nevertheless, procedures and formalities were kept few and simple to inspire confidence in these new entrepreneurs setting up industry for the first time. Unlike conservative, sceptical bankers, the organisation trusted the new entrepreneurs and counselled and guided them in obtaining information and know-how. The institution was built on a new "culture" of development banking rather than commercial money lending.

Some results achieved

This need-based finance opened wide the door for a variety of techno-entrepreneurs whose ownership potential and aspirations were previously prevented from fulfilment.

After 3 years, 500 techno-entrepreneurs obtained loans of Rs. 75 million. In the following 2 years 300 more projects were sanctioned. Within 6 years 800 projects were sanctioned of which 700 units are now in production representing an investment of Rs. 105 million. Their annual output is Rs. 137 million and paid employment is 7,000 workers in addition to the self-employment of the technicians and young engineer graduates.

The need-based finance facility has been subsequently extended to all new entrepreneurs (technicians and non-technicians) setting up industry for the first time, but lacking sufficient funds and securities to approach commercial banks. A wide variety of non-technical employees such as salesmen, managers, accountants, purchasing officers, and non-technical graduates are also eligible.

The New Entrepreneurs' Scheme (NES) has promoted 350 additional projects in the last 3 years, bringing the total of innovative schemes to 1,150 projects involving 1,500 entrepreneurs. Partnerships between technical and commercially experienced persons are growing and performing well.

Types of projects

These are small, modern manufacturing units ranging in investment from Rs. 30,000 for a repair-cum-maintenance workshop to Rs. 500,000 manufacturing precision jigs, fixtures or mini-computers. Principal industries are engineering 40 percent, chemicals 30 percent, plastics 15 percent and electronics 10 percent. Markets are spread over the entire State while many units compete nation-wide while others export their products.

Characteristics of entrepreneurs

Some 70 percent were previously employees in industrial and business concerns; 10 percent were professionals such as executives, managers, researchers and teachers in technical and science institutes; 15 percent were science, engineering or pharmaceutical graduates or diploma holders; while 5 percent were small traders under the NES.

Approximately 40 percent had more than 5 years of experience in industry; another 22 percent had worked 3-5 years; 20 percent had a limited 1-2 years experience, while the rest were inexperienced young graduates.

Whereas increased income and profit was described as the main motive for taking up business, almost a half were inspired by a desire to be self-employed (be my own boss), to use their skills and competence and to "achieve something in life".

Educationally, 46 percent had only reached matriculation or received less education, while 50 percent had degrees or diplomas. Average income prior to setting up industry was Rs. 700/- per month (see Table 10.2).

Performance of the units

The Corporation's faith in the competence, motivation and integrity of the new entrepreneurs has been justified. 65 percent of the units are making profits and paying back loans regularly. Some 20 percent are in difficulties with markets, working funds or production. The Industrial Extension Service of the Corporation is trying to diagnose problems and provide counselling to ensure that these problems do not lead to failures.

At present there are only 10 percent clear failures. Studies in Gujarat show that commercial banking failures are no less. Socioeconomic gains are pronounced in the innovative schemes since these new entrepreneurs come from non-business castes and non-industrial communities and are breaking traditional role-specialisations. There has been a multiplier effect on employment, income and production where employees leave jobs to set up industries.

10.2 ENTREPRENEURSHIP DEVELOPMENT PROGRAMME

Entrepreneurs are not simply born, they can also be developed. On this assumption, the Gujarat State Industrial Corporation launched the first Entrepreneurship Development Programme (EDP) in India in 1970.

Inspired by the success of the Technicians' Scheme, it was felt that there must be many employees such as workers, engineers, executives, managers, supervisors, small traders, salesmen and accountants who might have entrepreneurial potential and a desire to be on their own. However, they might be lacking self-confidence; their enterprises not fully developed and their motivation weak. With guidance, industrial information, and their ability to manage the enterprise developed by a comprehensive programme, many of them could become well-rounded, fully developed entrepreneurs setting-up new industries. A 3 months training-cum-development programme was started which now covers 15 centres of the State in developed and backward areas, large and small towns and some selected villages.

Selection and identification

Through sustained local promotional campaigns, advertisements, public meetings and door to door contacts, interest in thinking about one's own small industry by joining the development programme is generated. There are no educational, income, experience or know-how barriers when applying. Comprehensive entrepreneur selection, identification tests are applied with an assumption that not everyone and anyone can be developed into an entrepreneur.

Through behavioural-psychological tests in local languages, the potential entrepreneurial level is assessed[1]. A group of industry experts from the State industrial agencies and banks, successful entrepreneurs from the area and entrepreneurship trainers then explore the individual's potential for a manufacturing industry venture. Those who can be developed because of their experience, knowledge and attitude are selected for the programme.

Development inputs

A small scale industrialist has to be both an entrepreneur and a manager. His entrepreneurial capability may be enhanced through a 5 days full-time behavioural-psychological input package conducted by experts. The package covers:

The need to achieve: Motivation to achieve has been identified as an important input in entrepreneurial behaviour. This is evident in an individual's desire to compete with some standard of excellence and success in performance.

Risk-taking: Involves an inclination to taking calculated, moderate, intelligent risks. While avoiding both excessively high and low risk situations.

Positive self-concept: Includes self-confidence, self-efficiency, and a positive image of one's own abilities and achievements.

Initiative and independence: Showing initiative and independence in day-to-day behaviour. Capable of acting on one's own. A tendency to approach problems in order to solve them.

Hope for the future: A tendency to look at the future with hope. There may be dissatisfaction with present working conditions, but there is hope for a reasonably bright future.

Searching environment and time-bound planning: Not given to taking things for granted but searching the environment to seek answers to questions. Goals are time-bound with a desire to fulfil them.

---

[1] *Relevant entrepreneurial traits identified by research as relevant and measured by tests are listed under development inputs.*

Basic managerial understanding is developed in evening programmes of 2 hours covering aspects of setting-up and running one's own small industrial enterprise. Practical, down to earth basic concepts and "tricks of the trade" are discussed in the local language by practicing experts and successful entrepreneurs.

Initial counselling on industrial opportunities and preparing a project plan is provided by State Corporations industry experts, suppliers and traders. Each trainee is linked to a suitable project and is expected to develop a project report before training is finished.

Young engineers and fresh graduates, lacking in industrial experience, are placed in suitable factories during, or after, the programme to gain 6 to 12 month's shop floor experience. A Technical Training Workshop for engineering skills is part of the programme intended to develop technical skills, product development, experimentation and trial production.

Field visits for trainees to relevant small scale industries are organised to improve the information and motivation building. A full time specially selected project leader possessing industrial experience, training knowledge and leadership qualities is attached to each centre to act as the guide for each trainee responsible for individual development and meeting information and motivational needs.

At the programme's end the project report should be completed and submitted to the State Industrial Corporations and GIIC with its innovative finance scheme[1], where it is assessed objectively on merit, but processed on priority.

Performance

So far 1,240 new entrepreneurs have completed training and 667 units have already started production, many financed by the Technicians'Scheme/New Entrepreneurs' Scheme of GIIC. 230 projects are expected to begin production soon. Thus 897 net new industrial units, ranging in size from Rs. 20,000 to Rs. 1 million should be in operation employing an average 15 workers, with average investment of Rs. 200,000/- per project.

These newly developed entrepreneurs have performed well. 80 percent of them are making profits and only 10 percent are failures. Their return on investment averages 25 percent. Apart from developing those who otherwise would not have set up industries, the EDP provides a regular supply of informed entrepreneurs having viable projects for sponsoring financial institutions.

---

[1] *EDP is a joint venture of four major industrial state corporations: GIDC, the industrial development corporation for infrastructure; GIIC, the investment corporation for new entrepreneurs finance; the GSFC, the financial corporation for medium-scale projects; GSIC, the small industries corporation for raw materials and machinery purchase assistance.*

Sources of potential entrepreneurs

The Scheme has further widened its base for entrepreneurship. 45 percent of entrepreneurs were employees possessing work experience but lacking either confidence in managing a project or in setting it up. Another 20 percent were merchants of traders desiring to diversify into manufacturing but lacking motivation, risk-taking behaviour or knowledge about setting-up a unit. 20 percent have been fresh engineers, graduates or the unemployed who obtained work experience in the programme, project ideas from the project leaders and were prepared for relatively small industrial projects of an average investment of Rs. 50,000/-. 10 percent have been agriculturists mainly from small town programmes, some had capital surplus, others were motivated to diversify operations for economic and others to set up agro-based industries.

Strength of the programme

The success of the Gujarat EDP is attributed to:

(i)   the care taken in spotting persons with potential rather than relying on a mass training approach;

(ii)   a comprehensive, practical package of training inputs;

(iii)   dedicated, enterprising and qualified project leaders;

(iv)   a direct link with supportive financial and industrial agencies so that the trainee entrepreneur is not left on his own to struggle for finance and infrastructure. The GIIC provides 100 percent finance to resourceless trainees. The GSFC covers medium scale projects of traders and agriculturists who can contribute the required margins. The Gujarat Industrial Development Corporation provides ready factory sheds on liberal hire-purchase basis and the Gujarat Small Industries Corporation helps in raw-materials and machinery purchase;

(v)   the entrepreneurship development organisation is led by an entrepreneurship expert, with a team of project leaders and experts given freedom and flexibility to innovate and experiment in this complex new field. The programme is relatively inexpensive. The cost per trainee works out to Rs. 1,100 in developed areas and Rs. 1,500 in backward areas. The cost per factory has been Rs. 1,800 and Rs. 2,600 respectively for developed and backward areas.

10.3   READY INDUSTRIAL INFRASTRUCTURE

Organised small scale industry needs infrastructure such as land, factory buildings, power, water, roads, drainage, communications and services. For small enterprises, the cost of developed land with a building usually amounts to 30-35 percent of the project cost. While renting premises in cities is difficult and costly, purchasing land and construction factories is a time consuming, frustrating process for a new entrepreneur.

Realising the importance of ready infrastructure at carefully selected industrial locations, an exclusive organisation has been set up in Gujarat. The Gujarat Industrial Development Corporation

(GIDC) is a State government undertaking under autonomous management. With loans from the State Government, open-market borrowing and project loans from banks, GIDC has developed 79 industrial estates throughout the State taking up 10,000 hectares of land and 4,000 ready factory buildings, having full facilities of power, water, roads and communications. A new entrepreneur can choose from 10 different types of sheds (700 sq.ft. to 4,000 sq.ft.) available on hire-purchase to avoid tying up funds in unproductive assets. Easy terms are offered to new entrepreneurs:

(i)   no down payment;

(ii)   moratorium on repayment for 3 years;

(iii)   9 years to pay for price of land and shed;

(iv)   interest payable during moratorium at $4\frac{1}{2}$ percent and later at 9 percent.

Benefits to entrepreneurs

The availability of sheds has saved entrepreneurs 12 to 18 months in starting production. Using a different link to the Gujarat Industrial Investment Corporation, which appraises the loan applications of new entrepreneurs, a shed of suitable size in a sound location is automatically allotted when the GIIC sanctions a loan. With 100 percent finance for plant, machinery, working funds and pre-operative expenses, and no down payment on ready sheds the entrepreneur can begin production without further initial investment. Liberal terms, selected by the moratorium on land and building, ensures enough time to settle down to production before repayment starts. Arrangements of power, water, telephones, banking and postal services are taken care of by GIDC the catalyst for the industrial estate. Banks hesitant to finance new entrepreneurs for land and building are brought in to finance the Corporation on a long-term loan basis for industrial estate projects.

Results to date

2,500 units are in production in the GIDC estates, of which 96 percent are small scale. Of some 3,500 sheds constructed, 3,000 are all allotted. Apart from some 5 to 7 estates, there is no problem of unoccupied factory buildings. The significance of the GIDC's achievements in small scale industries development is that in most States in India, estates with ready sheds have remained idle, massive investments in land, sheds, power and water schemes are unproductively tied up. Some state agencies avoid sheds programmes altogether or construct facilities *after* the demand is registered thereby taking away the 'early start' advantage of ready facilities. Most operating estates provide sheds at highly subsidised rents.

GIDC has not subsidised sheds for sale. Its ready supply and soft repayment terms have been attractive to entrepreneurs. However, demand assessment in specific locations is the key to advanced construction and lack of idle sheds. This requires the appropriate organisation of a development economist, a planner, a marketing expert, several engineers, an architect and regional development officers. The planning team works on an area development approach by which even for the smallest towns, careful demand assessment based on industrial-cum-entrepreneurial potential analysis is carried out and, if

necessary, entrepreneur training programmes conducted before an estate
is set up and shed construction starts. In industrial cities where
a large number of small enterprises are located, demand projections
for 2-3 years are made and sheds prepared ahead of time.

10.4 CONCLUSIONS

The performance of new entrepreneurs financed and developed
under these innovative schemes has shown that faith in their abilities
and support on only marginal tangible securities can be justified.
Sources of entrepreneurship can be diversified and supply of entrepreneurs accelerated if conventional banking approaches to industrial
finance are substituted with need-based finance.

Business or industry experience is a key to motivation, skill
and confidence development, and exposure to opportunities.

Promotional agencies, using a development approach, can facilitate new enterprise formation with organised inputs of pre-investment
counselling on industrial projects, preparation of bankable proposals
and in liberally financing them to use entrepreneurs' skills and
enterprise setting up small scale units.

It may be necessary to set up State sponsored specialised organisations for enterprise development and promotion functions since
small scale industries development, through new and diverse sources
of entrepreneurs has an implied high risk. These functions are not
likely to be undertaken by commercial banks or private lending agencies which have the ready option to cater to the needs of established
businessmen and entrepreneurs with high return and low risk. Creation of new development agencies could be complementary rather than
competitive to conventional agencies. With imaginative inter-insti-
tutional coordination, even conservative banks can be brought in to
provide working funds and financial support for development projects.

The Gujarat experience indicates that this unconventional method
of promoting entrepreneurs is not as risky as some skeptics would
make it appear. The new (resourceless) small scale entrepreneurs
have proved to be highly competent and reliable, and their failure
rate has been low.

The success of a small enterprise, however, depends upon the
entrepreneurial and managerial competence of the man behind the project and the soundness of his proposal. All three must be adequately
assessed. Commitment to new entrepreneurs must be supported by
sound, objective assessment by mature industrial experts if it is not
to turn into a "welfare programme". A large number of failing units
does not contribute to development, nor does it benefit the entrepreneurs concerned.

Adequate, well-tested tools and techniques are available to
assess entrepreneurial potential and develop new entrepreneurs
through comprehensive development programmes.

The key to success lies in the package of assistance provided to
the new entrepreneurs. Co-ordination among various development agencies has to be smooth, otherwise, multiple promotional agencies can
cause as much frustration among entrepreneurs as would their absence.

TABLE 10.1: COMPARATIVE MEANS OF FINANCING FUNDING BY INNOVATIVE TECHNICIANS' SCHEME VERSUS CONVENTIONAL BANKING

Project Component Costs (Rupees)	Innovative Technicians' Scheme					Conventional Bank Scheme		
	GIDC	GIIC	Bank	Entre-preneurs	Total	Bank	Entre-preneurs	Total
Land and building	60 000 (100%)	-	-	-	60 000	42 000 (70%)	18 000 (30%)	60 000
Machinery and equipment	-	1 55 000 (100%)	-	-	1 55 000	93 000 (60%)	62.000 (40%)	1 55 000
Working capital	-	20 000 (25%)	55 000 (75%)	-	75 000	55 000 (75%)	20.000 (25%)	75 000
Preliminary and pre-operative expenses	-	5 000 (50%)	-	5.000 (50%)	10 000	-	10 000 (100%)	10 000
Total (Rs)	60 000	1 80 000	55 000	5 000	3 00 000	1 90 000	1 10 000	3 00 000
Percentage	(20%)	(60%)	(18%)	(2%)	(100%)	(63%)	(37%)	(100%)

TABLE 10.2: CHARACTERISTICS OF THE TECHNICIAN ENTREPRENEURS BY AGE, EDUCATION, OCCUPATION AND EXPERIENCE

Age

	20 or less	21-30	31-40	41-50
Total No.	3	249	325	144
% of total	0.42	34.54	45.08	19.96

Education

	Below SSC	SSCE	College drop-out	Diploma holders	Degree holders
Total No.	257	75	25	116	248
% of total	35.64	10.40	3.47	16.09	34.40

Previous occupation

	Un-employed	Stu-dent	Employed in factory	Trade or sales	Professionals	Other
Total No.	18	8	515	14	136	30
% of total	2.50	1.11	71.43	1.94	18.86	4.16

Years of experience

	None	Less than one year	1 to 2 years	3-5 years	More than five years
Total No.	33	101	140	158	284
% of total	4.58	14.01	19.42	21.92	40.07

Note (1) Total number of technician entrepreneurs = 721.

(2) Total number of factory units = 458.

PART IV

SMALL ENTERPRISE DEVELOPMENT IN SELECTED COUNTRIES

ALGERIA

Mohamed Arezki Isli[1]

11

The development of small- and medium-scale industries (SMI) in Algeria has been embodied in the national general economic and social development policy needed for planning investments based on intense industrialisation.

The first three National Plans permitted the setting up of a large number of SMIs managed by various promoters in the public (National Societies and local communities) and private sectors.

The expanding SMI sector, essential for integrating other economic sectors, now requires more adequate promotional, financial and technical assistance, in the form of studies, project development and training, if existing development objectives are to be met.

11.1 POLICY FOR DEVELOPING SMALL AND MEDIUM INDUSTRIES

In order to give a clear image of the place occupied by SMIs in Algeria and their objectives, it will be necessary to describe some of the features of the country's economic system.

The economic setting

The Algerian economy is a planned one in which the public sector predominates, especially in industry, agriculture and in providing infrastructure. The state controls the economy through a centralised system of financing investments.

The public industrial sector is organised into National Societies which generally control all production units in a given branch. These National Societies constitute the machinery through which the State applies its economic policy. Consequently, they act as sectoral planning units. Since 1966, communes have been playing a very important role as basic economic, political and social units in the planning system.

---

[1] *Directeur Général, Institut National de la Productivité et du Développement (INPED), Algiers, Algeria.*

Immediately after gaining independence, Algeria decided to base its development strategy on industry. Therefore, when allocating investment funds, priority was given to the industrial sector during the Three-Year Provisional Plan (1967-69) but more particularly during the first Four-Year Plan (1970-73) which devoted 45 percent of over-all investments, namely 12,400 million dinars (1 dollar = 4.5 dinars), to industry.

During the period of the Plan, this amount increased by 4.129 million dinars. Thus, at the end of the first Four-Year Plan, 46 percent of investments were devoted to industry. This major investment effort produced an average annual growth rate of 9.5 percent in the gross industrial product.

In the second Four-Year Plan (1974-77) industrial development continued to take first place, as this sector received 24,500 million dinnars or 45 percent of all planned investments during the period of the Plan. This large-scale industrialisation effort in the two Plans has three main objectives:

- to satisfy domestic demand for equipment and consumer goods;

- to establish the foundations of a modern economy by industrialising through setting up basic industries conducive to growth;

- to increase currency reserves by extracting and marketing hydrocarbons.

This large-scale industrial sector investment has involved setting up certain privileged points in the country of "growth nuclei" or industry-propagating industries (ANNABA, ARZEW and SKIKDA concerned mainly with gas, oil and iron and steel) which are known to exert a force of attraction on surrounding economic spheres. These "nuclei" have made it possible to achieve high growth rates in industrial output, as shown by the following results (expressed in real terms):

Year	Growth rate
1970	9%
1971	13%
1972	12%
1973	20%

However, despite the benefits in growth of industrial output and resulting economic independence, the setting up of these industries is impeded by various factors which it is appropriate to mention. These can be summarised as follows:

(i)   Algeria inherited an unbalanced economy from the colonial period. Furthermore, because the disjointed state of the economy at the beginning of industrialisation, the attraction forces were weaker than the polarisation (or concentration) forces. Consequently, there was a risk that development based exclusively on the privileged points constituted by these "growth nuclei" might actually accentuate initial regional disparities and imbalances.

(ii)   The basic industries set up at these "growth nuclei" use sophisticated capital-intensive production techniques, for which there are few, if any, efficient alternatives. A direct result is that these industries have very little job-creating capacity.

(iii) Concentration of industrial activity at certain points in the country is likely to bring about over-rapid and excessive town development with the heavy social costs which that usually implies.

Algerian planners, taking these various factors into account introduced in 1967, side by side with development plans based on industry, a series of regional development programmes called "special programmes" (not included in the Plan), covering regional, social and economic measures with respect to agriculture and infrastructures, involving the creation of small industrial units. Examples include the following special wilayate programmes[1]: Oasis (1966), Aures (1968), Tizi-Ouzou (1968), Titteri (1969), Tlemcen (1970), Setif (1970), Saida (1971), El-Asnam (1972), Constantine (1973) and Annaba (1973).

Systematisation of these special programmes and their incorporation in the Plan led to the SMI programmes of the two Four-Year Plans (1970-73) and (1974-77).

Objectives of the SMIs

Prior to the first Four-Year Plan 1970-73, SMI were already recognised as essential to the economic and social development of the country, and not merely as a marginal and secondary sector. In 1969, the Ministry of Industry and Power had already accepted the principle of launching an SMI programme.

The harmonious development of this sector, vital for the industrial future of the country, called for a coherent and sustained promotion policy taking into account the global industrial development strategy with particular regard to:

- consolidating the countrywide industrial network;

- strengthening the regional equilibrium policy;

- increasing integration of the national economy.

The second Four Year Plan (1974-77) established four specific objectives for the SMIs:

(i)   distributing industry throughout the country, by decentralising economic activities outside the already over-developed industrial centres;

(ii)   satisfying local needs by local production, thus improving incomes in rural areas;

(iii) stabilising local resources;

----

[1] A wilaya is one of the 31 administrative divisions of a territory, equivalent to a French province or département.

(iv) choosing appropriate technologies to provide local jobs, thus minimising migration.

The development strategy of SMI programmes

Having established the objectives of the SMI programmes, the economic measures taken to achieve them can now be examined.

The first requirement is that programmes shall be coherent; it is not a question of setting up units indiscriminately, anywhere, at any price. The various projects constituting a programme must not only attain their economic projection, which reflect the general orientation the planner has for the programme, but they must also be compatible with one another. The programme must also harmonise with other sectors and branches of the national economy as follows:

Industrial sub-sectors

A small industrial enterprise cannot be set up in just any branch. It is well-known that economies of scale and technical efficiency thresholds give a clear advantage to large industries in certain areas of production. It is, therefore, necessary to adopt viable projects for SMIs for which there exist both an adequate domestic market and operating conditions suitable for small industries rather than the concentration of production in large units.

Geographical distribution

Special site criteria must be established for each project to determine the possible impact of SMI development on the decentralisation of employment and regionalisation of development.

Within and between industrial sub-sectors

Algerian SMI programmes are not branch programmes. They are designed to rationalise and complement programming in fields which do not constitute large scale industry (National Societies).

Consequently, the SMI programmes take the form of priority programmes for SMI units, complementary to the development projects of the National Societies. These units provide backing, in some branches, for large scale industry production, or collaborate with those industries, by subcontracting, in producing a given final product.

For this reason, SMI projects within a given branch of industry must first of all be coherent one with the other and, secondly, coherent with other units of the National Societies constituting the branch. This constitutes an essential macro-economic coherence. This coherence must obviously also exist between the SMI units of a branch in relation to the SMI units or National Societies of a complementary branch.

Economic complexes

The final type of coherence stems naturally from the preceding one and relates to the balance to be established between supply and demand of goods and services and the labour market.

Goods and services. In order to determine the outputs required from SMI projects in the various branches of industry in which these can be programmed (coherence requirement), it is obviously necessary to know the estimated final and intermediate demands for the various products during the Plan period, the supply planned by the National Societies during the same period and the degree to which the SMIs and National Societies have achieved the outputs foreseen in the previous Plan.

If there is sufficient balance between supply and demand, there is obviously no need to plan the output of SMIs in the branch. Where demand exceeds supply, some standard or basic projects have to be planned. The distribution of basic projects over various local units will depend on the shortfall of supply. This procedure is determined by the complementary nature of the SMI programmes.

Labour market. The procedure described for the goods and services market also applies to the labour market, except that it is unlikely that there will be a balance between labour supply and demand if only National Society projects are taken into account. It must be remembered that creating jobs remains one of the main objectives of the SMI programmes.

11.2 FINANCIAL AND TECHNICAL ASSISTANCE STRUCTURES

Responsibility for promoting SMIs is shared by many executors.

SMI promotion bodies

For public SMI's the promotion bodies include technical ministries, National Societies, local communities, co-operatives, and mass organisations.

The Secretary of State for the Plan centralises all projects of these bodies and draws up a programme which is discussed by an interministerial committee before being incorporated in the general economic and social development plan for the country.

SMIs in the private sector are set up by national entrepreneurs supported by chambers of commerce and industry. Private investments have to comply with the private investments code adopted in 1966. Consequently, such investments require the approval of the regional commissions and the national private investments commission.

SMI-financing bodies

Generally speaking, the financing of public investments in Algeria is closely centralised. Projects can be financed by reimbursable assistance, in the form of external loans granted by national financial institutes, or in the form of external loans.

By applying standard procedures, a financing plan is drawn up for each project and submitted to the technical investments financing committee of the Banque Algérienne de Développement (BAD). Once a financial plan is approved for a project, loan agreements are signed by the firm and local financial institutes to permit expenditure. The Banque Algérienne de Développement has a monopoly on long-term loans and finance investments.

The primary banks (CPA and BNA) virtually hold a monopoly over short- and medium-term loans and, therefore, are responsible for financing exports.

Each enterprise is associated with only one bank. As a result, the state is in full control of the public and private sectors. The centralisation of export financing by primary banks and the abolition of self-financing means that undertakings must take out bank loans.

Technical assistance bodies

Technical assistance for public SMIs is provided by national planning offices answerable to technical ministries. These include INPED, SNERI, SOMERI, ECOTEC and the engineering services of the National Societies.

Because of the extensive need for technical assistance, it is also sought abroad, particularly engineering services. Since priority is given to the public sector, technical assistance to private SMIs is restricted to management and marketing assistance provided by chambers of commerce and industry.

11.3   RESULTS OF THE SMI PROMOTION POLICY

It is extremely difficult to assess accurately efforts to promote SMIs through the special programmes and the first and second Four-Year Plans. This difficulty arises because of the large number of activities and promoters operating in this sector. Some idea of these results can be provided by certain partial data such as those obtained from the programmes, the relevant budgetary appropriations, the number of units set up and the jobs created other than by the National Societies.

Special programmes

One hundred SMI projects, most of which are devoted to traditional crafts, have been planned within special programmes covering five wilayate.

SMI programmes under the Four-Year Plans

One hundred and fifty projects were included in the first Four-Year Plan. Local industry covers four major sectors:

TABLE 11.1: PROJECTS OF THE FIRST FOUR-YEAR PLAN	
Sectors	Number
The SMI (in practical terms) including mechanical construction, light chemical engineering, building materials, textiles, leathers and hides, wood and paper, food-crop industries	58
Traditional craft production	75
Tourism and local spa treatment	17
Total Small and medium-scale enterprises (SME)	150
Total budget: 110 million dinars.	

Sectors TABLE 11.2: PROJECTS OF THE SECOND FOUR-YEAR PLAN	Number
Building materials	216
Metal industry	62
Wood and paper	59
Food-crop industries	19
Textiles	5
Light chemical engineering	15
Total (Small and medium-scale industries)	376
Traditional crafts	15
Service crafts	55
Tourism and spa treatment	116
Total Small and medium-scale enterprises (SME)	562
Total budget: 1 128 million dinars.	

According to information supplied by the Secretary of State for the Plan, 200 public SME projects (SMI, crafts and service) were completed between 1969 and 1976, creating 12,000 new jobs in rural areas.

In addition, about 730 new projects were undertaken between 1967 and 1973 by the private sector, creating 23,000 new jobs. Private investment has concentrated particularly in textiles, light chemical engineering and food industries.

In addition, the National Societies have set up a large number of SMIs for their own purposes, especially for services such as maintenance and repair.

11.4   MAIN PROBLEMS AND SOLUTIONS PROPOSED

Financing

Financing SMI projects is governed by public investments regulations where authorisation of project expenditure is subject to many administrative formalities.

Although these provisions are intended to ensure better planning of the country's financial resources, in practice they constitute a major bottleneck in completing projects, because of delays caused.

Furthermore, the apparent conflict between profitability of SMIs and the social and economic objectives established for them handicap evaluation of the various projects. Their social and economic objectives may cause extra production costs because of excessive decentralisation or using obsolescent techniques to promote job-creation, issues which are not always completely rational from a financial viewpoint.

Cheaper loans

In order to popularise SMIs, a low interest rate merely covering bank costs, might be adopted for investment loans in place of the present rate which ranks national societies and SMIs on an equal footing.

Tax and customs relief

To reduce costs, the SMI units might be exempted from paying specific income and other taxes during their first years of operation.

Subsidies

Training SMI supervisors and technicians, unforeseen in the appropriations of past plans, is to be subsidised under the next plan. Subsidised raw materials prices used by local SMIs in special areas are to be maintained.

Appropriate support might be provided for exporting selected goods produced by SMIs.

Various measures should also make it possible to reduce the cost of SMI infrastructures by creating industrial zones. This should reduce the financial burden which SMIs have to face when beginning operations to provide such items as power supply systems and road building.

Technical assistance

Providing an institutional framework and suitable economic conditions are not enough to ensure the promotion and viability of SMIs. Such efforts need to be complemented by facilities support which these enterprises cannot provide for themselves.

This support may take two forms: technical assistance for establishing SMIs and management training.

Technical assistance for establishing SMIs

The SMI sector is very sensitive to the weaknesses of studies, design and execution presently existing at the national level and which may be explained for several reasons:

- The large number of units planned and their wide geographical scatter (604 projects spread over the country's 31 wilayate) necessitate a large number of studies and considerable building capacity.
- Conducting individual studies for SMI projects makes for prohibitive engineering costs relative to the total budget allocated to each project. Because of this, few design offices have taken an interest in this sector.
- There are no engineering firms with a structure adapted to the scale of the sector specialised in setting up SMIs.

- The shortage of resources for carrying out projects is particularly marked in the case of SMIs, as local communities (wilayate, dairate, communes) responsible for building have neither the human nor the technical means necessary, nor do they possess the experience needed to supervise projects.

In fact, the public works units of wilayate and communal works enterprises have difficulty in satisfying demands of housing, health and socio-educational sectors in studies and construction.

Measures required in this field are:

- reinforcing national design and engineering units participating in SMI programmes;
- reinforcing National Societies as technical counsellors for design and building of SMI enterprises in their respective branches. Those National Societies with experience in techniques and technologies should participate, directly or indirectly, in engineering activities associated with setting up SMIs. Such technical assistance can be encouraged by establishing legal relations facilitating service contracts between National Societies and SMIs.

National Societies, performing their normal role as leaders of their branches, should also carry out applied research programmes dealing with SMIs located upstream and downstream in their field of activity.

Services which National Societies could make available to SMIs could include: study and developing new products and processes, testing installations, standardisation and quality control, preparing technical specifications and assistance in acquiring licences.

The creation of industrial zones would facilitate the siting of SMIs having difficulties carrying out soil analyses, preparing site equipment such as roads, power and water. It would be possible to cut down costs of SMI premises considerably and, at the same time, to centralise marketing and certain supply functions for a group of SMI units such as bulk buying machine and spare parts.

Management training

The SMIs are, at present, inadequately managed. Due to the shortage of skilled managers, enterprises which have been set up are unable to develop an efficient management system rapidly enough.

Shortage of supervisors is the limiting factor in the launching and efficient operation of SMIs. Acceleration of the SMI programmes in the course of future development plans will merely increase the need for managers, especially since most new projects will be initiated by local communities possessing little industrial experience.

Therefore, it will be necessary to expand existing training programmes to provide the requisite projects managers, supervisors and skilled workers.

AUSTRALIA

Geoffrey G. Meredith[1]

12

Australia is a federal parliamentary state and a member of the
Commonwealth of Nations occupying the world's smallest continent as
an island nation with an area of 3 million square miles and a population in 1977 of 14 million. Population is concentrated on a relatively narrow coastal strip along the eastern and south eastern sea-
bord of the island from the northern city of Brisbane, capital of
the state of Queensland; through to Sydney in New South Wales;
Canberra, the national capital; Melbourne, capital of Victoria; to
Adelaide, in South Australia. A further concentration of population
in the south western corner is centred on Perth, capital of the
State of Western Australia.

Geographical features of the continent have a significant
impact on commerce and industry and the structure and performance of
small enterprises. Traditionally Australia has relied on natural
resources for its growth and development and its relatively high
standard of living. Australia is often seen as a "primary producer"
with an infant manufacturing sector and hence heavily relies on
imports of consumer products.

The advent of international conflicts, changes in the structure
of the Commonwealth of Nations, and shifts in international trade
have all led to significant changes in Australian industry. Recent
initiatives by government and the private enterprise sector in the
field of small enterprise policy and development suggest that an
increasing proportion of Australian industry will be taken up by
small scale non-rural enterprises contributing to the manufacturing
as well as retail and service sectors.

---

[1] *Professor and Head, Department of Accounting and Financial
Management, and Director, Research Centre for Small Business and
Professional Development, University of New England, Armidale,
Australia.*

12.1 SMALL ENTERPRISES IN THE AUSTRALIAN ECONOMY

Small enterprises identified

A uniform definition of a small enterprise has not been adopted as yet in Australia. One attempt to define a small enterprise was made by the national government's Wiltshire Committee - a Committee established by the national government in 1968 to examine small enterprises with particular reference to the manufacturing sector[1].

The Wiltshire Committee defined small enterprises as businesses in which one or two persons are required to make all critical management decisions - on financing, accounting, personnel, purchasing, processing or servicing, marketing and selling - without the aid of internal specialists and with owners who have specific knowledge in only one or two functional areas. The Wiltshire Committee assumed that this definition would apply to the majority of enterprises in Australia with fewer than 100 employees.

As various state governments in Australia have introduced programmes and policies for small enterprises, each has defined small enterprise for their own purpose. For example the Victorian Government identifies a small enterprise in its Small Business Development Corporation Act 1976[2] as one:

(i)   which is wholly owned and operated by an individual person or individual persons in partnership or by a proprietary company within the meaning of the Companies Act 1961, and which:

- has a relatively small share of the market in which it competes;

- is managed personally by the owners or directors (as the case requires), and

- does not form part of a large business or enterprise; or

(ii)   which is owned and operated by any person or persons, whether corporate or unincorporate, specified by a proclamation of the Governor in Council.

Given the level of interest in the 1970s on small enterprise programmes, it can be anticipated that a uniform definition will be adopted by all governments in Australia in the near future.

Australian industry statistics

Given the definitional problems referred to previously, official statistics available in Australia are deficient in that it is difficult to identify the significance of small enterprises in the Australian economy. An analysis of the data available from

---

[1] F.M. Wiltshire (Chairman): Report of the committee on small business (Department of Trade and Industry, Canberra, 1973).

[2] Legislative Assembly - Read April 1976: "A bill to constitute a small business development corporation to encourage and promote the development of small business." Reference 750/27.4.1976.

Taxation Statistics and from figures produced by the Australian
Bureau of Statistics does give an indication of Australian industry
structure and the broad place of small enterprises in that structure.

Table 12.1 is based on Taxation Statistics for the income year
1970-1971 and the figures suggest that small enterprises may account
for some 93 percent of manufacturing enterprises, 97 percent of
wholesale and retail enterprises and at least 93 percent of finance,
insurance, real estate and business service enterprises. While some
partnerships and private companies may not be regarded as small
enterprises, to offset this position, some public companies would be
regarded as small enterprise.

TABLE 12.1:   BREAKDOWN BY TYPES OF BUSINESS

Type of business	Manufacturing		Wholesale and Retail		Finance, Insurance, Real Estate and Business Services	
	No.	%	No.	%	No.	%
Sole proprietor	3,273	9.2	16,752	14.1	12,271	19.6
Partnership	15,823	44.2	78,359	66.1	15,693	25.0
Private Co.	14,104	39.4	21,041	17.7	30,504	48.6
Public Co.	2,563	7.2	2,449	2.1	4,259	6.8
Totals	35,763	100.0	118,601	100.0	62,727	100.0

Source: Taxation Statistics 1971/72 (Income Year 1970/71).

Based on figures available from the Australian Bureau of Statistics, Table 12.2 sets out an estimate of the contribution of
small manufacturing enterprises to the Australian economy in terms
of enterprise numbers, and the proportion of employment, turnover,
wages and salaries, and value added applicable to small manufacturing
enterprises. For purposes of Table 12.2 a small manufacturing enterprise is defined as one employing fewer than 100 persons.

TABLE 12.2: SIZE OF ENTERPRISE BY EMPLOYMENT, TURNOVER,
WAGES AND SALARIES, AND VALUE ADDED

Size of enterprise	No. of enterprises	Employment	Turnover	Wages & salaries	Value added
Enterprises<100	93%	38%	34%	35%	34%
Enterprises>100	7%	62%	66%	65%	66%
	100%	100%	100%	100%	100%

During the period 1968-1969 to 1973-1974 some industry subdi-
visions numbers declined, however the majority reported increases
indicating an overall growth in the number of enterprises during the
five years. Manufacturing enterprise numbers increased by 20.6 percent, wholesale trade enterprises by 17.1 percent and retail trade
enterprises by 15.6 percent. Highest percentage increases were

attributable to the smallest of the enterprises in each industry, and those enterprises employing fewer than 10 persons. In particular, the retail field is dominated by enterprises with fewer than 10 persons per enterprise. In 1973-74, 125,000 of the total of 134,000 retail enterprises employed fewer than 10 persons. Table 12.3 reports average employment per establishment for a selected group of retailing enterprises.

TABLE 12.3: RETAILING INDUSTRIES BY TYPE AND EMPLOYMENT		
SELECTED RETAILING INDUSTRIES		
Type of retailing	Number of establishments 1973-74	Persons employed per establishment 1973-74
Furniture and floor covering stores	2,686	5.9
Fabric and household textile stores	2,921	4.3
Menswear stores	3,250	4.7
Women's, girls' and infants' wear stores	8,173	4.0
Footwear stores	2,304	4.8
Household appliances stores	3,002	6.2
Electrical appliance repairers	1,560	3.9
China, glass and handware stores	2,142	4.3
Watchmakers and jewellers	2,211	4.1
Musical and record stores	819	4.3
Nurserymen and florists	1,918	3.1
Sports, bicycles and toy stores	2,302	3.2
Boat and caravan dealers	883	4.6
Cafes and restaurants	5,123	9.5

Source: ABS, Census of retail establishments, 1973-74.

In summary, available statistics suggest that small enterprises in the manufacturing, wholesale and retail and service sectors of Australian industry are significant in terms of the number of enterprises, contribution to employment, wages paid, value added and turnover. When the Wiltshire Committee was announced by the Minister of the day, the Minister commented

"small business plays a vital role in the Australian economy. It is a necessary element in the preservation and stimulation of competition, which is the main spring of economic efficiency. It provides a wide range of opportunities for the exercise of personal initiative and judgement, and scope for innovatory talents. In addition, it provides a wide range of employment opportunities - a particularly significant factor outside metropolitan areas. Because their resources are limited, small businesses face a number of problems which they must overcome if they are to flourish and to sustain their contribution to our development. It is clearly in the national

interest that small business management should receive guidance in the best ways to deal with these problems."[1]

The above comments confirm the view that small enterprises are significant for the Australian economy and Government initiatives are justified.

12.2 PROBLEMS FACED BY SMALL ENTERPRISE OWNERS

Numerous articles have appeared on this subject, the most recent being by Turnbull[2].

Lack of experience and/or management training

Individuals planning to set up a new business in Australia are not required to undertake any training or to produce evidence of experience before registering the new enterprise. It is not surprising therefore, that lack of experience and lack of training is frequently given as the reason for small enterprise failures in Australia. Until recently very few teaching institutions had introduced specific training programmes for potential small enterprise owners and operating owner/managers.

Isolation/lack of information

Australia is a large nation with a relatively small population. Small enterprise owners are often physically isolated in decentralized centres, while sources of information tend to be concentrated in state capital cities or the national capital, Canberra. Communication between owners and/or between governments and owners has remained a problem and recent government initiatives have attempted to overcome this problem.

Availability of capital[3]

Capital for business enterprises is usually supplied in Australia by private-enterprise, government-sponsored banks, or large financial institutions. The number of banks is closely controlled by government, interest rates are largely influenced by government policy, and lending policy is also closely monitored and controlled. Few specialised schemes for loans to small enterprises have been launched in Australia and therefore small enterprises in Australia tend to be under-capitalised and operating under aggravated financial conditions.

---

[1] *Press statement by the Minister for Trade and Industry, the Rt. Hon. John McEwen, Canberra, A.C.T., 16th January 1968.*

[2] *R.M. Turnbull: "Smaller businesses in the Australian Economy" in The Chartered Accountant in Australia, (Vol. 48, No. 2, August 1977), p. 4-8.*

[3] *R.G. Bird and D.J.P. Juttner: The financing of small business in the manufacturing sector (Australian and New Zealand Association for the Advancement of Science, 46th Congress, January 1975).*

High debt cost

Many small enterprises in Australia claim that loans when rene-
gotiated command high interest rates. As stated earlier, no special
loan schemes at controlled interest rates are operating in Australia
other than through a limited scheme by the National Government's
Commonwealth Banking Corporation Scheme for special loans to small
manufacturers. These loans have only been available in the past
"as a last resort" although recent action has been taken to modify
this restriction.

Inflation

During the 1970's Australia has experienced a relatively high
annual inflation rate. The national government hopes to reduce the
inflation rate to a single figure. Inflation - with its characteristic rising expenses - has caused problems for small enterprise
owners since there is often a reluctance (or an inability) to pass
on their rising expenses through the price system. In many cases
the problem is self-inflicted, since small enterprise owners have
inadequate information systems.

Declining productivity and high labour costs

Appropriate measures of productivity vary, but small enterprises
in Australia have been encouraged to measure the relationship between
turnover, gross profit, expenses and net profit and the number of
persons in the enterprise and total wages paid. While sales per
person and gross profits per person have been increasing for small
enterprises in Australia, expenses per person have been increasing
at a faster rate, so that net profit per person has declined. Sales
per dollar wages paid and profits per dollar wages paid have also
declined from year to year, indicating that sales turnover and profits
have not been able to keep pace with rising labour costs. These
factors have contributed to declining profitability.

Inadequate information systems

Accepting the Wiltshire Committee definition of small enterprises, owners generally do not have experience or knowledge of all
functional areas of management - in particular financial management.
Unfortunately, public (practising) accountants providing services
for small enterprises in Australia often restrict available services
to taxation and simple bookkeeping for taxation purposes. Few Australian small enterprises have adequate information systems.

Absence of counselling/consulting services

A number of private consulting firms are active in Australia;
however, few small enterprises obtain advice from these consulting
firms and few consulting firms have specialised in the field of
small enterprise advisory services. Banks have traditionally not
provided counselling services for small enterprise clients. Accountants in public practice have been overly concerned with taxation
advice. Solicitors concentrate on specialised legal advice, and
trade associations have been largely concerned with industry award
and trade matters rather than management counselling or advisory
services. Academics, as business consultants, have not made any
significant impact on meeting the needs of small enterprises.

Declining profitability

Evidence exists to show that small enterprises in Australia are technically efficient. Profitability however, has been declining. It has been estimated by the University of New England's Research Centre that more than 60 percent of all small enterprises fail to earn a profit which can provide owners with an adequate reward for time, skill, and responsibility; plus a return on investment in the enterprise. Declining profitability contributes to liquidity crises, restrictions in enterprise expansion and investment.

Absence of government policies

Only since 1973 have state and national governments given serious attention to policies and programmes for small enterprises. In the past, small enterprises have been given no special attention or privileges through legislation in the field of taxation, training, statistics, employment, or national development policy. Recent policy changes are discussed in this paper. Most commentators emphasise "taxation" as a major problem facing small enterprise owners in Australia[1].

Australian taxation laws levy a 46 percent taxation rate on proprietory (private) companies and a further levy is payable unless profits are "sufficiently" distributed to owners. The majority of proprietory companies in Australia are "small enterprises".

Perhaps many problems listed above arise from deficiencies in management, but some arise from the absence of government policy. As a result of these problems and recognition of the significance of small enterprises in the Australian economy, government initiatives have been taken.

12.3 GOVERNMENT INITIATIVES IN SMALL ENTERPRISE DEVELOPMENT

Initiatives at national government level

The first significant initiative taken by government in Australia was the establishment of the Wiltshire Committee in 1968 by the national government of the day. This Committee was established to assist the (then) Department of Trade and Industry in exploring ways of providing guidance for small manufacturing enterprise management in its attempts to improve efficiency.

The Wiltshire Committee presented its report to government in 1971 and concluded:

"The Committee is convinced that the magnitude and significance of small business, the quite special nature of its problems, and its potential, warrants active Commonwealth sponsorship of means to develop its efficiency and growth. Small business is a significant factor in all communities

---

[1] *B.L. Johns and W.C. Dunlop: The effects of income taxation on small business in Australia, (5th Conference of Economists, Brisbane, August 1975), p. 37.*

in Australia. Efficient small business is important to Australia's development, but because of its problems, its optimum efficiency will not be achieved without assistance by outside agencies. It is the Committee's considered belief that initiatives exercised by central government are the only way to bring this about."[1]

The Committee recommended that a "continuing body" be established to ensure that on-going effort achieved desired objectives in the field of small business development. The Committee further recommended that the continuing body work closely with multiplier agencies in the economy - trade associations, chambers of commerce, chambers of manufacturers, tertiary institutions, professional bodies and government - to achieve its specific aims.

A National Small Business Bureau was established in the national capital Canberra in November 1973 to develop and progressively implement a national programme of assistance in the secondary and tertiary sectors.

When the then Minister opened a national small business seminar in Canberra announcing the Australian Government's decision to establish the Bureau, the Minister made some significant points concerning policy for small enterprise development in Australia[2]:

"A national programme which encourages and facilitates the development of efficient and viable small enterprises should have the important long term effect of strengthening the development of efficient Australian industry in Australian hands. It should also be of great help to country areas, where, almost by definition, most businesses are small scale. Among our other reasons for being concerned with this sector is that small business is a source of much innovation and invention, is important in the supply side of the economy because of its adaptiveness and flexibility, and it enables Australian entrepreneurs with initiative. and independence to play a vital role in the community.
The small business programme the Government envisages will be comprehensive, balanced, and designed to have favourable impact on the long term viability of the small business sector, by
> *raising efficiency and profitability,*
> *strengthening the competitive position of small*
> *firms in relation to large (including overseas-owned),*
> *enabling small firms to cope better with structural*
> *changes in the economy,*
> *improving industrial relations and welfare of*
> *workforce involved."*

The Bureau's programme was to include research and policy, management assistance, and advisory services. A Small Business Advisory Panel, composed of small business owners, trade unionists,

---

[1] *F.M. Wiltshire, (see footnote 1, page 90), p. xx - xxi.*

[2] *Opening address by the Minister attending the National Small Business Seminar, Canberra, November 1973.*

consumer representatives and academics, was formed to assist the
Bureau in its work. Research initially undertaken by the Bureau
included an investigation into the adequacy of existing sources of
finance; research into taxation aspects of small firms; and research
into overseas provisions for financing of small businesses.

To evaluate the need for counselling and extension services, the
Bureau established offices in New South Wales and Western Australia
in 1975. These counselling services were used to identify small
enterprise problems, find solutions, and implement improvements.
Several thousand enquiries were handled by the offices until a change
in national government in December 1975 introduced a new policy of
federalism and a change in the respective roles of the national and
state governments for small enterprise development. New areas of
cooperation and decentralisation of activities were established for
small enterprise, and a national programme of assistance was planned
for counselling, management training, information services, research
and the availability of finance. As a result, the Bureau withdrew
from its previous direct contact with owner managers and closed its
separate offices in Sydney and Perth. Operational activities associated with small business counselling were taken over by state
government authorities and the former National Small Business Bureau
was absorbed within the Department of Industry and Commerce as a
Finance and Small Business Branch. The role of the Branch has changed
to one of co-ordination of national policy on small enterprise development, research, publications, investigation into management
training programmes and finance for small enterprises.

In its new role the Branch has produced publications summarising
current research into various aspects of small enterprise growth and
development, has commissioned specific research investigations, makes
submissions to government on small enterprise policy, has commissioned and produced publications on management accounting for small
firms, sources of finance, checklists for starting a business, marketing, importing, retailing, buying and selling a business - and
similar titles. The Branch holds a film library with training material supplied by the United States Small Business Agency, the
Australian Broadcasting Commission, the United Kingdom Central Office
of Information, the Swedish Institute and private enterprise groups.
Recently, the Branch has been successful in negotiating with the University of New England and the National Training Council of Australia
for the production of a management training package for small enterprises covering planning and starting a small business. The package
covers 8 sessions including factors in business success, business
ideas, industries and plans, the mechanics of starting and operating
a business, getting assistance, finance, financial management and
cash management, putting together a staff team, marketing and
selling and information systems and standards of performance.

From time to time senior staff of the Finance and Small Business
Branch meet with executives from state government departments to
assist in the co-ordination of small enterprise policy in Australia.
The co-ordinating role of the Branch can be expected to increase in
the future.

Initiatives at the State Government level

While the first important initiatives in the small enterprise development field in Australia were taken at the national level, the new federalism policy of government announced in 1976 encouraged initiatives at State Government levels. The New South Wales Government was the first to announce major new initiatives.

New South Wales

In November 1975, the then Premier of New South Wales foreshadowed the establishment of a Small Business Agency within its Department of Decentralisation and Development. The Agency began operating in March 1976 with a free counselling and referral service. A complementary subsidised consulting service was also introduced whereby firms paid designated consultants a standard hourly fee and apply to the Agency for a refund of 50 percent of the fee paid.

The N.S.W. Small Business Agency has been organised with an officer-in-charge responsible to the Assistant Director (Technical) of the Department of Decentralisation and Development with supporting staff including counsellors, a trade association liaison officer, training co-ordinator, and an information officer.

The Agency, as announced by the Premier of the day, was to have the following general charter:

(i)   To provide a Centre for the collection and collation of research data and statistics appropriate to small enterprise development.

(ii)   To collaborate with established trade and commercial and professional associations to identify the short and long term needs of small enterprises and to establish means whereby the Government might assist in meeting these needs.

(iii)   To bring about the establishment of an advisory committee representative of small business interests and to investigate the desirability of creating a State statutory authority to promote small enterprise development within the State.

(iv)   To provide the basis for the introduction of a subsidised counselling service aimed at meeting the management advisory needs of small enterprises.

(v)   To investigate the legal and financial problems facing small enterprises and in particular to investigate the possibility of establishing a State sponsored financial assistance programme designed to meet small business development needs, this programme to be potentially based upon a loan guarantee scheme supportive of the financial resources of the established banking system and applicable to expansion and conversion loans, machinery and equipment purchase loans, working capital loans, establishment and development loans, and disaster loans.

(vi)   To review and monitor existing future legislation with a view to providing advice thereon to both small enterprises and to Government on any aspects of such legislation which could be identified as having an inhibiting affect upon the well being of small enterprises and to formulate recommendations concerning steps necessary to alleviate such affects.

The Agency has initiated a publications programme with a wide range of publications available from a number of resources and including guidebooks, pamphlets, manuals and general brochures.

Recently, the Agency has co-operated with the State Government Department of Technical and Further Education for the development and implementation of small enterprise courses at technical colleges throughout the State. A number of courses have been introduced including an introductory programme for those comtemplating the start-up of a new enterprise, a general management course for managers of existing small enterprises, and a more advanced course in financial management for managers of existing small enterprises.

A Small Business Development Council has been formed to give advice and guidance to the Agency. The Council consists of a chairman and members drawn from business, professional and academic communities in N.S.W. The Council has formed six subcommittees covering information and statistics, education and training, finance and taxation, advisory services and assistance, legislation, and research and development.

Victoria

In the State of Victoria, following a Parliamentary sub-committee report on small enterprises, the Small Business Development Corporation Act 1976[1] was enacted by the Victorian Government to establish a statutory corporation to provide programmes of assistance to small enterprises.

The Corporation consists of a chairman and 4 members, all part-time. To assist them, the Corporation has appointed 4 advisory committees on multiplier organisations, finance, education and legislation. In establishing the Small Business Development Corporation, the Government expressed the intention that the Corporation should do everything necessary "for or in connection with encouraging, providing, facilitating and assisting in the establishing, carrying out, expansion and development of small enterprises".[2] The Corporation's Act defining small enterprises is set out on page 90.

The Corporation is specifically directed in the Act to establish an organisation to be known as a "Small Business Advisory Agency" which has a director and other staff engaged by the Corporation. The functions of the Agency are:

(i)   to establish a Centre to be known as the Information and Referral Centre;

---

[1] *See footnote 2, p. 90.*

[2] *Press statement on Committee Guidelines from the Chairman of the S.B.D.C. - based on Section 12(2) of the Bill.*

(ii)   to investigate the effect upon small enterprises
of the policies of Governments, Acts of Parliament, and
the rules, regulations, by laws made thereunder;

(iii) to arrange training and educational programmes for
small enterprises;

(iv)   to publish and distribute information for the
guidance of small enterprises;

(v)   to arrange financial assistance to small enterprises
and to make recommendations to the Corporation in respect
to applications for Government guarantees under this Act.

The Corporation's Central Information and Referral Centre is
in the capital of the State, Melbourne, and offices are located
throughout the State.   Counsellors have been appointed to the Centre
and advice is provided to small enterprise owners on matters raised
directly by owners, or in writing, or through telephone contacts.
The Agency provides information regarding training and educational
programmes and distributes and publishes information for small enterprise guidance.   It is envisaged that the activities of the Agency
will expand considerably in the foreseeable future.

Queensland

The Queensland Government has established a Division of Small
Business within the Department of Commercial and Industrial Development, to provide assistance to small enterprises.   The Division provides a counselling and referral service, produces and distributes
publications for small enterprises, and conducts seminars on small
business topics.   The Division actively draws on the total resources
of the Department, other Departments within the Government, professional and commercial groups and multiplier agencies.   The Division
is currently co-ordinating the introduction of courses in small enterprise management throughout Queensland with Department of Education authorities.   One College of Advanced Education at Toowoomba
has recently announced the establishment of a regional small enterprise referral centre and other Colleges of Advanced Education are
introducing specific awards for small enterprise management courses
or individual study units.   The Division has recently appointed additional staff and expansion is envisaged in the future as demand
for services increases.

South Australia

In South Australia, a Small Business Advisory Service has been
established within the Development Division of the Premiers Department.   This Service provides South Australian small enterprise owners
with a counselling and referral service and where necessary meets
the costs of consultants assisting owners.   The Service also assists
in providing improved management training facilities for owner/mana-
gers through the Government's Department of Further Education.

Western Australia

In Western Australia, counselling and referral services previously operated by the National Small Business Bureau have been
taken over by the Small Business Advisory Service of the Western
Australian Department of Industrial Development.   In addition, the

the Education Department in Western Australia has a number of courses developed for small enterprise owner/managers.

Tasmania

No Tasmanian government agency is at present exclusively directed to small business enterprises although the State Government is currently examining possible developments.

12.4 GOVERNMENT-BASED PROGRAMMES FOR SMALL ENTERPRISES

Initiatives taken by national government and various state governments since 1973 have been identified in the proceding section. What follows is a summary of programmes for small enterprises available from government departments, agencies or associated institutions. In Australia, this includes tertiary teaching institutions which are government funded.

Counselling/Information services

State governments of Queesland, New South Wales, Victoria, South Australia and Western Australia now provide free counselling and advisory services for small enterprise owners. Information services include the distribution of printed material and films, as well as programmes operating through the media - radio, newspapers and television.

Subsidised consulting

State governments in New South Wales and South Australia have introduced programmes which provide for subsidised consulting services from private consultants. Other states are considering the service. Certain limits and restrictions are placed on the service, however its introduction has encouraged private consultants to specialise in the field of small enterprise development.

Loan guarantee schemes

New South Wales has introduced a loan guarantee scheme and Victoria may introduce such a scheme in the near future. National Government is investigating the availability of finance for small enterprises and further announcements in this area are expected in the future[1].

Training packages/programmes

State government agencies in New South Wales, Victoria and South Australia have developed training packages which are available to any group wishing to conduct courses for small enterprise owners. The national government is coordinating training package preparation and has commissioned a series dealing with problems of starting and operating a small enterprise. These packages provide notes for the instructor, visual aids, details of bibliography as well as material to be used in presentation and provided to participants. Several

---

[1] *Press release issued by the Minister for Industry and Commerce, Canberra, 26 May, 1977.*

State Governments have produced films on small enterprise development and a film library is maintained in Canberra and state capitals.

Publications and publicity

Most state governments have produced specific publications for
small enterprises covering government services and technical matters
associated with industry sectors. The University of New England's
Research Centre has reproduced pamphlets originally made available
by United States Small Business Administration. These have been
modified to meet Australian conditions and are distributed largely
through state government agencies and corporations. National government agencies such as the Productivity Promotion Council, Industrial
Design Council and Materials Handling Bureau also produce publications for distribution throughout Australia.

Research

Research into small enterprise activity is largely undertaken by
staff attached to universities or colleges of advanced education. In
many cases, research projects are supported by government or semi-
government organisations. A unique research centre in the Australian
environment is attached to the University of New England in New South
Wales. The research centre specialises in small enterprises, rural
enterprises and professional practices. The centre is self financing and undertakes surveys, inter-business comparisons, monitors
small enterprise performance and expectations and conducts management
workshops on a resident basis. The national Finance and Small Business Branch of the Department of Industry and Commerce publishes
summaries of on going research[1].

Services from National Government Departments

A large number of national government departments provide services of interest to small enterprise owners. The Department of Productivity provides an inter-firm comparison service, controls the
Industrial Design Council of Australia, the Productivity Promotion
Council of Australia and the Material Handling Bureau. The Department of Overseas Trade provides information on exports and the
Department of Employment and Industrial Relations provides information for small enterprises on awards and employment. The Australian
Bureau of Statistics provides information on industry statistical
data, while the Australian Taxation Office provides information
relating to taxation for small enterprises. The National Training
Council, Commonwealth Scientific and Industrial Research Organisation
and National film library all provide sources of interest to small
enterprise owners.

Services from State Government Departments

Most state governments have established departments which encourage decentralisation and industry development. These departments
provide loans for purchase of land and buildings for manufacturing

---

[1] *Register of Small Business Research, (Department of Industry
and Commerce, Canberra, 1977).*

and processing industries in decentralised areas; make available subsidies to assist with removal expenses, rail freights and consultancies for decentralised industries; and often provide housing loans for key personnel in decentralised industries. Other state government departments provide information on awards, employment, training, small enterprise establishment and development, and technical advice on a wide range of matters including manufacturing opportunities, markets, raw material supply, utilities and related matters.

State government education departments provide formal and informal courses for small enterprise owners at the technical college level and both the national and state governments are committed to additional expenditure in this particular field.

Services from Local Government

Local government offices provide small enterprises with information regarding regional services available, zoning of land, building costs, health regulations, local environment, the provision of utilities such as electricity, water and sewerage and also offer assistance with planning developments on industrial estates. Many local government councils in Australia encourage new small enterprises by actively providing various incentives and finance or general assistance.

Tertiary institutions

As stated previously, funding for tertiary institutions in Australia is the responsibility of the national government. Universities make their own decisions designing specific courses at the undergraduate and graduate levels. Greater control is exercised by state governments and the national government over courses offered by colleges of advanced education and technical colleges. Although some encouragement has been given to tertiary institutions, these institutions have been slow to introduce specific programmes for small enterprise development in Australia. Some universities have one or two programmes at undergraduate or graduate level; a number of colleges of advanced education have also introduced specific programmes or are considering programmes; and technical colleges in New South Wales and South Australia have a wide range of programmes for small enterprise owners/managers. Some universities have established research companies - for example Unisearch Limited of the University of New South Wales, Technisearch Limited in Victoria - providing services (largely technical) for large and small enterprises, while the Financial Management Research Centre of the University of New England concentrates specifically on small enterprises, rural enterprises and professional practices. Given the preparation of training packages by state and national governments, it is to be expected that tertiary institutions in Australia will increase their involvement in small enterprise management development.

12.5 INITIATIVES BY THE PRIVATE ENTERPRISE SECTOR

Trade and commercial associations

Many industrial and commercial associations have been established in Australia to represent and promote the common interests of members including small enterprise members. The aim of most associations is to keep members informed of technical and commercial developments in particular industry sectors. Trade associations in Australia tend to offer members such services as advice on industrial relations, training, information services through journals and newsletters, standardization programmes, liaison with government departments, record keeping services, purchasing facilities, credit reporting facilities, technical advice, taxation and financial advice and to some extent market surveys.

A major problem in Australia is the large number of associations operating for a relatively small number of enterprises. Over 2,000 trade associations exist in all states with duplications between industries and between states. With this proliferation, it is unlikely that the majority of trade associations will be able to provide a wide range of services for small enterprise members. Trade associations are currently showing increasing interest in expanding services to small enterprise members, and it is possible in the future that government financial assistance will be provided to allow associations to make staff appointments as small business trainees.

Chambers of Commerce/Manufacturers and employer organizations

Chambers of Commerce have been formed throughout the length and breadth of Australia - they exist in all large cities and in small country towns. In general, Chambers of Commerce deal with local matters of interest to business owners - particularly matters which concern a community and the business within the community. While the major cities and the central organisation based in the national capital in Canberra have full-time staff, the majority of the Chambers are not equipped to provide on going advice or services to the small enterprise owner.

State-based Chambers of Manufacturers advise members on tariffs, domestic and export trade, the economy, taxation and finance. In addition to Chambers of Commerce and Manufacturers, most states have employer federations/associations. These play a significant role in industrial affairs in the fields of arbitration and conciliation, provide information on all industrial relations matters, make representations before industrial tribunals, give assistance in settling industrial disputes, take part in negotiations with trade unions, offer secretarial assistance for associations, and advice on insurance and superannuation. One or two employers' organisations have provided a counselling service for members as small enterprises.

The Australian Institute of Management has divisions in each state. The Institute is a non-profit, self-help organisation, making use of management resources amongst its members to provide publications and training programmes in all fields of business management. All divisions have a nucleus of full-time staff, quite often including a training officer. Members of the Institute provide services on an honourary basis and produce programmes which may include meetings and forums, services, courses, conferences, seminars and advisory services.

Service organisations

The many service organisations throughout Australia - Jaycees, Rotary, Lions, Apex, Y.M.C.A. - to mention a few, are active in providing services of one kind or another for local small enterprise groups. Services are in general restricted to the organisation of seminars or conferences and perhaps the distribution of the basic publications for small enterprises. Given that the national and state governments in Australia are to provide standardized course material for management training sessions, service organisations may become more active within small enterprise workshops, seminars and discussions.

Professional bodies/associations

Professionals actively concerned with services for small enterprise owners are accountants and solicitors in the public practice. As stated previously, accountants in Australia tended to concentrate on taxation and related services, and solicitors have generally restricted their activities to traditional legal services for owners. The professional institutes and associations have not provided services for small enterprise owners per se, but have concentrated on providing training and instruction for their own members who wish to provide services for small enterprise owners. In particular, the Law Foundation of New South Wales and the Law Institute of Victoria have established programmes and produced publications to encourage their members to expand their horizons beyond the traditional fields of interest of the legal profession. The accountancy profession is also attempting to produce training and continuing education programmes for its members on providing assistance to small enterprise clients.

Business consultants

Initiatives by government both at the national and state levels have created an interest amongst consultants in assistance to small enterprise clients. Prior to government initiatives being taken, few consultants were providing services for small enterprise owners and few small enterprise owners showed any interest in obtaining services from consultants. Given the national and state government counselling services, some medium size and larger firms of public accountants and some larger management consulting firms have recently taken initiatives to actively provide consultative services for small enterprise clients. An increasing number of specialists are establishing themselves as private small enterprise consultants and some tertiary institutions are establishing counselling or consulting groups in decentralised regions.

Banks and financial institutions

Traditionally, banks and financial institutions in Australia have provided small enterprises with financial accommodation in the form of overdraft facilities, term loans, lease financing, commercial bill financing, bridging loans, personal loans and a wide range of export and import financial assistance. Assistance and initiatives in the field of small enterprises have not extended beyond finance. In recent months, several private enterprise banks in Australia have investigated the possibility of introducing a small enterprise counselling scheme for clients. Such a scheme appears to operate effectively overseas[1] and it would seem to be a natural progression for the small enterprise owner seeking bank finance to also seek advice on general business management problems. Since the banking sector will need to recruit trained personnel for these purposes, it is likely to be some time before non-finance advisory services are available to small enterprises through the banking system in Australia.

Small enterprise organisations

Recent activity in the field of small enterprise development in Australia has seen the formation of a number of associations, institutes or groups to provide small enterprises with a voice particularly at the political level. Groups have been formed in several state regions and national bodies are now appearing. A self-employed business organisation has been formed in several states; a national smaller business association is based in Sydney; a small business association of Victoria; an Association of Australian Independent Businesses is based on the national capital of Canberra; and a Council of Organisations hopes to link together trade associations and other groups representing small enterprises. These organisations can be expected to become more active in the future and one national body may be formed with state and regional branches.

12.6 FUTURE DEVELOPMENTS

Material presented in this paper has attempted to describe objectively the position of small enterprise development progression in Australia. Comment on "future developments" must be largely subjective and requires an initial assessment of programmes as they stand at present.

Most critics would concede that significant progress has been made in Australia since the first major initiative by the National Government in November 1973 when the National Small Business Bureau was established. In less than 4 years,

- state small enterprise agencies, divisions and/or corporations have been established,

- legislative review has been accepted as necessary to eliminate discrimination against small enterprises,

- counselling/consulting services have been implemented,

- training packages have been prepared,

- some special financial assistance has been introduced,

- the need for further reforms is acknowledged,

- small enterprise owners are co-operating to form one voice.

The future is speculation, however, initiatives by national, state and local governments, professional bodies, multiplier agencies in general, and small enterprises are likely to increase in Australia

---

[1] *For example, initiatives by the Bank of America and Industrial and Commercial Finance Corporation Ltd. (in the United Kingdom) are often quoted.*

FIGURE 12.1: SUGGESTED REPRESENTATION OF GROUPS INVOLVED
IN NATIONAL POLICY IMPLEMENTATION

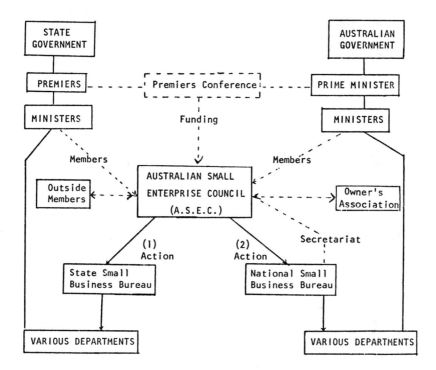

over the next decade. Activities at the government level will be coordinated; trade associations may amalgamate and strengthen their operational arms; professional bodies and professionals will become more involved with general management advice for small enterprises; banks will provide an increasing range of non-financial services; and small enterprise agencies and associations will unify. State government and national government officials associated with agencies, corporations or branches will increase their cooperative effort and a structured programme for small enterprise development is likely to emerge. Such a programme will probably recognise that certain segments can best be undertaken and implemented at the national level through national government and national multiplier agencies. Other segments of the programme will best be implemented through state government, regional bodies, and state or regional multiplier agencies.

A diagramatical representation of the various groups involved in a national policy for small enterprise development is suggested in Figure 12.1 (see preceding page).

Effective action in Australia will require direct involvement of government and it is suggested that the formation of an Australian Enterprise Council would act as a strategic coordinating body involving not only government but small business associations, professional bodies and other multiplier agencies.

At the state and regional levels, government and multiplier agencies would be involved in reviews of state legislation; management assistance programmes; small enterprise set-up and development; counselling services; referral and information centres; and financial assistance. At the national level, government departments, agencies and multiplier agencies would be involved in the review of national legislation, information documentation services, coordination of all programmes, training of counsellors, supplying finance through loan guarantee or other means; and the coordination of small enterprise research.

Australia has made progress in small enterprise development in 4 years, but still lags behing most developed nations in implementing a coordinated small enterprise development policy. Increasing activity is expected in the following decade to bridge the gap.

CAMEROON

Thaddeus Kinga[1]

13

For some considerable time the Cameroon authorities have been preoccupied with promoting small and medium-sized enterprises (SME). The principal means of action is entrusted to the national Centre for Assistance to Small and Medium-Sized Enterprises (CAPME).

Because of the wide range of problems to be dealt with, CAPME has opted for a sectoral approach. Activities focus on the environment within which the SME operate (fiscal problems, credit facilities and public contracts), on collective assistance to certain trades (associations and training), and on individual assistance to enterprises (assistance in administration, management or technical problems). To date, operations have been limited to Douala and Yaoundé, but will be extended to the entire country when resources become available.

13.1 POLICIES

For some time Cameroon authorities have considered it necessary to promote and develop SME to complement economic expansion of Cameroon.

President Ahidjo has often referred to this need. During the 1975 Congress of Maturity of the Cameroon National Union Party a special resolution was passed requesting the Government to redouble efforts in pursuing its policy in promoting national small and medium-sized enterprises.

It is now 10 years since two French organisations, "Société d'Aide Technique et de Coopération" (SATEC) and "Association pour la Formation des Cadres de l'Administration" (AFCA), financed by bilateral French assistance, began to assist small and medium-sized enterprises in Cameroon. In 1968, the United Nations Development Programme (UNDP) with assistance from the International Labour Organisation (ILO) and United Nations Industrial Development Organisation (UNIDO) established two projects to create a national Centre for Assistance

---

[1] *National Director, Centre for Assistance to Small and Medium-Sized Enterprises, CAPME, Douala, Cameroon.*

to the Small and Medium-Sized Enterprises (CAPME) which came into being in 1970.

Among the general principles basic to Government policy, are three of great importance in promoting small and medium-scale enterprises.

(i)   The principle of planned liberalism which permits and encourages the free operation of private initiative in line with the general policy fixed by the Five-year Economic, Social and Cultural Development Plan. This principle makes individual initiative and responsibility the cornerstones of development. Where the entrepreneur controls the future of his own enterprise is the best possible expression of this planned liberalism.

(ii)   The principle of self-dependent development (by and for Cameroonians) which leads CAPME to be interested only in Cameroonian enterprises, that is, enterprises owned and managed by Cameroonians.

(iii)   The principle of national unity which demands balanced regional development to encourage SME development throughout the country. This is a formidable task, of course, for a growing organisation such as CAPME which should avoid dispersing its efforts.

Actually SME are not specially mentioned in the 4th 5-year Development Plan. In fact, 10 years after the first pronouncement by the authorities, a gap still exists between the wish expressed and what is, in fact, carried out in their favour. This confirms that the real problems of SME ought first be known, so that the basic elements of a global policy can be defined. We are now entering this phase in Cameroon.

13.2 STRUCTURES

CAPME is the major institution established by the Cameroon Government for promoting small and medium-sized enterprises. It is a public corporation, created in 1970 and endowed with a civic personality and financial autonomy. It seeks to promote SME by:

- providing individual assistance to existing enterprises (to deal with technical and management problems);
- creating new enterprises;
- establishing trade associations;
- creating a favourable administrative and legislative environment;
- coordinating assistance to SME.

CAPME is made up of three departments:

The Department of Business Administration responsible for conducting, marketing and financial studies for new enterprises, and management assistance to existing enterprises.

The Technical Department comprising a mechanical workshop to carry out repairs and maintenance, and to fabricate spare parts for SME. The department is also responsible for technical studies for new enterprises and adapting new equipment for Cameroonian enterprises. The Service for Studies is presently being developed.

The Development Department responsible for collective interventions and environmental activities.

A fourth, *Training Department* responsible for pedagogics is just coming into being.

CAPME, now employs 53 people (22 located at the Workshop at Bassa). Its budget for 1976-1977 financial year is 223 million francs CFA[1].

Sub-contractors of CAPME

CAPME uses two sub-contractors SATEC and AFCA. These organisations have been operating in Cameroon for 10 years. Since July 1975 their expatriate personnel has been financed by UNDP, and their activities controlled by CAPME. The Cameroonian personnel of these two organisations will be incorporated within CAPME plus part of the expatriate personnel.

During the past two years AFCA has carried out sectoral studies and collective assistance, while SATEC has conducted research and developed new projects.

Other institutions

In 1975 the Fund for Assistance and Guarantee of Credit to SME was created to guarantee loans provided by public or private banks to SME. This Fund built up from banks profits and the state budget has been operating only since June 1976. It has, however, already guaranteed some 20 loans.

In addition, the Cameroon Development Bank (BCD), a company with mixed shareholding, seeks to provide financial assistance to all projects promoting economic and social development of Cameroon. A special SME Section has been created in the BCD which received a joint loan of 6 million U.S. dollars (half from the International Development Agency and half from the Central Fund for Economic Cooperation) to encourage the creation of 65 medium-sized enterprises. This section is assisted by 2 UNDP experts. The first loans from this line of credit were advanced at the end of 1976.

Small agro-industrial projects may also benefit from loans provided by the National Fund for Rural Development (FONADER).

The National Company for Industrial Sites (SONADIC) created in 1971 to build industrial sites, particularly for SME, has yet to become operational. However, it will be an important institution for promoting SME who often do not have the necessary funds for constructing suitable buildings without consuming what little working capital they have.

[1] *One US dollar = 238 CFA.*

Specific facilities for SME

Eligibility for a reduced global rate of 5 percent on all customs duties and taxes levied on imported material, machines and tools directly necessary for exploitation, production or transformation of certain products.

Granting of a regime of interior production tax where, instead of paying tax when purchasing raw material, the SME pays a compensatory tax on the finished product; the advantage being essentially deferring payment of tax.

On the financial side, the authorities have insisted that, since 1970, banks should provide loans to SME on the same grounds as to other enterprises. Because of the banks' reluctance, they are now obliged to allocate 20 percent of short term loans to SME.

Definitions

In Cameroon, as elsewhere, these are several definitions of SME. Amongst them are:

(i)   Fiscal definition

SME are exempt for tax purposes if annual turnover is less than 20 million francs CFA for commercial enterprises, and 5 million CFA for industrial enterprises. In addition SME are considered as handicrafts for tax purposes if employing 5 labourers at maximum, whether they be relatives or apprentices, and selling only their own products.

(ii)   Banking definition

The Ministry of Finance permits national enterprises, whose authorisation for rediscount with the central bank is less than 25 million francs CFA or whose own resources are less than 50 million francs CFA, to benefit from a special rate of interest for bank loans.

(iii)   CAPME definition

An operational, but not quantitative definition is employed, namely a small and medium-sized enterprise is one where one person takes all management decisions concerning the enterprise.

From a 1975 study it became clear that if a general classification of SME is to be made, it would be necessary to take into account:

-   turnover

-   number of permanent employees

-   investment

-   enterprise's own resources

It now appears that to derive a definition suitable for providing assistance, other criteria are also important. We need to know elements which distinguish the structured from the non-structured sectors such as payment of taxes, respect of labour legislation and relationship of the entrepreneur with the local economic milieu. These elements mark the boundaries which the enterprise has to break through to obtain eventual development.

How large is the SME sector in Cameroon? If we take the figures of the Business Tax Register, a very rough calculation would be 40,000 SME in Cameroon.

According to estimates in the National Accounts the traditional sector (comprising mostly national SME) contributes 30 percent of the non-agricultural gross domestic product, and the national SME contribute approximately 15 percent of the modern non-agricultural sector. As a whole, the national SME accounts for 45 percent of the non-agricultural gross domestic product which is quite considerable.

In daily operations CAPME deals particularly with enterprises having a certain stable structure, namely

post box number

telephone

bank account

name and office

The number of enterprises so far benefiting from CAPME's assistance is only a small fraction of the total referred to above (less than 10 percent).

Concerning the question of conducting a general census of SME, which has been emphasized on numerous occasions both by foreign visitors and some local authorities, CAPME's policy is:

- to avoid a strictly quantitative census whose cost would be out of proportion with the results expected, and outside the competence of CAPME;

- to conduct in-depth analyses of sectors, limited sectorally and geographically, commencing with the most structured sectors;

- to use current socio-economic techniques to establish the best critera for quantitative classification.

These methods have the advantage of rapidly furnishing data of immediate use to CAPME for its activities.

13.3 PROGRAMMES

Operational for two years CAPME receives about 15 applications for management assistance and about 40 applications for assistance in maintenance and repairs, per month. It directly monitors the daily management of some 30 enterprises and is in contact with some 50 promoters through its sub-contractors. In the latter cases either continuous or regular repetitive assistance is provided.

CAPME's operations are fivefold.

(i) Knowledge of the SME milieu

Three sectoral studies have been completed for Yaoundé and Douala in bakery, furniture-making and building construction. Two other studies are currently underway in photography and printing. Others envisaged include: manufacturing ready-made clothes and iron-foundry.

(ii) Environmental aspects of SME

Access to credit

In spite of pressure by public authorities on banks to increase credit to SME, a 1976 study showed that banks are still reluctant to grant credit to the SME, at times, one is bound to say, for good reasons.

Banks complain of SME's lack of internal funds, lack of sufficient guarantees, absence of accounting systems and lack of bank accounts which prevent banks assessing the managerial capacity of loan applicants. Following a Round Table (organised by CAPME involving banks and SME) an information campaign has been undertaken in order to improve relationships between SME and banks.

Access to public contracts

The same round-table approach of enquiry and discussion has been employed with the different parties involved (Administration - Banks - SME - CAPME). Discussions included: how to improve the technical competence of SME so that a greater number could tender for public contracts? How to help SME to rapidly obtain advances needed for executing contracts? How to modify legislation to facilitate and increase the access of SME to public contracts?

Fiscal system

CAPME has proposed to the public authorities adjustments to turnover tax which, by double incidence, inhibits sub-contracting.

CAPME has also proposed that salaries of partners in companies should be deducted from taxable profits so that the tax incurred does not interfere with development of Cameroonian SME, which is the case at the moment.

(iii) Collective assistance

This concerns training activities such as seminars for bread-makers and furniture-makers which began in 1976 and are being continued. For bread-makers in Douala, a collective maintenance programme is under study.

Collective assistance also concerns establishing trade organisations and credit unions or buying cooperatives. CAPME is in discussion with 4 groups on this subject, namely bread-makers, garageners, building contractors and a mixed group of industrialists.

(iv) Individual assistance

Individual assistance takes two forms:

- Applications for assistance are screened by the Development Department and submitted to a Management Committee (made up of Heads of Departments) which may ask for further information, or send it to another Department, usually to the Department of Business Administration. Only a small number of applications (about one-third) eventually receive assistance. A greater part of the applications have to be abandoned because, often, the applicant cannot or does not wish to supply the minimum information required for screening the dossier, and many projects are unrealistic. This, also, is an important CAPME activity - avoiding the launching of projects doomed to certain failure.
Assistance provided by CAPME is intended to be global. It not only aims at soliciting credit, obtaining exoneration from taxes for the enterprise concerned or establishing an accounts system but, above all, at enabling the head of enterprise to appreciate his role and fulfill it better.
A particular aspect of CAPME's individual assistance is creating new enterprises.

- Applications for assistance in repair and maintenance of equipment. It is necessary to point out that this form of assistance extends beyond the Cameroonian SME; since jobs are also accepted from larger enterprises in Douala with a view to using the Workshop to capacity and training our own personnel.
Assistance provided by CAPME is free for general advice and diagnosis. But fees are charged for handling well-defined problems, in such cases, contracts are drawn up between CAPME and the enterprise concerned.
On technological matters, CAPME calls in outside specialised technicians to advise the enterprise in improving production.

(v) Coordinating assistance

This mostly revolves around the two organisations, AFCA and SATEC, who have a fixed programme with CAPME.

However close collaboration is maintained between CAPME and FOGAPE, and the SME Section of BCD on financial matters.

Finally, CAPME coordinates miscellaneous inputs such as governmental and non-governmental assistance to the rural and handicraft sectors.

13.4 PROBLEMS AND PROPOSED SOLUTIONS

The enormous dimensions of this sector and its wide dispersions make it difficult to manage in its totality.

Inadequate economic statistics make it difficult to define markets for given products. In this respect CAPME:

- carries out sectoral studies to try to understand the fringe of the most structured sector of SME, and to extend the findings to other trades and provincial capitals;

- uses data available from some ten diverse censuses, such as labour, finance, chamber of commerce and general census of the population to make a synthesis of the SME sector;
- participates in socio-economic studies of the non-structured sector such as the ILO programme for the acquisition of qualifications and self-employment in the urban non-structured sector;
- creates impact substitution studies where efforts are made to exploit available customs statistics and to collaborate with import-export firms;
- in the medium-term will carry out studies on household consumption and its evolution as a function of the standard of living, such studies should define potential markets for certain products and possible localities for new SME. For example, a study on bread consumption would enable localisation of bakeries.

Credit

Present measures are sufficient for promoters having their own funds and guarantees, they are insufficient in all other cases. CAPME proposes:

- To study possibilities of investment companies advancing a fraction of the share capital when floating the company, which would eventually be sold back to the promoter.
- To extend leasing and facilitate disbursing loans based on mortgaging materials or merchandise.
- To grant credit on criteria other than the traditional "own" funds, pledges and guarantees. The system of credit unions, based on personal knowledge of the borrower by his colleagues, has been sufficiently successful to warrant further study.

Fiscal measures

Obligations to pay current taxes discourages SME from keeping accounts. CAPME intends:

- To enable reforms proposed to Government be accepted and applied.
- To ask for temporary fiscal exoneration of newly created enterprises (as in Senegal and the Ivory Coast) for the first 5 years. By this time, the enterprise should be sufficiently developed and structured to pay taxes.

Public contracts

Only few SME can obtain public contracts. Therefore CAPME intends:

- To ensure the widest publicity when calling for public tenders among the SME.
- To upgrade the technical competence of SME and assist them in preparing submissions.

- To obtain a legislation assuring SME part of public contracts, or obliging tenderers, who are not SME, to sub-contract a fraction of their contracts to SME.

Training

The level of managerial and technical knowledge of most SME owners is inadequate. This causes many of their difficulties. CAPME is setting up a Training Department to analyse SME needs and to implement programmes in on-the-job training combining training with assistance.

Collective assistance

Most trades making up the SME sector are unorganised which hinders collective actions such as: training; common purchases; product specialisation, standardisation and quality control. CAPME attempts:

- To assist existing trade associations.
- To encourage meetings of entrepreneurs in the same trade groupings, particularly by seminars, to provide opportunities to confront their problems, to know one another better and, as a result, to group themselves if possible.

Individual assistance

CAPME is not yet sufficiently recognised among existing enter-prises. For new enterprises feasibility studies encounter two diffi-culties:

(i) market studies relative to the products envisaged,

(ii) choice of materials suitable for production covering the markets envisaged.

In this respect CAPME intends:

- To conduct market and feasibility studies by establishing these services in the Development Department.
- To assemble and exploit existing documentation on intermediate technology.
- To create enterprises in sectors with potential markets, where the Plan envisages future investment.
- To train personnel of the Centre in better approaches and understanding of SME by adopting an attitude of salesmen for the Centre and not that of civil servants.

13.5 CONCLUSIONS

The entire system of assistance has only been operational for two years. It is, therefore, too early to assess its effectiveness.

Assistance to SME can only yield positive results if it is global, that is to say, if progress is made simultaneously in the five areas discussed earlier. This implies an all-embracing policy for promoting SME be made by the public authorities. It is one of the future tasks of the centre to make such recommendations to the Government.

The development of SME ought be made within the framework of the Plan. That is to say, investments envisaged in the latter should be made directly or indirectly, perhaps by sub-contracting with SME involvement.

In the long term SME should form a special chapter of their own in the 5th Plan.

To extend activities throughout the country the Centre could create regional branches in each Province. However, these may assume a different structure to those in Douala and Yaoundé, particularly for industrial sites.

Developing SME should harmonise with large enterprises and not be in competition with them.

There is the problem that large enterprises are normally subsidiaries of foreign companies, this ought become the subject of special study to the Centre.

CANADA

Rein Peterson[1]

14

John J. Shepherd, the Executive Director of the Science Council of Canada recently presented frightening evidence which claimed that the Canadian economy is in decline[2]:

"1. Canada, relative to the rest of the world, is rapidly deindustrialising.

2. Canada's current economic problems are not transitory, but longer term in nature, being widespread and chronic.

3. Canada's debilitating economic condition can only be reversed by radical shifts in what currently passes as industrial strategy, both at the federal and provincial level."

Was he calling wolf, as some of his critics claim? No! replies Shepherd, pointing out that Canada has been declining over the last 20 years as an industrial power, by any standard we wish to name. In 1955, we were second only to the U. S.A. in terms of our standard of living. Since then we have been overtaken and passed by Australia, Finland, France, Japan, Sweden, and West Germany, and within the next 5 years, Brazil and Korea will overtake us if current trends persist.

Between 1970 and 1975 our share of world exports dropped from 5.4 percent to 3.1 percent (most of which was unprocessed raw materials) while our imports expressed as a percentage of domestic demand rose 26 percent to 33 percent (mostly manufactured goods). In spite of protective tarriffs, all sectors of our domestic economy are being flooded by imports because we are unable to compete. If the current trends continue, we may soon see the complete destruction of several sectors of manufacturing industries in Canada:

---

[1] *Professor, Faculty of Administrative Studies, York University, Toronto, Canada.*

[2] *J.J. Shepherd in Remarks made to the Ontario Engineering Advisory Council, Guild Inn, Toronto, June 27, 1977.*

"Over the last decade we have witnessed singularly
unsuccessful attempts to formulate industrial strategy
in Canada. At the federal level, thoughts of one
overall strategy have metamorphised to a sectoral
approach, with failures developing faster than strategies
emerge."[1]

Many Canadians (including this writer) agree that the lack of
a comprehensive Canadian national industrial policy is at the root
of many of our social and economic problems. They have started to
enquire, "would as many residents of the Province of Quebec be
considering separation from Canada if our economic future as a
country looked brighter?" It is clear now that many people voted
for the separatist Parti Quebecois during the November 15, 1976,
election because they felt that the former Government was making a
mess of managing their economy in the Province of Quebec.

There is less agreement on what action needs to be taken immediately. While Shepherd claims that he is not unaware of the need
to enhance the innovative dynamic among smaller Canadian-owned
companies, he represents a group of Canadians that believe that we
must press immediately for the creation and fostering of large
Canadian-owned corporations. "Size is a corollary of being competitive and successful in the international arena, and Canada has no
depth in large firms." The government policy which Shepherd advo-
cates is based on "Technological Sovereignty" which links Canadian-
developed (as opposed to foreign-branch plant imported) technology
to industrial and economic goals, through an alliance between government and industry. "Only governments are Canadian-owned and strong
enough to develop the momentums for the change which is required."

"Public entrepreneurship" in bold, large-scale, development
schemes is a Canadian tradition. The Quebec economy for years has
been fueled by large projects: aluminium in Arvida, iron ore in
Gagnon and Schefferville, Expo 67, The Olympics, and now the James
Bay hydro-electric project. In New Brunswick, we recently saw the
demise of the Bricklin automobile venture. Resettlement and retrain-
ing have been a feature of economic programmes in P.E.I. In Nova
Scotia, we have the Glace Bay heavy water plant. In Manitoba, the
government promoted the big Churchill Forest Industries project.
In Saskatchewan, two large pulp mills at Prince Albert and Meadow
Lake are often cited as classic examples of how not to develop
Canada. Currently most of our focus is on Alberta, the Yukon, and
the Northwest Territories where oil, tarsands and pipelines are
touted as important to our future economic development.

The point of these examples is that we have almost totally
ignored alternative approaches, such as developing and encouraging
private, entrepreneurial, self-sufficiently in Canada. Too many in
government have accepted this "big is modern" philosophy, without
seeing technology as something that must be selected to fit the different social, cultural and economic realities of the diverse regions
in our country. Technology is not a fixed and given commodity to be
imported from abroad. The Japanese and most of the developing
countries understand this - why can't we?

---

[1] *J.J. Shepherd, IBID.*

14.1 BUILDING A BALANCED ECONOMY

A growing number of people believe that we in Canada should not expect governments to take all the initiatives to lead us out of our dilemna. More and more of us have to learn to become self-reliant and self-sufficient: individually, regionally, and as a nation. We have to restore the *balance* between those activities that do need to be centralized, concentrated, planned for, and those for which each individual should take responsibility. We need to restore the *balance* between government intervention and individual initiative. We need to restore the *balance* between small and big business.

All over the world, and especially in Canada, small business faces seven tough challenges to its survival. It will need better access to capital, raw materials, qualified labour, markets (including government purchases) and appropriate-scale technology. The managers of small and medium-sized businesses will need to be more broadly qualified and effective than is the case now; in particular, we shall need more entrepreneurs who specialize in the management of risk. Finally, and most importantly, small business will need a strong, more supportive social and economic environment, one guaranteed by law and sparked by imaginative government policies, policies free from unnecessary harassment and burdens imposed in the past by ill-conceived regulations. Some believe we will fail to meet these seven challenges and small business in Canada will be overwhelmed and snuffed out. This writer presents a more optimistic prognosis: *Small business and individual initiative does not have to disappear in Canada.* We do have a choice to make as to what kind of society we wish our children to live in[1].

"1. We need in Canada to increase our awareness and understanding of the various roles to be played by both large institutions and individuals in a more dispersed and balanced economy and to stress innovation, entrepreneurship and self-reliance as social goals."

"2. We propose that separate industrial policies be developed for the big, foreign-owned and small business sectors in Canada."

"3. Of primary importance to a small business policy would be the establishment of this measurable goal: *To increase the rate of new business formation, the number of persons employed, and the amount of Gross National Product produced in the owner-managed small and medium-sized business sector.*"

"4. Linked to this must be a clear conceptual definition of small business: *A small business concern is one which is independently owned and managed. For statistical and financial purposes, unless otherwise limited by specific regulations, a small business has at most 500 employees.*"

1

See R. Peterson, Small Business: Building a Balanced Economy (Press Porcepic, Erin, Ontario, Canada), p. 178-181.

"5. The proposed goal and the definition of small business
     should be ensconced in Canadian law, so that their
     importance is not easily forgotten and overlooked by
     future generations of civil servants, politicians and
     Canadians in general."

"6. Small business needs more than just a political voice
     in cabinet. The recently created federal Minister of
     State for Small Business needs permanent, departmental-
     level, civil service support."

"7. Greater emphasis needs to be placed upon encouraging
     true regional self-sufficiency which is based on appro-
     priate-scale technology. Measures of industrial produc-
     tivity should be developed to reflect the effective
     use of *all* inputs into the production process. The
     blind substitution of capital for labour must be
     discontinued."

"8. A number of specific policies and programmes need to be
     adapted to the Canadian milieu by the federal and
     provincial governments. These include the institu-
     tionalisation of the following:

     - a Law on the Establishment and Operation of
        Consortia. Small businesses should be advised
        and assisted financially to form consortia.

     - a Law on Subcontracting to protect all parties
        involved. Governments should demonstrate that
        subcontracting makes good economic and organi-
        sational sense through reprivatisation of many
        of their own services.

     - a Law on Government Purchasing. A fair proportion
        of all government purchases should be reserved for
        small owner-managed firms as is the case in the
        United States.

     - a Law on Guaranteed Loans. Lending to small
        businesses through the private sector chartered
        banks should be made an attractive alternative
        to all parties concerned through establishment
        of loan insurance processes as in Japan.

     - the existing tax laws need to be changed so that
        succession within an owner-managed business is
        encouraged to ensure long-run continuity of
        smaller business concerns.

     - the existing tax laws need to be changed so that
        medium-sized manufacturers pay taxes that are
        equivalent to those paid by smaller and larger
        firms.

     - a Law on Industrial and Apprenticeship Training.
        A well-defined attractive set of steps that lead
        to highly-qualified craftsman status needs to be
        established as an alternative to the currently-
        existing, academically-oriented, education system.

- a Law that provides incentives for small businessmen to upgrade their workforce and themselves.
  Education credits should be provided to employers
  for distribution to employees key to the firm's
  survival and/or expansion. This in turn would
  encourage more responsive educational programmes
  in the private sector, the colleges and universities, as well as greater use of in-house training,
  and ultimately should stimulate replacement hiring.

- a Law Establishing University Small Business
  Development Centres. Universities should be encouraged to establish research, teaching, and student-
  based consulting programmes that strengthen and
  contribute to the understanding of the small
  business sector.

- a Permanent Committee on Small Business of the House
  of Commons and Senate. A yearly airing of the concerns
  of the Canadian small business sector, along the
  lines of the Hearings carried out in the United States,
  would be useful as a means of informing and educating
  the politicians, the civil servants and the general
  public."

The above changes represent a considerable rearrangement in the
Canadian economic landscape. In November, 1976, the Toronto *Globe
and Mail* reported on a private international conference of economists
that urged the world's industrial nations to reverse the "anti-infla-
tionary slow growth" policies agreed to by President Gerald Ford and
six other heads of state at a summit conference that had been held
in Puerto Rico in June. According to the economist "The slowdown
(philosophy) is gaining so much momentum it is scaring everybody."[1]

14.2 PROGRESS TOWARDS A SMALL BUSINESS POLICY IN CANADA

The miracle of Japanese economic growth is often presented as
being due solely to Japan Incorporated - a monolithic industrial
complex[2]. But the large Japanese multinationals represent only the
tip of an iceberg. Without the diversity represented by the 68 percent of the work force working in Japanese smaller firms that support
these multinationals through subcontracting, would the rapid growth
have been possible? The Japanese experience is often discarded as
irrelevant. It is true that there is a large chasm between their
culture and ours, but the lessons to be learned do not lead to direct
emulating or copying of the Japanese systems. The lessons to be
learned are as subtle as the Japanese culture itself: *it is possible
and desirable to build an environment where small and large firms can
work effectively together.*

In the past it has been generally assumed that the problems and
dynamics of small business are similar to those of *all* businesses

---

[1] *Economic Conference Urges Slow-growth Policy Reversal (The
Globe and Mail, November 9, 1976).*

[2] *As for example in Herman Kahn, The Emerging Japanese Super-
state: Challenge and Response.*

and therefore no special attention nor understanding for the former was necessary. While this is true to an extent, some important differences have been overlooked. Also, small manufacturers, wholesalers or retailers, whether individually or in groups, have in the past not been organised to defend their own interests successfully, especially in comparison with larger groups such as government or big business. Owner-managers are not by nature the types who join groups easily. They prefer to operate individually. But the politics of small business has changed considerably and we can expect to hear a great deal more from them in the near future.

To start with, the speech from the throne, at the Opening of the Second Session of the Thirtieth Canadian Parliament, October 12, 1976, assures us that:

"The Government ... places a very high value on the contribution small businesses make to the economic and social well-being of Canadians. Small owner-managed firms are a mainstay of employment in cities and towns across the country. They supply goods and services essential to consumers and to other business, and they demonstrate the innovation and entrepreneurship from which successful enterprise must spring. More than that, small business, and the people who own them, manage them, and work in them, are the economic backbone of countless communities throughout Canada."

In *The Way Ahead*, a Liberal party working paper, this sentiment was echoed, but with an added dimension, when it was acknowledged that "bigger is not necessarily better... efficiencies of scale may be overestimated"... (and) "opportunities may arise, where it is possible and desirable to lean against centralizing forces."[1] In Canada, as in many other countries, the political commitment to small business is nonpartisan. All federal and provincial parties support, admittedly to varying degrees and for different reasons, the strengthening of this sector of our economy.

The Liberal opposition party in the Province of Ontario (Canada's most populated and industrialised region) will introduce in the next session of Legislature a Private Member's Bill called *An Act Respecting Small Business in Ontario*[2]. The Bill proposes:

(i)   an independently owned operated definition of small business;

(ii)   a government purchasing programme from small business;

(iii)   a government subcontracting programme with small business;

---

[1] *The Way Ahead: A Framework for Discussion, (Government of Canada Working Paper, Oct. 1976), p. 29*

[2] *T. Eakins, (MPP, 1st session, 31st Legislature, Ontario, 1977, starting in November 1977).*

(iv)   a government Small Business Certification programme that declares, upon investigation, certain small businesses to be"... in sound financial and productive position."

(v)   a government programme to encourage the formation of small business consortia (co-operatives);

(vi)   a standing committee of the Assembly that reports annually "... with respect to all aspects meriting legislative attention with respect to small businesses..."

Because of the minority government in Ontario this Private Member's Bill has an excellent chance of passage.

The Federal Government's support of Canadian small business can be seen as beginning in 1944 when the Industrial Development Bank (IDB) was established to provide debt financing to small firms and to help small business adjust to post war economic conditions. The Federal Business Development Bank (FBDB) replaced the IDB in 1975 with expanded powers in the direct lending area, as well as being empowered to make equity investments in small firms. The FBDB also offers advisory services to small business for a nominal fee.

The Small Business Loans Act (SBLA) is another programme which helps small firms to meet their debt financing requirements through government guaranteed loans acquired from private chartered banks. In June, 1977 Parliament passed legislation which made the programme available to a larger group of smaller businesses. Although the revised legislation failed to resolve the most difficult issue of how to establish an interest rate on individual loans that made such loans attractive to chartered banks.

Probably the most important measure which helps small businesses is the preferential tax rate paid by private, Canadian-controlled firms with taxable income less than $150,000 per year. Such companies may pay tax rates as low as 25 percent compared to the normal corporate rate of 46 percent.

In economically disadvantaged regions small businesses have benefited from industrial incentive programmes offered by the Department of Regional Economic Expansion. Recently (Summer, 1977), the Federal Department of Industry, Trade and Commerce announced a revision in its aid programmes to small business. The new Enterprise Development Programme (EDP) is intended to help small firms produce and market new products and implement innovative production techniques. EDP will be administered on a decentralized basis through regional boards consisting of both private sector and government personnel.

In addition to these federal initiatives, all the 10 provincial and 2 territorial governments are involved in small business assistance, typically through provincial development corporations and counselling services run through provincial departments of industry and commerce. Considerable overlap, duplication and gaps exist between federal and provincial programmes. This lack of coordination has resulted in confusion among small businessmen and wasted expenditures of the taxpayer's money.

The Small Business Secretariat, in the Federal Department of Industry, Trade and Commerce has created a significantly improved climate for small business policy measures among civil servants in Ottawa, since its formation about a year ago. Although considerable work remains to be done in the political arena.

On September 19, 1977 at the Annual Meeting of the Canadian Chamber of Commerce the Federal government announced a series of directions and initiatives it intends to pursue in the future[1]:

(i)   the Federal government will improve coordination among federal and provincial programmes;

(ii)   the Federal government will create easier access by small business to information available from government sources;

(iii) the Federal government will study the applicability of small business investment company mechanism to the Canadian economic content;

(iv)   the Federal government will study the feasibility of pilot projects to provide a meeting-point mechanism to bring together entrepreneurs, investors, academic-techno-logical sources, government agencies, and other elements whose activities have a bearing on small business;

(v)   specific tax measures that have a bearing on small business will be studied, including inter-generational transfers, the tax treatment of spouses'incomes, and non-arms's length gains and income, as well as the general effect of tax measures on venture financing;

(vi)   the Federal government will study the feasibility of encouraging closer and mutually beneficial relationships between small and large firms;

(vii) the Federal government will examine means to assist small business through government procurement policies;

(viii) the Federal government will analyse the collection of data by all levels of government, with the aim of deter-mining the utility and dispensibility of data collection forms;

(ix)   a statistical handbook on small business will be prepared and published by the federal government, and efforts will be increased in order to make useful statis-tical information available to assist small business in making business decisions.

A significant omission from the above initiatives is the mention of a Small Business Act, such as proposed by the writer and being introduced into debate in the Ontario Provincial Legislature by the Opposition Liberal Party. The unresolved major difficulty remains the definition of what constitutes small business in the Canadian economy which is dominated by foreign owned companies.

---

[1] *Small Business in Canada: Perspectives, (Minister of State Small Business, Government of Canada, Cat.No.C2-55/1977, Sept. 1977)* p. 30-31.

In the years ahead we shall see a continuing battle in the political arena on the issue of Canadian ownership. The Canadian Federation of Independent Business, representing considerable political influence through its approximately 50,000 company members is expected to lead this fight.

The central philosophy which dominates the actions of the CFIB is the diffusion of power in all sectors[1]. The CFIB is convinced that small businessmen must become increasingly politicised if they are to provide the stimulus to bring about the necessary structural changes that will reinforce the natural forces of decentralisation. If small business organisations do not take this leadership, "overly centralised Western societies will become increasingly difficult to govern by democratic means; and our democracies will be replaced in differing degrees by various forms of bureaucratic authoritarianism and central planning".

In September, 1976, Prime Minister Trudeau named Len Marchand (replaced in September 1977 by Tony Abbot) as the first Federal cabinet minister with special responsibilities for small business. This was a clear acknowledgement by the government that the needs and interests of large and small business are not identical. Furthermore, small business is expected to play a major role in reversing the deliterious economic trends described by Shepherd at the beginning of this chapter.

Based on J.F. Bulloch : The Politics of Small Business, (International Symposium on Small Business, Washington D.C., 1976). See also J.R. Conrad: La politique des petites et moyennes entreprises, (Club Richelieu, Victoriaville, P.Q., 1976).

FRANCE

Will E. Straver[1]

15

Introduction

The richness and variety of public and private organisations which have as their explicit goal the fostering of the cause of the small business makes the preparation of a global overview a challenging proposition. This task is further complicated by multiple sets of beliefs or attitudes prevailing among the various agents involved in the life of small business such as owners, managers, employees, bankers, government officials and the general public. Finally, the author of the overview must seek an equilibrium between subjective opinion and objective facts while also seeking to equilibrate stereotyped opinions with specifically identifiable strengths and weaknesses of small business in France.

In this article, we have elected to go from the general to the specific. After a brief review of possible reasons explaining the absence of a general public policy towards small business, we provide a review of institutions, public and private, that assist the development of small business in the field of finance, technology and management. Finally, we provide a description of the set of government initiatives developed in 1976 and implemented that same year through pilot operations.

15.1 SMALL BUSINESS IN FRANCE - THE ABSENCE OF A GENERAL POLICY

One basic observation we can make is that small business has not really been treated as a significant factor in the establishment of national economic policy. In the preparation of national economic plans, policy development for small business has occurred at the level of sub-commissions. Further, the historical centralisation of political and economic power and structures in Paris has made it difficult to respond to the needs of small business in the various regions. Governments have been accused of being insensitive to small business needs as a consequence. The close grip that the government has over the banking system, particularly via the major

---

[1] *Professor, Institut Européen d'Administration des Affaires (INSEAD), Fontainebleau, France.*

nationalised banks, has a strong influence upon their credit policy. Furthermore, many banks are said to act more as a no-risk source of credit than as a partner in the development of a business. Finally, the lack of a co-ordinated policy at national level concerning financing, technical and managerial assistance apparently makes it difficult for many small business owners to fully utilize the wide range of services available.

We may propose a number of reasons to explain why the cause of small business has not been supported at national policy level. A quote from the Mialaret report[1] already goes a long way in helping understand the status of small business:

"Today's society doesn't appreciate the classical motivations of the entrepreneur nor the kind of success he achieves. The expression of the entrepreneurial personality goes against the current evolution towards socialisation of society. Further, entrepreneurial success is of an economic character with profit as its measure, which is considered immoral by an influential segment of the population (academicians, government officials, writers, economists)."

A second reason we propose is the lack of political clout on the part of small industrial enterprises (SMI). Whereas commercial enterprises have been quite active politically through their national association CGPME (Confédération Générale des Petites et Moyennes Entreprises), SMI have depended greatly on the national employers' federation CNPF (Confédération Nationale du Patronat Français). SMI consider the CNPF and its national sectorial federations too passive vis-à-vis the development of small business interests. At the level of government structure, the winds have not always blown in favor of SMI. In 1969, the Ministère de Développement Industriel et Scientifique (today the Ministère de l'Industrie, du Commerce et de l'Artisanat) created the position of Secretary of State for SMI. However, this function was eliminated in 1973. The new position of "Délégué à la PMI" was created only in April 1976 as part of a new government program which we will discuss later.

A third reason we propose is the lack of urgency. Prior the 1974 economic crisis, small *industries* were actively participating in the economic boom. We observe that small *commercial enterprises* were affected by the creation of hypermarkets and discounters. Their political might helped pass the 1973 Loi Royer which installed a more balanced approach to implantation of such mass distribution centres. Industrial firms were particularly touched by inflation, high raw material costs, energy costs and labour costs when orders started to fall around 1974.

A fourth reason may well be related to the problem of political continuity. France has a history of rapidly changing governments causing frequent periods of uncertainty. We mention in particular the political crisis of May 1968 as new venture creations which had run at 4 percent of the existing park, declined that year to

---

[1] *Pour Entreprendre, (Commission Mialaret, 1973).*

1.5 percent and went as low as 1 percent in 1970. The rate of creation of new business now runs about 3.5 to 4 percent[1]. This presents roughly 10,000 creations in an average year. This rate of creation is still low as compared with the German Federal Republic (5 to 6 percent) and the United States (8 to 10 percent)[2].

The above comments suggest that the general situation of small business has not received full attention at national policy level. In the absence of a specific government policy they find themselves in the maelstrom of the competitive markets. Yet, as we shall point out in the next sections of this paper, many public and private initiatives have been taken to foster the development of small business. But as there has been no central force to coordinate these efforts. structures and programmes available to small business, the entrepreneur is faced with a maze of services through which he has trouble finding his way

Finally, a major problem in the formulation of initiatives in favour of small business is that such initiatives often result more from political pressures by a number of powerful interest groups, rather than being based on research into the causes of the problems which the government is asked to alleviate.

15.2 STRUCTURES SUPPORTING SMALL BUSINESS DEVELOPMENT

These are numerous organisations in France that are fully or partially implicated in the development of small business. They are public, private, non-profit, and voluntary in nature, covering a wide range of philosophies and objectives. Their assistance may be a combination of financial, technical, managerial and developmental programmes.

In order to facilitate comprehension of the structures that provide assistance to small business, we have created Figure 15.1. Horizontally, this Figure shows the various Ministries involved in small business programmes, the organisations that fall under their responsibility, the direct or indirect way in which help is given, and the type of assistance supplied. Vertically, on the right hand side the Figure indicates the major professional organisations participating in the enhancement of the small business cause: technical centres, chambers of commerce, chambers of trade, financial structures, professional associations and educational institutes.

In our subsequent discussion of these structures, we analyse the individual structures and their relationship with other structures according to the predominent type of assistance they provide: financial, technical, managerial and developmental.

---

[1] *Les Echos, (18 avril 1974).*

[2] *Pour entreprendre, (Commission Mialaret, 1973).*

(i)   Financial institution

(a)   Public and semi-public institutions

- The DATAR (Délégation à l'Aménagement du Territoire et
à l'Action Régionale) of the Ministère de l'Equipement
et de l'Aménagement du Territoire plays a major role
in the decentralisation of large programmes and firms
away from the Paris area. Through association with
regional industrialists, DATAR seeks to enhance the
erection of new ventures in certain regions. It
provides subsidies of up to 80,000 Francs per creation
under the condition that the new enterprise create at
least 10 new jobs.

- The ANVAR (Agence Nationale de Valorisation de la
Recherche) is a public organisation under tutelage
of the Ministère de l'Education Nationale. It was
created in 1967. Although primarily having a vocation
to bring public (in particular those of the CNRS -
Centre National de la Recherche Scientifique)   or
private inventions to commercialisation this organisation does provide some financial help to individuals
desiring to create their technology-based firm (or to
existing firms). This financial assistance averages
300,000 Francs and is designed to bring the inventor
to the prototype phase of his new venture.

- The DITEIM (Direction de la Technologie, de
l'Environnement Industriel et des Mines) (1969)
provides financial assistance at the pre-development
stage of new processes. Access to these firms is open
to projects presented by enterprises and public
laboratories or professional technical centres. An
average of 200,000 Francs, to finance between
50 percent and 70 percent of the project cost, is
made available to research centres that are associated with a firm that can eventually commercialise
the invention. Clearly, individual inventors must
insert themselves in this structural set-up of they
are to be eligible for these funds.

- The DGRST (Délégation Générale à la Recherche
Scientifique et Technique) (1959) makes available
an average 1,500,000 Francs per contract to help a
public or private laboratory or an enterprise to
develop an innovation, covering a maximum of 80 percent
of the project cost.

- The FDES (Fonds de Développement Economique et
Social) (1955) under tutelage of the Ministère de
l'Economie et des Finances has as objective to foster
the development of small business by providing funds
indirectly via the private banking system, particularly the CCCHCI (Caisse Centrale du Crédit Hôtelier,
Commercial and Industriel) and the Crédit Populaire.
These two structures play a major role in financing
the development of small business. They get a
government subsidy on interest rates.

- The CNME (Caisse Nationale des Marchés de l'Etat) under tutelage of the Ministère de l'Economie et des Finances indirectly finances innovation and development by making funds available to banks. The MICA (Ministère de l'Industrie, du Commerce et de l'Artisanat) makes a technical survey of the proposed project and the CNME approves financing by issuing a "Lettre d'agrément" which recognises the innovative value of the project (or product) and the need to help the firm commercialise it. With this letter, the firm gets access to bank loans made available by the CNME from a special fund. The loans are reimbursed over a period varying normally between 4 and 5 years. As of January 1978, a project may be financed 100 percent. This CNME procedure aknowledges a certain risk factor that requires more in-depth study and guarantees that go beyond the realm of the clearing or merchant banks.

- The CN (Crédit National) is not a bank but a semi-public financial organisation that is the principal re-discounter in medium-term financing and the main distributor of long-term financing of industrial investments of larger firms. The CN actively participates in SDR's (Sociétés de Développement Régional) and has played a major role in setting up of SOFINNOVA, a venture capital firm in Paris.

- The IDI (Institut de Développement Industriel) (1971) was created by the Government (48 percent), the Crédit National (13 percent) and main public and private banks. This structure has an objective to make available investment funds (300 million Francs in 1977) for regional or sectorial development programmes. Most enterprises benefiting from IDI intervention (mostly between 1 and 5 million Francs) are medium to large in size (10 to 150 million Francs turnover). Less than 10 percent of the interventions are with small enterprises having less than 10 million Francs turnover. In principle, IDI plays the same role as a venture capital firm in that it gets out of its participation after 5 years.

- The three major French banks, Banque Nationale de Paris, Crédit Lyonnais, and Société Générale are nationalised. Branch activities in regional areas are closely controlled by Paris Headquarters to ascertain implementation of government financial policies. The Société Générale created the SOGINNOVE in 1970 to assist in financing innovation.

(b)   Private Structures

- The SDR's (Sociétés de Développement Régional) (1955) are private corporations created with the co-operation of the Ministère de l'Equipement et de l'Aménagement du Territoire as part of the government effort to

encourage enterprise creation and development in
the various regions, away from the Paris hub. The
primary purpose of an SDR is to take a temporary
equity position with a firm or to provide loans.
In practice, SDR's do not attract local savings
but are financed by large (often nationalised) banks
and large corporations. They lend mainly to large
and medium-sized enterprises and are not very active
in lending to small businesses. Today the 15 SDR's
have taken 250 million Francs in participations and
have granted 11 billion Francs in long-term loans.
Their combined capital and reserves amount to
480 million Francs.

- Aside from its nationalised banks, France has a large
  number of private clearing banks, the most important
  among which are the Crédit Commercial de France, the
  Crédit Industriel and Commercial (grouping regional
  banks) and the Banque de l'Union Parisienne-Crédit
  du Nord. Of particular interest to small business
  are the Crédit Agricole which plays a special role,
  assigned by the government, in the development of
  rural enterprise and artisanat and the Crédit Populaire de France (Groupe de banques populaires)
  financed by the FDES and driving force of the CCCHCI
  (Caisse Centrale du Crédit Hôtelier, Commercial et
  Industriel). CCCHCI is the source of funds specialised
  in medium and long-term financing for small and
  medium-sized firms. The Banques Populaires also
  provide loans to artisans, with interest rates subsidised by the FDES (Fonds de Développement Economique
  et Social).

- Further, a number of merchant banks take participation
  in or provide loans to new or developing enterprises.
  Among the best known are La Banque de Paris et des
  Pays-Bas, la Banque de Suez, la Banque de l'Union
  Européenne and la Banque Lazare.

- Venture capitalism, although present in France, has
  never boomed. Two firms, EED (European Enterprises
  Development) (1968) and SOFINNOVA (1971) have as objective to take temporary participations going from 10
  to 50 percent in a new venture or in the expansion
  of the equity base of an existing venture. SOFINNOVA
  works closely with ANVAR, IDI and SDR's but is really
  too small to make a clear impact on new venture
  creation with about 100 participations of an average
  400,000 Francs, among which 25 percent constitutes
  real new venture creations. EED, which has generally
  taken fewer but larger participations is currently
  undergoing a financial restructuring.

- A certain number of financing corporations has been
  created by banks to explicitly assist small business
  development. We mention as examples SOPROMEC (of
  the Groupe des Banques Populaires) which may take an

143

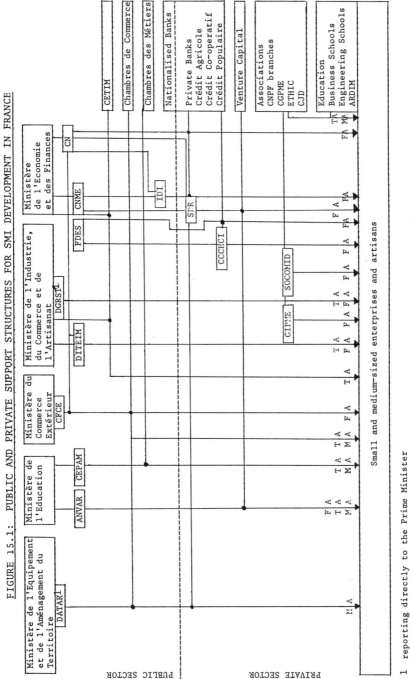

FIGURE 15.1: PUBLIC AND PRIVATE SUPPORT STRUCTURES FOR SMI DEVELOPMENT IN FRANCE

1 reporting directly to the Prime Minister
FA financial assistance
TA technical assistance
MA management assistance

equity position in 50 percent of its interventions
and provide personal loans to firm owners in the
other 50 percent. The BANNEXI (created by the Banque
de Paris) is designed to assist industrial enterprises needing financial restructuring. Two-thirds
of its capital goes to dealings in property or with
large enterprises, with one-third going to holdings
in small and medium-sized enterprises. In 1974,
BANEXI had 70 holdings with a total of 320 million
Francs[1].

- A number of private enterprises, associations and
  educational institutions make available start-up
  capital or loans to new or existing enterprises.
  The CGPME (Confédération Générale de la Petite et
  Moyenne Entreprise) has created with a number of
  banks the ACPME (Association pour Favoriser la
  Distribution du Crédit aux PME). It has also created
  the SOCOMID-PME (Société de Caution Mutuelle pour
  le Financement des Industries Diverses) which
  guarantees loans made to small businesses provided
  the CNME has given its agreement.

- Leasing has become a favored method of financing
  equipment as it enables small business owners to
  maintain control over their company by avoiding
  outside participation to expand the firm's capital
  base.

- The regional stock markets at Lyon, Nancy, Lille,
  Marseille, Bordeaux and Nantes account together for
  only 3 percent of total movements in France. Their
  role in financing small businesses, even those that
  would want to go public, is very limited.

(c) Problems prevailing in financial assistance

As is evident from the preceding text and Figure 15.1,
the system of financing available to small business is
very complex and lacks guidelines for the user. The
author has observed in interviews with SMI managers
that their knowledge of potential sources of financing
is fragmentary, reflecting both their own preference
to contact a local banker and the absence of a clear
information system on the part of the financial
institutions.

SMI access to medium and long-term loans is difficult.
Bankers hesitate to engage in costly project evaluation
procedures for small loans, considering the risk-
reward trade-off insufficiently attractive. They
substitute for the lack of knowledge concerning

---

[1] *National Reports on the Equity Financing Problems of Small
and Medium-sized Enterprises, (EEC, Brussels, 1975).*

the SMI with a demand for collateral. The efforts by
institutions such as CNME, CCCHCI, SOCOMID, Crédit
Populaire and Crédit Agricole have been very beneficial for SMI on the other hand.

One major financing problem persists: expansion of
SMI equity base. Whereas self-financing through
retained earnings has been a favoured practice, the
current economic conditions make this difficult to
achieve. As SMI managers wish to maintain control
of their company, limited alternatives exist. The
SDR's, with their objective to create larger-scale
operations, are of some help. However, many SMI
managers turn to leasing which has turned out to be
problematic in periods of recession (heavy charges;
overcapacity).

Finally, whatever observations we may make on the
inadequacy of the financial system, bankers insist
that the major problem SMI encounter is that of
appropriate management policies and strategy formulation.

(ii)   Technological assistance

(a)   Public or semi-public structures

-   The ANVAR already mentioned before, annually takes
    about 2,000 outputs from public laboratories (such
    as CNRS), universities and private laboratories with
    the objective to bring the innovation to the point
    of industrial exploitation. Through its Small
    Business Unit, it sells new techniques to new or
    existing enterprises and diffuses these techniques
    nationally and internationally. Its information
    service called SICANVAR tries to match innovations
    with the profile of companies subscribing to its
    service. It also helps inventors to obtain patent
    protection via the INPI (Institut National de la
    Propriété Industrielle) which registers designs and
    patents.

-   The DITEIM and DGRST, also mentioned before, provide
    technical assistance to the projects which they
    partially finance.

-   As an example of technological assistance at the
    industry sector level, we may mention the CETIM
    (Centre d'Etudes Techniques de l'Industrie Mécanique).
    This structure has links with the Ministère de
    l'Industrie, du Commerce et de l'Artisanat and the
    Ministère de l'Economie et des Finances. Its
    audience consists mainly of artisans and small busi-
    nesses with a turnover of less than 500,000 Francs.
    By means of personal visits by technical specialists
    and through travelling trucks equipped with latest
    technologies this organisation tries to keep its
    dues-paying members informed.

- The Chambers of Trade (Chambres de Métiers) have a
  major responsibility in ascertaining the proper
  technical qualifications of artisan apprentices who
  receive a diploma "maître-artisan". All enterprises
  in the chamber must send their apprentices through
  such programs. At the level of the owner/manager,
  technical assistants are sent into individual enterprises or hold regional meetings to help them keep
  abreast of new technology or to assist in solving
  technical, operational problems. These technical
  assistants receive their own schooling at the CEPAM
  (Centre d'Etudes et de Perfectionnement de l'Artisanat
  et des Métiers), created in 1967 by the chambers
  with government help (Direction de l'Artisanat) and
  under the supervision of the Ministère de l'Education.

(b)   Private institutions

- Assistance is provided to enterprises seeking innovation in products by DRI (Délégués aux Relations
  Industrielles) who work at the A.D.E.R. (Associations
  pour le Développement de l'Enseignement et de la
  Recherche). These associations are of a regional
  nature and are created by groups of academicians,
  bankers and business men. The first DRI was appointed
  in 1972; today there are 18 DRI. They are selected
  by their region and appointed by the Ministère de
  l'Industrie, du Commerce et de l'Artisanat.

(c)   Problems prevailing in technological assistance

A number of problems seem to persist in the area of
technology. First of all, the French SMI manager is
said to be a good inventor but lacking the knack to
commercialise his ideas. The author has found in his
interviews with SMI that the majority have engineering
and technical background, which tends to explain why
they would be production-orientated rather than mar-
keting-orientated. Also, such background may lead
to a tendency to overinvest in new technology not
adapted to the style and scale of SMI operations.

Secondly, the diffusion of innovative technologies
to SMI has only recently been accelerated by institutions like ANVAR. It is obviously extremely
difficult for this organisation to cover the entire
fabric of SMI in France with new ideas, although
subscribers to SICANAVAR find help in technology
transfer.

We must also acknowledge that professional associations
may not be successful in feeding technological information to SMI. Particularly those associations which
operate at a national level are sometimes accused of
an attitude of waiting for the businessman to come to
them. The role of the DRI who go to SMI on a
regional basis should be beneficial.

(iii)   Managerial assistance

A large number of public and private structures, many
of which have already been referred to when discussing
financial and technological assistance, are active in
France.

(a)   Public and semi-public structures

- The DATAR plays a co-ordinating role via regional and
  local institutions such as préfectures, chambres de
  commerce etc.

- The ANVAR, in addition to its major role as diffuser
  of innovation, gives limited financial help and assists
  inventors in the process of setting up their firm.
  For example, it helps obtain patent protection, it
  puts an inventor in contact with a venture capital
  firm such as SOFINNOVA, and it helps evaluate over-all
  commercial aspects of the project.

- We reported before that the Chambres de Métiers
  have created the CEPAM to train technical assistants.
  In addition, they train specialists in business administration ("moniteurs de gestion") who then teach
  small businessmen, either on an individual or on a
  collective basis, to deal with general management
  problems.

- The Chambers of Commerce (Chambres de Commerce et
  d'Industrie) have recently started to play an active
  role in counselling small businessmen. Many have
  set up "Bureaux de Promotion Industrielle" which
  organise regular discussion groups among a dozen
  entrepreneurs or so, but also offer complete training
  programmes for small business owners ("cycles d'initiation à la gestion"). A BPI may also look into
  specific problems of an individual firm. Implementation of new materials and programmes at the enterprise is sought with the assistance of outside
  consultants. Collectively, the 150 Chambers of
  Commerce in France now have 180 AGI (Assistant Technique en Gestion Industrielle) who have received
  special training at the CEFAGI (Centre d'Etudes et
  de Formation des Assistants en Gestion Industrielle).
  The government plans to add 50 AGI per year as of
  1977.

(b)   Private Structures

Managerial assistance and education is available from
a large number of organisations, including venture
capital firms, professional and interprofessional
associations, and from business schools.

- The venture capital firms - EED and SOFINNOVA - have
  put heavy emphasis on evaluating the managerial capacities of an inventor. Where necessary, they may well

have suggested that the inventor join forces with an
entrepreneur. As part of the agreement to take an
equity position in a firm, SOFINNOVA assist the new
manager in the general operation of his venture. This
aid may vary from financial control to marketing
program implementation.

- The CGPME provides managerial assistance via SOCOMID,
  already discussed before.

- The ETHIC (Mouvement des Entreprises de Taille Humaine
  Industrielles et Commerciales) nurtures a committee
  that responds to questions from potential entrepreneurs
  and makes frequent interventions in new venture
  creation programs at universities and business schools.
  ETHIC was created in 1975 by 25 creators/managers of
  medium-sized industrial enterprises with the objective
  to better foster the cause of SMI.

- The CJD (Centre des Jeunes Dirigeants) groups about
  2'500 managers/owners of small industrial firms. Among
  the members, 1/3 have created their own firm. Most
  members open up their enterprises to help new venture
  creators. Over 150 case histories have been written
  for use in pedagogical curriculae. Special task forces
  on new venture creation are available for counsel.

- Within the CNPF (Conseil National du Patronat Français),
  the French employers'federation, assistance programmes
  for small business exist mainly at the regional level,
  In technical and economic matters, the first branch has
  national federations of industry sectors as members.
  A typical example is the CETIM mentioned before which
  was created with the co-operation of the Ministère de
  l'Industrie, du Commerce et de l'Artisanat. The second
  branch is more concerned with social matters. It is
  organised by industrial sectors at national level but
  also has regional and local inter-professional associations. At the local level, such organisations are
  quite active in providing managerial training programmes.
  to their managers. For example, the GGIISM (Groupement
  Général Interprofessionnel Interentreprise de Seine-
  et-Marne) near Paris has just created with INSEAD
  (European Institute of Business Administration) a
  total programme of need identification, programme construction and diagnostic operations.

- Many of the universities and business schools who work
  within the framework of the FNEGE (Fondation Nationale
  pour l'Enseignement de la Gestion d'Entreprise) provide
  some type of education for small business creators
  and managers. Whereas only a few have a specific
  programme on new venture creation and management, most
  cater to small business managers in their education,
  research and consulting programmes. The ARDIM (Association pour la Recherche et le Développement des
  Moyens Pédagogiques favorisant la Création et le

Développement de Petites, Moyennes et Nouvelles
Entreprises) is a non-profit organisation which tries
to enhance new venture creation through development
of appropriate curriculae at member institutions.

(c)   Problems prevailing in managerial assistance

A major problem raised by many SMI managers inter-
viewed by the author is that post-management education
programmes on the market are not adapted to the needs
of small business. Programmes such as developed recently by the GGIISM should help overcome part of this
problem.

Secondly, managerial assistance provided by public
or semi-public institutions is not always welcomed as
it is seen as government-sourced intervention by some
SMI managers. Others question the real experience
and knowledge of these consultants of SMI operations
and needs.

In the area of preparing new entrepreneurs, programmes
at business schools, schools of engineering, and
universities are said to be too theoretical and too
general. Efforts made by ETHIC, ARDIM and CJD should
help improve contact with reality by enterprise visits,
interventions by business men and the use of live
case histories.

Finally, as stated in the Mialaret report, very
frequently new ventures are created by technicians
who have technological expertise but who do not
possess appropriate managerial and administrative
capacities. On the other hand, those generalists
with appropriate management education who want to
start a new venture often lack a precise idea of
what they want to produce and how to produce it.

(iv)   Development institutions

There are many institutions among those mentioned
before that are very active in developing small
business. The DATAR by definition tries to use the
fabric of regional and local business activity to
decentralise business from the Paris region.

The development associations (A.D.E.R.) now have
18 delegates (DRI) whose responsibility includes to
assist regional and local enterprises to acquire
new technologies.

The regional and local Chambers of Commerce, via
the technical assistants (ATI) at the promotion
centres (B.P.I.), support small business development
in multiple ways: providing information; supporting
programmes on new venture creation at local business
schools; assisting businessmen with management

problems; and holding regular meetings and seminars
where SMI managers exchange information and are exposed
to new management techniques. The ATI are to play a
significant role in expediting the paperwork process
in new venture creation.

Both the technical and social regional and local
branches of the employers'federation (CNPF) play very
active roles in the creation and development of SMI.

In the financial arena, both IDI and SDR's are trying
to improve the industrial structure in the various
regions by enlarging the scale of operations or by
trying to merge enterprises to create more viable units.
We must acknowledge that these institutes could expand
their role with small industries.

Finally, the financial institutions which have a
particular role to play in the development of small
business - Crédit Hôtelier (CCCHCI), Crédit Agricole,
Crédit Populaire (Banques Populaires) and Crédit
Coopératif are almost functioning as regional development banks.

15.3 MAJOR INITIATIVES TAKEN TO ENHANCE SMALL BUSINESS DEVELOPMENT

The period of energy crisis and stagflation which started in
1974 showed how vulnerable small businesses are to environmental
threat. Costs sky-rocketed and markets disappeared in many sectors.
The new government which arrived in 1974 under President Giscard
d'Estaing faced the challenge of reviving the fabric of small business in France in order to preserve and improve the country's economic
competitiveness.

Plans were developped that led to the presentation by the Ministère de l'Industrie, du Commerce et de l'Artisanat of a full action
programme in favour of small and medium-sized industrial firms (SMI)
in March 1976. The principal details of this action programme are
outlined below.

First of all, the action programme established the socio-
economic importance of SMI in France. For purposes of defining the
target group of the programme, only small industries (6 to 49
employees) and medium-sized industries (50 to 499 employees) were
included. (A small firm employing between 1 and 5 persons was considered an artisan operation.) The importance of the SMI concerned was
established: in 1973 these 400,000 firms represented 96 percent of
all enterprises, 41 percent of all employees, 33 percent of all
turnover, 35 percent of total value added, and 24 percent of all
investment.

Secondly, the action programme starts with the premise that SMI
have a particular function in the economy and offer specific advantages that are of a unique character:

-   SMI have the flexibility to respond to very personalised
    demands: their small production units are well-adapted to the
    specific needs of certain sectors (e.g. precision tools).

- SMI have a great ability to innovate in products and processes (e.g. energy saving; new energy; small computer equipment).

- SMI may be more profitable than many large enterprises. Figures show that the rate of bankruptcies has increased least for small business in 1974/75.

- SMI help maintain a competitive market system, as shown in the United States.

- SMI assist in the achievement of social promotion: at least 90 percent of new venture creators have been employees before; about 50 percent are self-made men without advanced degrees.

- SMI contribute to regional development.

As a third point, the action programme recalls the environmental threat that weighs heavily on SMI, demanding therefore measures to alleviate the situation:

- SMI have limited access to the growing marker of large export contracts. Figures show that large firms export an average 16.1 percent of their turnover as compared with only 6.4 percent for SMI.

- SMI spend relatively less on R&D than large firms: 0.8 percent of value-added as compared with 4.1 percent.

- SMI suffer disproportionately from administrative obligations and formalities.

- Notwithstanding some specialised financial organisations, the over-all structure and methods of financing are not favourable to SMI.

The action programme which takes into consideration the preceding text, covers four major areas of concern to SMI: new venture creation; financing; management education; and subcontracting.

(i)   New venture creation

First of all, in order to simplify the formalities and steps to be taken in creating a new venture, the technical assistants at the Chambers of Commerce will assist entrepreneurs in pre-start-up and start-up procedures.

Secondly, more attention will be given to the formal education of new venture creators by business schools, engineering schools, permanent education programmes (Chambers of Commerce will play an important role to train 1'000 persons a year to obtain their "brevet professionnel") and by technical high schools so as to better prepare entrepreneurs to create and manage a firm.

Thirdly, a 1000 Francs tax which is a compulsory forfeit for any firm since 1974 is abolished for the first three years of operation of a new venture, provided its shareholders are physical persons.

(ii)   <u>Financing the creation and development of SMI</u>

This part of the programme is geared to alleviate two major problems faced by SMI: access to short-term credit in periods of recession and expansion of their equity base.

First of all, the SDR (Sociétés de Développement Régional) will be allotted special funds to take equity positions in regional enterprises that are not quoted on the stock market and are not subsidiaries of quoted firms, provided also that their turnover is less than 100 million Francs. These funds can cover 25 percent of the participation in existing firms and 50 percent in the case of new ventures. In selecting projects and participation rates the SDR are to work within the government programme of regional development.

Secondly, a study will be made to create closed small business investment companies (SICAV's) that would take equity positions in non-quoted SMI.

Thirdly, managing partners of SMI as defined above may now deduct interest on their advances to the firm's current accounts, provided these accounts do not exceed 150 percent of the firm's equity.

Fourthly, in order to accelerate payments to SMI on government contracts, the CNME (Caisse Nationale des Marchés de l'Etat) will pay 90 percent of the invoice after a two months delay.

(iii)   <u>Help in managing SMI</u>

Firstly, the role of the Chambers of Commerce is expanded. Technical assistants (Assistants techniques à la Gestion Industrielle) will do more counselling and diagnostic work. Further, 50 assistants will be trained each year by the CETAGI (Centre d'Etudes et de Formation des Assistants en Gestion Industrielle).

Secondly, a system will be created where appropriately trained administrators help firms in difficulty overcome their deficit situation prior to the starting of the legal procedure required by law. Their guidance will also be available to healthy firms.

Thirdly, an effort will be made to co-ordinate the action programmes of SDR, Crédit National, Caisse Centrale du Crédit Hôtelier, Industriel et Commercial, and the Caisse Nationale des Marchés d'Etats with those of the Chambers of Commerce.

Fourthly, the various SMI associations are to collaborate closely with the government programme started in 1969 to train potential entrepreneurs and to assist firms in the management of their operations.

(iv)   <u>Export assistance to SMI</u>

Export credits made available to finance investments that will lead to exports are brought to 10 billion Francs. Priority is given to SMI which export directly or indirectly as subcontractors to exporting firms.

Secondly, the regional programme "New Exporters" aimed at improving SMI access to foreign markets will be continued in 1977.

Thirdly, the funds of UFINEX (Union pour le Financement et l'Expansion du Commerce International) are augmented by 5 million Francs to facilitate foreign investment by SMI (loans are granted over 15 years provided exports follow at a rate of 3 to 4 times the investment over 5 years).

Fourthly, French international commercial counselors will play a greater role in facilitating SMI access to foreign markets.

Fifthly, following the successful decentralisation of export aid facilities to Lyon, other cities will be added: Lille, Bordeaux, Marseille, Nancy, Nantes and Strasbourg. This decentralisation will be executed by local offices of the Customs Department, the Banque de France, the CFCE (Centre Français du Commerce Extérieur) and the COFACE (Companie Française d'Assurance pour le Commerce Extérieur).

Finally, a reorganisation of the CFCE will give more information and assistance to SMI.

(v)   Sub-contracting

A commission (Commission Technique de la soustraitance) will be created to study the subcontracting market, information about which is still scarce. The objective is to increase information flow between order-letters and order-takers, to encourage firms to subcontract on a wider basis, and to help order-takers to diversify their clientele.

Secondly, SMI will be encouraged to create temporary structures (such as GIE - Groupement d'Intérêt Economique) to make it possible to submit bids on projects with a group of SMI.

Finally, the Ministère de l'Economie et des Finances and Ministère de l'Industrie, du Commerce et de l'Artisanat will develop measures that will facilitate SMI access to government contracts and will create a system adapted from the experiences in the United States and the German Republic.

(vi)   Creation of a new office: "Délégué à la PMI"

To facilitate the co-ordination of government policy towards SMI, a new office will be created within the Ministère de l'Industrie, du Commerce et de l'Artisanat. This delegate for SMI will co-ordinate action programmes with other Ministries, regional, local, and consular services. He will also preside the commission on sub-contracting. At the regional level, he is represented by the "Chefs de Services Interdépartementaux de l'Industrie et des Mines" (S.I.M.).

15.4 CONCLUDING COMMENTS

The implementation of the action programme has taken place by means of making available credits and by starting pilot operations. In April 1976, a delegate for SMI was appointed. Pilot operations were launched in a number of regions and departments. In August 1976, the Technical Commission on subcontracting came to life. In October 1976, 3.5 billion Francs (le Prêt Barre) were directed specifically to help SMI with a turnover of less than 100 million Francs which were not quoted on the stock-market nor a subsidiary of a quoted company. Loans are granted under the condition that the investments lead to the creation of new job or to the saving of energy. An additional 2 billion Francs were made available in May 1977 via the following institutions:

SDR (Sociétés de Développement Régional)	500 million Francs
CCCHCI (Crédit Hôtelier)	450 " "
CN (Crédit National)	250 " "
GIPME (Groupement Interprofessionnel PME)	250 " "
Banques Populaires	250 " "
CNME (Caisse Nationale des Marchés de l'Etat)	100 " "
Crédit Agricole	100 " "
Crédit Coopératif	50 " "
IDI (Institut de Développement Industriel)	50 " "
Total	2 billion Francs

The government initiative to start developing a clear policy toward small business has gained momentum today. All programmes underway in pilot operations now have a central control point at the delegate level. Co-ordination and concertation with national socio-economic objectives is sought.

IVORY COAST

M. T. Diawara[1]

16

Despite international competition and acceleration in the development of new technologies necessitating industrial gigantism and world-wide market uncertainty, small and medium-scale enterprises (SME) have been able to retain an important place in modern economies, because their human dimension provides for individual development and social integration needed by all types of society.

Young African economies, still at the formative stage, have to retain, in their development strategies, the contribution to social and economic balance provided by small and medium-scale enterprises.

In the Ivory Coast we have set up structures for promoting and financing SMEs, there are also problems to be overcome. Provision is made for assisting the sector during the 1976-1980 economic and social development plan.

The Ivory Coast development strategy for the present decade is based on transition from a growth economy to a promotion society. One of the most effective ways of achieving this objective is to develop SMEs, which is the basic element of the policy for achieving a true Ivory Coast economy.

This approach enables nationals to participate in economic activity at employment, capital and decision-making levels. It also generates income and satisfies Ivoriens' aspirations by offering products and services adapted to market conditions while maintaining flexibility in setting up enterprises by encouraging regionalisation.

Furthermore, efforts to achieve strong growth are necessarily accompanied by an increase in density of industrial networks and service activities tied to economic and social progress. Control of this progress must remain in the hands of nationals who will provide future generations of entrepreneurs.

---

[1] *Minister of Planning, Government of Ivory Coast. Address delivered at the opening of the ILO's Abidjan Symposium on small enterprise development schemes in Africa, 21 March 1977.*

16.1 PAST ACTIVITIES

In order to facilitate the creation of this SME network, the Government conceived a technical and financial system comprising:

(i)   a "National Office for the Promotion of Ivory Coast Industries (OPEI)";

(ii)   a Guarantee Fund providing State surety for credits granted by the banks to Ivory Coast entrepreneurs;

(iii) a Special Fund to assist entrepreneurs raising initial contributions when seeking credit from banks.

OPEI

OPEI was founded in 1968 and placed under the aegis of the Ministry of Planning, illustrating the Ivory Coast Government intention to embody national enterprise promotion policy within the over-all development process.

The responsibilities entrusted to OPEI were far-reaching since, according to its statutes, it had to conceive and undertake any studies, activities or measures which could contribute to creating and developing genuine Ivory Coast trading, industrial and agricultural enterprises, as well as organising associations and enhancing productivity improvement in both individual enterprises and business sectors.

Because these wide terms of reference resulted in scattering of OPEI's efforts, it was reorganised in 1975 in order to concentrate on sectoral activities.

Tasks were divided into two distinct groups. One group responsibility for preparing plans and programmes, supervising implementation and evaluating results, reports directly to the Director-General. A second group takes on programme execution, and acts as an Operations Department responsible for:

- operational units specialised in specific branches such as food, building, timber, mechanics and garages, textiles and clothing, and a "miscellaneous industries" unit;

- a sub-directorate synthesesing results and providing support to sectoral cells through specialised advice following up financial arrangements with banks.

OPEI's staff consists of 200 persons of whom 100 are responsible for promotion and support.

Since 1968, OPEI has contributed to setting up more than 250 enterprises representing three billion francs CFA investment and creating 2,500 jobs. Indirect contributions made by OPEI in developing national enterprises, by assistance and follow-up, management training and building institutions such as unions, associations are, obviously, more difficult to evaluate, but undoubtedly have been stimulating.

The Guarantee Fund

The Guarantee Fund was also established in 1968 to supply surety for bank advances necessary for entrepreneurial development. The fund guarantees up to 80 per cent of a loan for a modest guarantee charge of between 0.5 and 1.5 per cent varied according to the type of credit guaranteed.

In the case of medium-term bank loans, where the borrower's contribution is set at 10 per cent, the Special Fund can make up the difference to respect the central bank's rule of 20 per cent borrower participation. In this way, the Guarantee Fund had made a notable contribution to the financing of SMEs.

Since its inception, 135 Ivory Coast enterprises have benefited from Fund Guarantee to a value of 2.6 billion francs (capital and interest included). The commitment accepted by the Fund on these loans amounts to 1.5 billion, at a guarantee rate of 59.3 per cent.

The Special Fund

The Special Fund for SMEs conducted by the Société Nationale de Financement, was founded in 1970 to help that SMEs unable to provide sufficient capital for foundation or expansion to qualify for loans from banks and financial bodies.

Support from the Fund takes the form of a loan at central bank rate to sum equal to 15 per cent of total investment. The loan is not reimbursable until the principal loans granted by commercial banks have been fully paid back.

Such structures as these can obviously be improved but to do so requires an analysis of the numerous obstacles holding up SME development in the country.

16.2 PROBLEM AREAS

These obstacles are associated with such factors as: human factors, financial arrangements, the form of enterprise, the market and the environment, be it economic, technical, administrative, legal or political.

(i) Concerning human factors, true entrepreneurs are still rare, greatly sought after, yet poorly prepared to run an enterprise. Examinations of managerial practices disclose serious weaknesses threatening the life of the enterprise.

(ii) Another fundamental problem facing small enterprises at the time of their foundation and continuing throughout their existence concerns financial matters. These require special attention and arrangements adapted to given situations. The entrepreneur's own capital contribution is often inadequate to permit setting up, ot expanding a modern enterprise, especially when trade based. Even where some capital is available, it is often only the minimum and most investments have to be covered by bank loans.

(iii)   Legal structures of small enterprises are not
always adapted to the needs of small undertakings, either
due to ignorance of available opportunities, or to lack
of sound appreciation of the economic situation.

(iv)   The acquisition of industrial land undoubtedly
constitutes a major obstacle to setting-up and promoting
small enterprises. These problems lie in the high cost
of developed land, the complexity of administrative procedures and the unsuitability of plant for activities in
urban settings.

(v)   In addition, markets present problems for small
enterprises due to:

-   lack of information of markets for manufactured goods,
    or those lending themselves to manufacture;
-   the lack of "slots" for priority allocation to small
    enterprises;
-   that access to public markets is made difficult, if
    not impossible, by administrative regulations and
    requirements;
-   lack of access to publicity and the possibility of
    displaying goods; many consumers distrust the products
    of smaller enterprises and artisans;
-   access to markets also becomes difficult because of
    competition from larger enterprises, forcing smaller
    and medium-scale enterprises to develop markets amongst
    expatriates and the informal sector.

16.3   PROPOSED SOLUTIONS

Attempted solutions to the main identified obstacles are
provided for in the Ivory Coast plan for economic and social development.

Firstly, the maximum development of small enterprises in urban
and rural areas is explicitly established as an objective. Far from
being an all-embracing objective, it is designed to promote activities lending themselves to modernisation which can be integrated in
the economy and play an active role in development.

With this in mind, three major orientations are possible:

-   integrating craftsmen and SMEs in industrial and service
    activities to facilitate creating small enterprises
    whenever economic and social situations permit;
-   regional promotion of SMEs, in conjunction with land-
    development policy;
-   integrating craftsmen and SMEs in rural development to
    modernise and promote rural areas to satisfy basic and
    related needs (improving living conditions, supporting
    agricultural development and improving local resources).

To attain these objectives, plans have been made to establish requisite facilities as part of general and environmental policies and operational programmes.

16.4 POLICIES

Concerning general policy, six ways of creating the environment necessary for successful promotion have been considered. These are:

(i)   Creation of a co-ordinating structure.
The diversity of activities; the numerous administrative departments and bodies concerned with promoting the sector; the optimum use of these agencies and the need for a policy integrated with the general development strategy necessitate the creation of a co-ordinating structure.
The Plan, therefore, provides for establishing an Inter-Ministerial Committee for Craftsmen and Small and Medium-scale Industries.

(ii)   Improved knowledge of the sector.
The shortcomings noted make it necessary to set up a coherent statistical system for synthesising available information, especially for effective programming of sutides, surveys and inquiries.

(iii)   Regulations.
Drawing up and introducing appropriate sets of taxation, financial and other regulations.

(iv)   Promotion.
Promotion of sectoral activities and resultant goods and services.

(v)   Training facilities.
The specific needs of the sector, which must expand considerably in view of the programmes foreseen, plus the necessary liaison between assistance and training at the enterprise level call for close consultation between the promotion bodies and training structures to ensure optimum use of existing training facilities by adapting them to the requirements of the sector. Special emphasis must also be placed on apprenticeships for small qualified and organised enterprises. Priority support must be given to the training of instructors, particularly national executives specialising in promotion work and assistance for SMEs.

(vi)   Research.
Planning and carrying out research and experiments on technologies, products and production methods.

16.5 PROGRAMMES

OPEI has drawn up a procedure for programming by objectives for the immediate future, comprising five major programmes:

Sectoral development

The promotion and organisation of occupational sectors. This consists, firstly, of creating or expanding enterprises in selected sectors such as garages, wood-working shops, ready-made clothing and tailoring shops and food. Funds for this programme are available as a loan of one billion four hundred million francs CFA from the World Bank to the Crédit de la Côte d'Ivoire, in 1975. The latter is one of Ivory Coast's development banks, and will provide bank loan guarantees for more than 100 entrepreneurs.

Criteria will be established for the installation of plants in each sector and trade regulations will be issued following the establishment of employers' associations.

Regional development

Regional development will include the creation of industrial zones. These industrial zones will bring together craftsmen and small entrepreneurs by providing them with infrastructure necessary for business, under very favourable conditions.

Subcontracting

Firms responsible for designing and setting up major agricultural or industrial development projects prefer to entrust contract work to large enterprises installed in the Ivory Coast or abroad, mainly to ensure sound construction. It is, therefore, necessary to enable Ivory Coast enterprises access to these large markets by creating a national subcontract exchange.

Purchase of foreign firms

OPEI has recently set up a purchasing unit which, at the request of Ivory Coast purchasers, provides expertise, cost estimates of firms for sale and helps with negotiations.

Management and technical assistance

General assistance and follow-up and to national enterprises is provided by management and technical training.

Since policies for promoting national enterprises in developing economies depend mainly on accumulating human capital, their effects cannot be assessed before the end of a generation. Choices made during this decade will, therefore, have far-reaching effects and will determine future results. We hope that the exchanges of opinion and careful study will enable our young planners to avoid a dichotomic view of industry, in which giant industries plan the activities of man, and allow small enterprises to survive only in marginal sectors offering low profits. From this and other studies we hope to produce a joint philosophy for industrial development which, for the African, is a condition for mastery of his destiny.

SWEDEN

Yngve Svensson[1]

17

Sweden's business life is a typical market economy. Free enterprise is one of its fundamentals. Despite a long term of socialistic government, the country's efficient industry has been able to function fairly freely, and provides a high living standard for Swedish people. Many Swedish companies, founded on great inventions, have important world-wide markets.

17.1   THE SWEDISH SETTING

The country's industrial life is drawn from a base of

- 8,200,000 population
- 4,100,000 labour force
-   400,000 enterprises made up of:

          160,000 farming and forestry
           70,000 distributive trades
           35,000 manufacturing
          100,000 service sectors

Ninety per cent of total industrial employment is found in private enterprise. As in most countries, small enterprises are the largest group of all registered businesses. Most of the very small companies, say less than 5 employees, are in farming and forestry (95 per cent of the total), and building, transport and services (80-87 per cent of the total).

However, most research and services have been devoted to the industrial sector. In this context small enterprises are taken as those up to 50 employees. In most cases these are family owned and managed. There are about 300,000 family entrepreneurs in Sweden (of which 125,000 are farmers).

There are no formal obstacles preventing anyone starting a business. Despite this the number of family companies is decreasing. In recent years sales and liquidations of family companies have increased rapidly.

[1] *Director, Swedish Employer's Confederation (SAF).*

In the last 10 years new business start-ups in the manufacturing industry have decreased. This trend is attributed to a deteriorating business climate in Sweden. Many laws have come into being, which more or less confine the freedom of movement of enterprises. As a result, profitability declines and financing becomes more and more difficult.

Family companies are particularly burdened by capital and inheritance taxes. Recent opinion polls have shown that the majority of Swedish people favour family businesses. Since 1976 the liberal and conservative government has created a somewhat more friendly business climate.

17.2 POLICIES

In reality there are no clearly formulated government policies for small business. There are many statements about the need for small enterprises to complement large ones, and that small enterprises are a valuable asset. Some assistance is provided. For example, several forms of credit using state money are available solely for small enterprises. There are also certain service and training facilities provided by government, as well as specific institutions to assist in developing new products.

However, there is little effort to promote new business development. This has worried private business organisations who, jointly, have recently written to the Government suggesting a concrete programme to stimulate new businesses. These suggestions include improved capital supply, special establishment loans, reasonable guarantees, decreased employment tax for the very small firms, changes in certain laws dealing with security of employment and introducing public information to create a positive attitude towards small enterprises and similar issues.

During 1975-76, the year before the election, small companies reacted sharply to the existing trend. They arranged large meetings, made harsh statements about the Government, and demanded new and better attitudes towards small business. These manifestations were later co-ordinated with the more organised actions of established business organisations who, in cooperation with small enterprises, formulated their demands in an official statement. They emphasized issues such as protecting free trade, the need for changes in capital and inheritance taxes, and that the new law about co-determination at work should have special interpretations. In particular, the smaller companies objected to the trade unions' proposal for wage earners' funds, suggested adjustment to the law about security for employment, stated that non-wage labour costs should not be increased, that new laws on taxation of family firms needed changing, that obligations to submit particulars to authorities should be reduced, and a request for improving the general understanding of how a business functions.

The present government is expected to develop a common package of actions affecting small enterprises which will incorporate several of their demands. Therefore, it can be taken that an official policy for small business may soon be formulated.

17.3 STRUCTURES

Governmental and private institutions both serve the small enterprise sector.

Government and parastatal structures

For industrial matters the National Industrial Board, answerable to the Ministry of Industry, promotes technical and economic development of industry, with particular attention paid to small and medium-sized companies. It advises and carried out investigations for the parent Ministry. In addition, the Board coordinates government activities, grants loans, and organises training for small businesses. A Council to handle small and medium-sized enterprise matters, with representatives from business and political circles is also attached to the Board.

In each of Sweden's 24 counties there is a so-called Trade Development Association. These are not state organs but independent, economic associations whose main task is to support and expand the development of industry, handicraft and enterprise and to provide continued employment and sound working environment. These associations, governed by state rules, obtain grants for their administration from state and county councils. State representation makes up the majority of their boards. The principal state service to small enterprises is performed by these associations. The developing and supporting work of the National Industrial Board is carried out through the associations which can be considered, more or less, to be controlled by the Board.

For technical and industrial development there are particular state institutions, which support research and new product development by means of financial grants and advisory services. Some institutions are created particularly to provide services for developing areas, as in the Northern part of Sweden.

Exports are very important for Sweden's economy. There is a special Swedish Export Board with both government and private enterprise represented. The Board gathers and distributes marketing information and provides advice in international marketing. The Board has a special section for small and medium-sized business, which directs and stimulates their exports.

Some credit institutions are specifically designed for lending money to small and medium-sized enterprises, mostly on terms of up to 15 years. In several cases they are owned jointly by Government and private banks.

Within several universities there is emphasis on research into problems of small enterprises. In some cases these become projects of international interest. The National Industrial Board also contracts investigations to universities on such topics as the volume and causes for liquidations or possibilities of establishing new businesses. There is an increasing interest in small enterprises as shown by the large number of student papers dealing with small business problems.

Private structures

In Sweden there are hundreds of business organisations, whose membership is composed of enterprises and entrepreneurs. Only a few of them have enough resources to provide tangible services. Some organisations show increasing interest in small and medium-sized business, particularly in efforts to attract the authorities' attention to business policy questions.

Some organisations deal only with small enterprises particularly in such fields as law. The largest such organisation is the Swedish Federation of Crafts and Small and Medium-sized Industries (SHIO) of nearly 30,000 members. It has a regional administration which does a great deal in bringing small firms together, disseminating information, and arranging cooperation between member firms. It plans to amalgamate with another small business organisation, which will mean even better business policy safeguards in favour of small and medium-sized businesses. Other organisations act for such groups as farmers, tradesmen and drivers.

Employers' organisations have a particular role to play. They safeguard employers' interests mainly by negotiations with employee organisations. Furthermore, they work for a free enterprise system and higher productivity of members. The most important such organisation in Sweden is the Swedish Employers' Confederation (SAF) which has more than 33,000 member firms of which 94 per cent have less than 100 employees.

Apart from labour market questions SAF has, during the last 10 years, also developed programmes for increasing efficiency and profitability, particularly in the small and medium-sized business. The technical department has prepared the material "Look after your firm", specially devised for small and medium-sized business. To a large extent this has improved the managerial control of these businesses. The material has also been translated and adapted to several languages.

A Swedish Institute for Management (IFL) has been created to cater for management training. It was an amalgamation of training activities conducted by universities, professional organisations and SAF who remain the constituents of the institute. Within IFL, a special training programme for small business has also been developed, which started as a continuation of SAF's material "Look after your firm".

Important bodies for developing small enterprises include accountants, book-keepers and auditors. These professionals frequently contact small firms and also cooperate with development associations and the business organisations to improve companies. They use the "Look after your firm" material often with entrepreneurs.

17.4 PROGRAMMES

Varied programmes exist for small firms. In fact, there might be too many for entrepreneurs to understand and use properly. Three important activities are herein reviewed dealing with services, training materials and training courses.

Trade development associations

The original task of the associations was to prepare state loans and guarantees for smaller firms experiencing difficulties obtaining sufficient loans from ordinary credit institutions for investment and purchase of current assets. They attempt to complement normal credit institutions.

Small firms usually have less collateral than big companies and, therefore, need more credit. Development associations investigate the development potential of enterprise in the country and evaluate needs for loans. In principle, they only invest in companies likely to prove profitable even if only in the long run.

The credit offered can consist of direct loans up to 300,000 Swedish Crowns, or a state guarantee to a bank up to 800,000 Sw.Cr., even more under certain circumstances. Loans are granted to build new workshops or extend and modernise older ones, as well as to buy new machines and similar improvements.

Credit supply remains one of the two main tasks of these associations. The most important task is known as company service (extension service). It includes (i) information and contact, (ii) general advice and business analyses, (iii) consulting, (iv) training and (v) other services. The first two activities (i) and (ii) are the most common.

(i)   *Information and contact:* Meetings are arranged in various parts of the country, where information is provided about services available from various bodies. Such meetings may deal with specific topics as product development, exports, or work environment. Information can also be received through bulletins. Efforts are made to reach all enterprises concerned. Associations have prepared detailed lists of all manufacturing companies in the country providing such details as sub-contracting capacity, types of services available and vacant premises. Other activities include sales missions for sub-contractors, visits of suppliers to buyers and participating in trade fairs.

(ii)   *General advice and business analyses:* Associations carry out in-company exercises where officers visit companies, find out about problems, and appraise potential resources.

A business analysis may be conducted when one or two officers visit an enterprise. In some counties individual officers are allocated specific regions, which means maintaining constant relationships with those enterprises. On other occasion the analysis may be carried out during conferences of several entrepreneurs. On these occasions, the SAF-material "Look after your firm" is often used. In addition, the association offers one free consulting day for each company.

Among the most pressing identified problems are product development and marketing. As a result, some associations employ marketing specialists. In a few countries there are also special product development councils of various specialists.

(iii) *Consulting:* To a small extent direct consulting is carried out. It mainly takes place where conventional consultants are difficult to find. Some associations feel that it is valuable to keep in contact with real-life problems with consulting work. Others feel this is not their task. Consulting fees are charged at competitive rates.

(iv) *Training:* Associations do not carry out training. However, it is important to show entrepreneurs the importance of training, to analyse training needs and to inform about central and regional training opportunities. Further they need to ensure that the courses offered are suitable for small and medium-sized business. Each association has a training adviser to carry out these tasks.

(v) *Other services:* Associations may engage in other activities depending on need and interest. Hence, they may organise industrial health services, act as agents for purchase or hire of industrial sites and premises and gather data about persons in keeping with their role as advisers and board members of small and medium-sized business. Furthermore, they may conduct investigations about localization (in certain areas state support is offered), business economic investigations regarding labour market questions, and examine factors affecting public purchasing.

Development associations obtain central services and support from their superordinate National Industrial Board. Although associations are not governmental they must follow the state's terms of reference. Their administrative support has gradually increased while Parliament has correspondingly given them more tasks. During 1977 new directions for the associations are expected to be agreed. They will receive larger resources, growing from the present 400 employees to 800 by the 1980's. The organisation may also change into a foundation with the state and the county councils as constituents. Thus, they will become public regional agencies for the business and political activities of small and medium-sized business. In the main, they will serve the Industrial Board, the Export Board and a Board for Technical Development.

Particularly urgent questions to be considered are the promotion of new businesses and regional sub-contracting systems. Other high priority items are product development, marketing and export.

"Look after your firm" materials

In 1970 the Swedish Employers' Confederation (SAF) published the analysis material "Se om ditt företag". It was intended as a simple and practical aid, which entrepreneurs could use to help themselves. However, it was also intended to analyse the whole business, by viewing its strengths and weaknesses. The name of the material was carefully chosen to indicate that a layman's approach was being directed to the entrepreneur. When translated into English the title "Look after your firm" is felt to best reflect these objectives. The material has been adapted in Britain under the title "Know your business".

The Business Analysis material, first published in 1970, consists of a binder containing forms and comments for financial surveys plus an overall analysis of the company's operations. It is designed to function in a simple routine way.

This analysis kit has been successful and accepted by entrepreneurs and organisations working with small business. Several countries have translated and adapted the material.

Why was it successful? Analysis suggests that

- The material deals with the entrepreneur in his own language. It was based on in-depth interviews with 50 companies.
- The material is adapted to the needs of small companies. Important items were selected while working with the entrepreneur.
- During its development entrepreneurs had opportunities to test and reshape the contents before publishing.
- Development was carried out in close contact with bodies frequently dealing with small business, such as banks, accountants and small business organisations.

An important feature is that the material is based on a strict set of rules without the need to carry out special investigations in advance. The material is also visually stimulating.

Because entrepreneurs requested additional information with hints and advice on planning for the future Part 2 entitled "Action Programme" was published in 1974. It naturally follows on from Part 1. This material assists the entrepreneur to examine his company systematically and consider what steps should be taken in order to safeguard its future.

Very small enterprises requested a simplified version of the material. In 1974 SAF then published an edition called "Mini-version" which embraced both the analysis and action programmes in extremely simple terms. It can be used to introduce the basic material, or as a very rough business analysis and guide for suitable programmes of action.

Much effort has been made to make this material easy to use. In particular, it employs a concise and colloquial text as well as many illustrations. It consists of two parts, a work booklet and a handbook. Both parts are used in parallel. In the work booklet reference is occasionally made to the corresponding text in the handbook.

The "Look after your firm" material is a system for analysis and planning in small and medium-sized business. One can start with the Mini-version and, if it is too simple, one can transfer to the basic material. The main idea is to provide the entrepreneur with an overview and control over the whole business activity. It presupposes that the entrepreneur is not a professional manager.

It is important to realize that "Look after your firm" has a Swedish bias, adapted for small and medium-sized business in Sweden governed by particular laws and regulations. Although the principles

may be common to other countries, introduction of the material into
a new country requires not only translation but a total adaptation
to the conditions in that country. It can be mentioned that such an
adaptation of the Mini-version is underway in Africa under the auspices of ILO and the Swedish International Development Authority
(SIDA) as a pilot stage preparing the material for developing
countries.

Training for managers in small enterprises

"Develop your company" is the title of a training course specially designed for managers of small and medium-sized companies.
It was introduced by the Swedish Institute of Management (IFL) in
1971 built on the framework of "Look after your firm". Before commencing the course, participants should have completed the SAF-kit.
This means that all participants will be thinking about their own
companies in the same terms, so that discussions during the course
should benefit accordingly.

The essential aim of the course is to help participants become
more efficient in managing their companies. With this in view the
course has 7 sections.

1. Analysis of your company

2. Market and products

3. Management accounting and taxes

4. Financing

5. Personnel planning

6. Top management and board

7. Long range planning in your company

The programme comprises 21 residential days split up into 7 sets
of 3-day sessions. There is about a month interval between sessions.
During that time the participants work through subjects dealt with
in the previous session. In this way the course suits top executives
of small companies who find it difficult to be absent for long
periods at a time. Another advantage of month-long intervals is that
participants have time to introduce changes to achieve greater efficiency in their companies. Up to 30 participants from one course
where working in groups of 5 or 6, they function as boards of
directors.

Emphasis is laid on economic and administrative questions starting with company analysis and appropriate actions. The trainers have
practical experience in such matters. During the course participants
develop long-range plans for their companies. The knowledge acquired
is directly applicable to management and board level activities.

"Development programme for smaller businessmen" is another course
designed by IFL. It is a fairly new project for very small firms.
This course also commences with the "Look after your firm" material,
in this case the Mini-version. Participants should have worked
through that material before starting the course.

The programme lasts 20 days, made up of 4 residential sessions of 3 days each plus 8 days in the participants' own companies according to the following schedule:

Location	Session title
Residence 1	The company and the environment
In-company	Your own company 1
Residence 2	Market and products
Residence 3	Management accounting
In-company	Your own company 2
Residence 4	The possibilities of the company

Trainers have practical experience in small enterprises. The programme is adapted to the needs and problems of small firms and provides participants with the basics of modern management. By the end of the course participants work out action programmes for their companies. Thus the training relates to experiences and knowledge directly useful in daily work.

Both training programmes have proven successful, especially where own company material is used. Groups which work together during the programme often decide to meet again to follow up what happened in their companies.

General conclusions

To develop small and medium-sized business there is first of all the need for basic systems to provide finance. Next, questions of project proposals and product development raise difficulties. These three fields are natural areas for state intervention. Other difficulties facing small enterprise include marketing and introducing new products and methods. Again, the state can provide assistance through its development associations.

Education and training is a general function requiring central control. There is an enormous range of courses making it difficult for the entrepreneurs to choose what best suits their needs. It is, therefore, important that the IFL takes charge of management education.

Concerning courses for small firms the institute cooperates with the National Industrial Board which has a section for small business training. There are also other in institutes with access to state subsidies which arrange evening courses throughout Sweden. In addition, several private institutes and consultants conduct training courses. An overview of available training should be maintained by training advisers in development associations.

In addition to these central and more general services there are wider services on offer to small enterprises. Most are provided by professional private service companies. There are about 16,000 such companies. The most important private service companies include law offices, architect bureaus, banks, accounting and auditing bureaus, computer service bureaus, consulting engineers and patent bureaus.

There are also special debt-collecting agencies, leasing and factoring companies as well as general management consultants.

Development association advisers need to know the types of services available in their respective counties. Advisers have, basically, two types of managers to reckon with. There are the progressive, smart, strong and self-dependent types open to everything new and wanting to develop further. Such types look for qualified contacts and require clever and experienced advisors. They seldom turn to development associations, except for help with loans, since they would rather contact business organisations or private consultants.

The second managerial type is more laborious, even if skilled in his trade, with less of a general outlook. These types accept common services, and are satisfied if the business manages to break even. They must be approached more intensely by development associations, training institutes, and others qualified to help.

Common to most small enterprises is that, perhaps more than in larger ones, they need to know exactly what results can be expected from a training course before they subscribe. Such services need to have general recognition, to emanate from well-known sources and be backed up by reputable bodies. It is this support which lies behind the success of the "Look after your firm" material where all parties such as the state, business organisations, business schools and banks acknowledge the material as sound and appropriate. These are important contacts for services and training institutions.

Another important aspect is availability of services and training, as a result decentralisation becomes essential. A problem remains in that services are usually applicable in specific situations only, which tends to narrow their availability.

Entrepreneurs normally do not want to be spoon-fed with assistance. They like to act for themselves and to have access to resources. The training task should be to motivate them to use services and training, in particular situations, with emphasis on practical matters.

Personal development for entrepreneurs embraces a choice of means and responsibility for allocating time for it. They rely on it to be useful, easy to carry out, to be seen as fun, and to provide a real break from the daily grind.

Small business managers can feel very lonely. Therefore, there is need to arrange meetings with colleagues to provide opportunities for them to check if there is something new which they may have missed, to get fresh views on their own situations and help in evaluating various alternative solutions to actual problems. They will also find they often have common problems and, by getting together, they are better equipped to handle them. In the hard work of running businesses profitably and efficiently, entrepreneurs need the most positive supporting conditions possible.

UNITED STATES OF AMERICA

18

Robert E. Nelson[1]

Because of the significant number of people who own their own businesses or who are interested in business ownership and management as a career, there is a growing need to make available formal education and training that will provide the necessary skills for this career option. The most discouraging fact about people who begin new businesses is that approximately 50 percent of them fail within the first two years of operation. Most of these failures result from: (i) lack of training and experience as a manager; or (ii) lack of personal qualifications to operate a business. Educational institutions need to be more actively involved in developing total programmes that will adequately prepare young people to successfully pursue careers in small business ownership and management.

Government involvement

The Small Business Administration (SBA) was created by the United States Congress in 1953 to "aid, counsel, assist and protect the interest of small business concerns ...". The primary function of the SBA was assisting small businesses to borrow money.

18.1   THE SMALL BUSINESS ADMINISTRATION (SBA)

During the past few years, however, the SBA has recognized the growing importance of management assistance as another important aspect of the total SBA program. As a general rule, most small businesses fail during the first five years they are in existence. Results of research studies have indicated that the primary cause of small business failures is a lack of managerial skills.

The U.S. Small Business Administration (SBA) has identified five personal characteristics which appear to be essential for small business success. These personal characteristics include:

(i) *Thinking ability* - original, creative, critical and analytical.

---

[1] *Chairman, Division of Business Education, University of Illinois, Urbana, USA.*

    (ii)   *Drive* - the will to succeed; includes vigour
           responsibility, initiative, persistence and health.

    (iii)   *Technical knowledge* - of products, process,
           equipment, materials and business methods.

    (iv)   *Communications ability* - competence in giving and
           receiving information and instructions.

    (v)   *Human relations ability* - the capacity to interact
           favorably with other people and to motivate them.

In order to prepare for potential careers in small business
ownership and management, students should develop the above personal
characteristics identified by the SBA while they are in school.

The SBA continues to provide for the building of "inner
resources" among actual and potential small business persons by means
of training courses, conferences, workshops, and business problem-
clinics. In co-sponsorship arrangements with communities, colleges,
chambers of commerce, and others, valuable training for business is
made available in every state. From July 1975 through June 1976,
more individuals sought and received training help than ever before
- 183,630 as compared to 154,829 in the previous year. With special
recruitment efforts by the SBA, attendance increases were achieved
among minorities, women, and veterans.

In particular, the one-day Pre-business Workshop programme was
received enthusiastically. Not only did the attendance increase
nationally, almost 32 percent over the previous fiscal year of
1974-75, but an independent evaluation indicated they were extremely
valuable for persons facing the issues of starting a new business.
In some cases the workshops were tailored to special situations.
For example, when the Californian Department of Transportation faced
an 800-person reduction in its workforce, a special workshop was
arranged to help the employees decide if an independent business
venture was a viable career option.

More than five million copies of 250 different business management publications, produced by SBA, were distributed during the
past year. The bulk of these publications are distributed free of
charge to persons interested in particular issues or problems of
managing a business. Others are available as "for sale" items from
the Government Printing Office. New publications that meet specific
business needs are continually being developed. Among these in 1976
were "Tourism and Outdoor Recreation", and "Training Salesmen to
Serve Industrial Markets".

18.2   THE SMALL BUSINESS DEVELOPMENT CENTRE (SBDC)

The Small Business Development Centre provides a framework for
interrelating the resource strengths of American universities with
those of government and business in a partnership-for-growth. Its
basic objective is to impact upon the economic welfare of society
while at the same time providing students with superior learning
experiences.

These learning experiences arise out of combining the best
academic knowledge with the best experiential understanding and

relating these to the innovative inquiries of today's youth in the
search for optimal ways to solve problems and create opportunities.

The Small Business Development Centre rests upon the philo-
sophic assumption that the proper role of the university is to be
engaged in both knowledge growth and knowledge sharing and upon the
belief that through knowledge sharing one finds a great simulus to
knowledge growth.

Objectives of the SBDC

The overall objectives of the Small Business Development Centre
are threefold. First, it is intended that each will be the principle
factor in developing the economy in the area it serves and corpora-
tely SBDC's will be the primary mechanism for developing the economy
of the nation in a planned way. Unlike the centrally controlled and
planned development mechanisms, the SBDC programme is developed and
controlled by the university to respond to local needs. It uses a
multiplicity of federal programmes to accomplish its objectives. This
objective of developing the economy in the region around the university is accomplished by developing existing small and medium size
businesses and industries and in fostering the development of new ones.

The second major objective of the SBDC is to provide a resource
that will enable the participating university or college to provide
more meaningful educational mechanisms, and to develop new knowledge
through research. In doing these things, many of the objectives of
the Government, education, and private sector will be satisfied as
illustrated in the Figure 18.1.

The Small Business Development Centre provides a framework for
cooperatively relating the resources of our universities and colleges
with those of government to strengthen the small business community
and to contribute to the productive welfare of the American people as
illustrated in Figure 18.2.

Small Business Development Centres can be divided into two
general categories according to the services offered: Basic Services
SBDC's, and Full Services SBDC's. which are illustrated in
Figure 18.3.

The orientation of the SBDC is not upon what the university can
get out of the government, but rather it is upon addressing the
basic problems of unemployment, inflation, and productivity through
the educational experiences afforded students across the span of
their adult years, and through direct assistance provided to the
business community.

In doing this, the SBDC utilizes as a point of departure the
agricultural partnership, established more than 100 years ago by the
passage of the Morrill Act and the setting up of the nation's Land
Grant Colleges system. This and the Smith-Lever Act established a
basis for bringing university schools of agriculture together with
government and the American farmer and farm community through the
Agricultural Experiment Station, the Home Economist, and the Agricultural Extension Agent. This agricultural partnership has resulted
in the United States becoming preeminent as a world food producer.

FIGURE 18.1:   SMALL BUSINESS DEVELOPMENT CENTRES (SBDC)

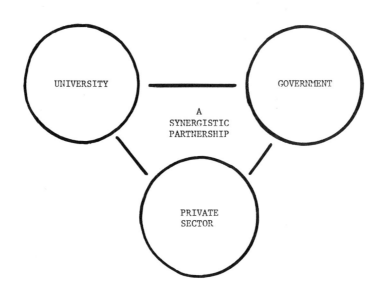

TO BENEFIT:

. The Nation's Economy
. Small Business
. University, Faculty
. and Students

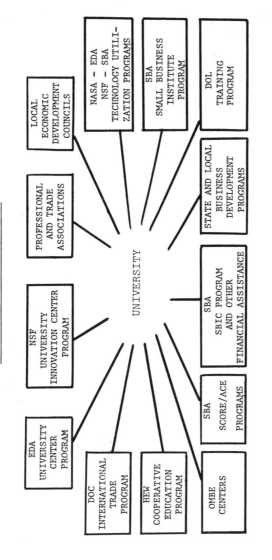

FIGURE 18.2: THE SMALL BUSINESS DEVELOPMENT CENTRE

A SYNERGISTIC LINK-UP OF:

UNIVERSITY

EDA UNIVERSITY CENTER PROGRAM

NSF UNIVERSITY INNOVATION CENTER PROGRAM

PROFESSIONAL AND TRADE ASSOCIATIONS

LOCAL ECONOMIC DEVELOPMENT COUNCILS

NASA – EDA NSF – SBA TECHNOLOGY UTILI-ZATION PROGRAMS

SBA SMALL BUSINESS INSTITUTE PROGRAM

DOL TRAINING PROGRAM

STATE AND LOCAL BUSINESS DEVELOPMENT PROGRAMS

SBA SBIC PROGRAM AND OTHER FINANCIAL ASSISTANCE

SBA SCORE/ACE PROGRAMS

OMBE CENTERS

HEW COOPERATIVE EDUCATION PROGRAM

DOC INTERNATIONAL TRADE PROGRAM

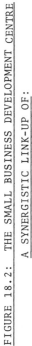

Small Business Development centres can be divided into two general categories according to the services offered: Basic Services SBDC's, and Full Services SBDC's, which are illustrated in Figure 18.3

Editor's note: In this, and the following figures in this Chapter, we have used the accepted American spelling of center for centre and program for programme.

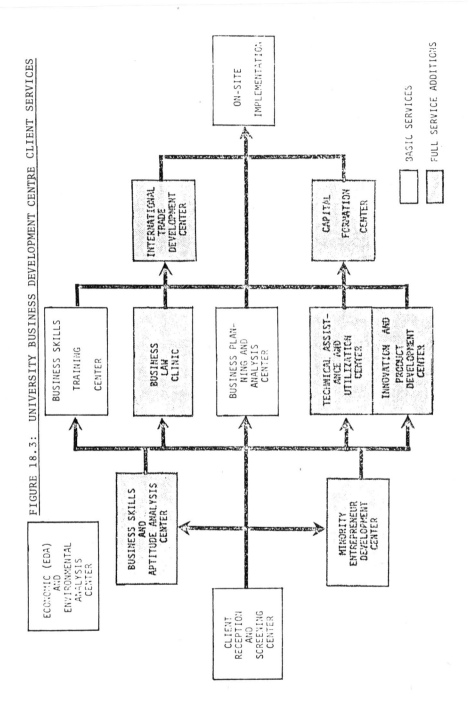

FIGURE 18.3: UNIVERSITY BUSINESS DEVELOPMENT CENTRE CLIENT SERVICES

In relating the resource strengths of universities to the needs of society, emphasis must be placed upon those areas that bridge existing academic and professional schools such as Engineering Management, Agri-Business, Business Law, Industrial Psychology, and Environmental Economics.

A major focal point of activity within the SBDC will be on the one-half of the economy classified as small business. The reasons for this are multiple. It is the small business sector that has been basically neglected, heretofore, by American universities in their academic and professional emphases. It is the small business sector where we have the greatest opportunity to increase our national productivity through assistance in the technological, financial, managerial, and marketing areas.

It is the small business community to which we look, in large part, for innovative approaches to the resolution of current problems, and it is to this community that today's young people are increasingly orienting in the fulfillment of their personal and career goals.

In this regard, particular emphasis will be placed upon assisting minority groups and women in the realization of their dreams and desires to become effective economic contributors. It has often been observed that minority group business is small business. Most certainly both women and minority groups place their hopes for economic expression upon this sector of the economy.

The educational and impact areas of the SBDC, as currently visualized, are depicted in the circular Figure 18.4.

Curriculum Development[1]

Many community colleges and four-year institutions offer isolated courses in small business management. The value of these courses to students is questionable, however, because of their apparent reliance on textbooks and lectures. It may be inappropriate to offer small business management courses in M.B.A. programmes, because many of the students in these programmes are developing management skills that apply to large organizations. Instead, comprehensive programmes relating to small business ownership and management should be developed in community colleges and other post-secondary institutions.

Recommendations have been made at the national level to integrate business ownership and management concepts into the curriculum at the elementary, secondary, and post-secondary levels. Recently, the U.S. Office of Education has completed the following curriculum development projects:

Business Ownership Exploration (Grades 7-9). The National Business Education Association has developed a course of study to acquaint seventh, eighth, and ninth grade students with business ownership and management as a potential career choice.

_____

[1] *See also Chapter 8 Education and Entrepreneurial Initiatives, Part 8.3.*

FIGURE 18.4:   EDUCATIONAL AND ECONOMIC IMPACT AREAS

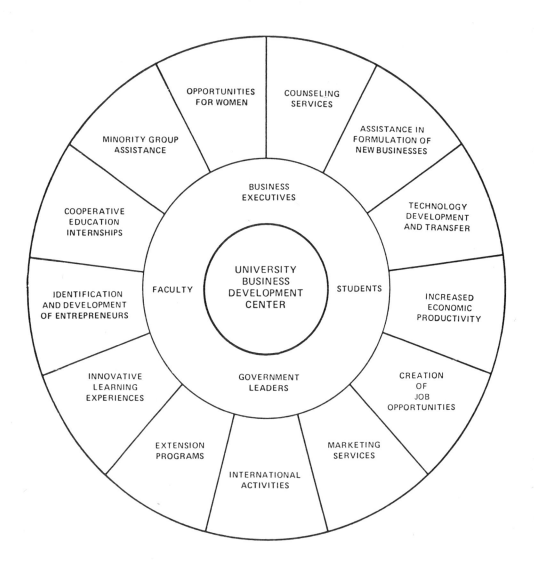

Preparation for Small Business Ownership (Grades 10-12).
Approximately fourteen instructional modules have been
developed for teaching small business topics in grades
10-12. Several simulations were also prepared.

Development of Curriculum for Minorities in Small
Business Ownership and Management (Post-Secondary Level).
Materials for a two-course sequence were prepared to
teach minority students the opportunities and skills
necessary for small business entrepreneurship. The
introductory course provides students with an awareness
of the requirements and demands inherent in owning a
small business. The actual skills and knowledges
(how to) necessary for successful minority ownership
and management of small businesses are presented in the
second course.

Adult Education Programmes for Small Business Entrepreneurs,
including Minorities. A complete adult programme has been
designed to assist instructors in setting up adult
education programmes pertaining to small business management.

In the near future, the curriculum materials develop for
(i) Grades 10-12 and (ii) Post-Secondary Level will be revised
under an Office of Education, Department of Health, Education, and
Welfare grant entitled "Field Test and Diffusion of Entrepreneurship
Instructional Materials". The primary objectives of this grant
include:

(i)   To determine the effectiveness of course materials
developed to prepare secondary and post-secondary school
students in the skills of business ownership and management.

(ii)   To improve the format and content of the course
materials on the basis of the field test findings to make
them more effective for preparation of secondary and post-
secondary students in business ownership and management.

(iii)   To develop a selective list of potential users
(teachers) in entrepreneurship courses.

(iv)   To disseminate the revised curriculum materials to
secondary and post-secondary institutions who will offer
programmes to prepare students for small business ownership
and management.

In addition the Office of Education has funded a variety of
projects relating to entrepreneurship and small business ownership.
These projects include:

1.   *"Individualized Employee Training for Small Rural*
      Businesses"

2.   *"Personnel Development for Entrepreneurs"*

3.   *"Vocational Education Programme development in*
      Entrepreneurship"

4.   *"Competency-based Individualized Instruction Modules*
      for Owner-Managers of Small Business Firms"

5. *"Entrepreneurship Education for Adults-Programme
    Development and Implementation"*

6. *"Instructional Materials for Adult Entrepreneurship
    of Apparel Shops"*

7. *"Entrepreneurship for Post-Secondary Institutions"*

8. *"Compentency Based Instructional System for Adult,
    Post-Secondary, Special Needs, and Entrepreneurship
    via the Interstate Distributive Education Curriculum
    Consortium (IDECC) System"*

9. *"Adult Education for Women's Entrepreneurship"*.

It appears evident from the actions of the U.S. Office of Education
that one of its current major priorities is the development of
entrepreneurship materials for use at the secondary and post-secondary educational levels.

State Involvement

Various states have also prepared materials for teaching small
business ownership. In Illinois, a curriculum guide *Owning and
Operating a Small Business*[1] was prepared at the University of Illinois for the Illinois Department of Vocational and Technical Education. The curriculum guide was developed in a manner that allows
the material to be utilized wherever it is desirable to emphasize
the subject of small business management; whether in adult and
continuing education classes, at the community college level, or as
career information at the high school level. The flexibility of the
materials presented in the guide promotes its usage in various ways.
In its entirety, the guide can become the catalyst for developing a
course in small business management or it can be used as either a
primary or supplemental resource for an existing course in small
business management. The guide can also be used most effectively
to integrate small business concepts into other business courses.

The curriculum guide consists of fourteen units including
topics which are relevant to the establishment and successful operation of a small business. Each unit contains: a) an introduction,
b) objectives, c) content, and d) suggested activities. The suggested general and special activities include projects, simulations,
role-playing, case studies, and assignments. The purpose of the
general activities is to familiarize the students with the knowledge
and skills necessary to own and operate a growing and successful
business.

A number of special activities designed to enhance human or
attitudinal factors which are necessary for successful business
ownership and management appear regularly throughout the guide. Each

---

[1] *The curriculum guide, Owning and Operating a Small Business
was developed by Dr Robert Nelson, James Leach and Thomas Scanlan,
Department of Vocational and Technical Education, University of
Illinois, at Urbana-Champaign. The guide may be obtained from:
Curriculum Publications Clearinghouse, Western Illinois University,
Macomb, Illinois, 61455, U.S.A., at a cost-recovery basis of $3.50,
plus postage.*

special activity can be categorized under one or more of the following areas:

> *Creativity and Innovation* - *Creativity and innovation are complementary. In order to be innovative one must be somewhat creative. Creativity has been defined as a combination of new and old ideas which will better satisfy a need. The application of creativity may be an important reason for the success of any business. The formation of the business itself is a creative act. Creativity can help in long-range forecasting of the future role of the business and of the future environment in which the business will operate. Creativity can be useful in surmounting problems in many business activities.*

> *Coping with Change and Competition* - *Effective business owners must look ahead and, to greater or lesser degree, prepare plans for the future of the business. It is possible to get some idea of the extent of future change when one reflects on the tremendous changes that have occured within the past ten years. Changes in the future will continue at an accelerated rate. In order to be successful in the future, the business owner must become adept at coping with change.*

> *Achievement Motivation* - *The successful entrepreneur has high need achievement. A need achiever is one who takes moderate risks, takes responsibility for his or her actions, and looks actively for feedback to improve performance. The need achiever has a propensity to action. He or she does not wait for things to happen. Achievement motivation can be developed among individuals.*

> *Problem Solving and Decision Making* - *The success of the business owner depends to a great extent on his or her ability to solve problems and make decisions quickly. Students should be given the opportunity to understand and practice the decision making process.*

> *Human Relations ability* - *Human factors, both in relation to employees and the general public, are an important ingredient for success. Ability to have personal contact with customers and employees is a decided advantage which the small business has over its larger competitors.*

> *Developing a Positive Self-Image* - *A positive self-image begins with an awareness of self. The prospective business owner must be willing to spend time evaluating his or her own personality. Personal strengths and weaknesses must be identified and understood. The business owner must be willing to change or modify any negative personal traits.*

18.3   THE SMALL BUSINESS INSTITUTE (SBI)

One of the newest SBA management assistance programmes is the Small Business Institute (SBI). In 1972, the SBI programme began in 37 colleges, and by 1977 had expanded to over 425 colleges and universities. A primary purpose of the SBI program is to provide small business enterprises with management assistance. College students, usually seniors or graduate students, serve as consultants to assist businessmen in solving various problems relating to the operation and management of a business enterprise. Most of these consulting cases with actual businesses are use to supplement a regular course in the business administration curriculum. The faculty member who teaches the course is usually the director of the SBI programme.

In a recent study of SBI programme directors, 89 percent of all respondents indicated that SBI cases were used in regular business administration courses[1]. The purpose of integrating SBI cases into the business administration curriculum is to provide students with opportunities to accomplish the following:

(i)   develop problem-solving procedures which would be useful in managing a business;

(ii)   provide alternative recommendations for solutions to actual business problems; and

(iii)   understand that uncertainty and ambiguity are involved in most business problems and that risk taking is an important element in any business enterprise.

Education at the post-secondary level, and especially in four-year institutions, is in a transition period. In order for education to be meaningful it must be compatible with the rapidly changing conditions of a highly technological and business-oriented society. The SBI may be viewed as an exemplary program because it combines classroom instruction (theory) with experiences for students in working with business (practice). Table 18.1 below, indicated the results of a recent survey of seventy SBI programme directors regarding the primary teaching objectives of the programme[2].

TABLE 18.1:   MAJOR OBJECTIVES OF THE SBI PROGRAM

Number of Institutions	Percentage of Institutions	Objective
31	44	Practical experience in real life situations
20	28	Application of business principles
7	10	Consulting techniques
5	5	Capstone (General business policy)
3	5	Analysis of business problems
2	3	Exposure to small business
2	3	Development of business acumen
70	100	

[1] A. Pabst and W. Stahlecker: An Evaluation Analysis of the Small Business Institute Program Survey, (School of Business, St. Cloud State College, 1975).

[2] W. Stahlecker and A. Pabst: The Role of SBI Cases in the Business Curriculum, (presented at the Region V-Small Business Institute Project Director's Workshop, Cincinnati, Ohio, 1975).

In-Service teacher education via the SBI

During the spring semester, 1975, a Small Business Institute was established in the College of Education at the University of Illinois, Champaign-Urbaba Campus. The purpose of the Institute was to provide business instructors with opportunities to work on a continuing basis as consultants to small businesses.

In many instances, instructors who teach business subjects have had limited involvement in the actual operation and management of small business firms. Typically, instructors have completed business administration programmes which emphasized (a) formal classroom instruction and (b) the development of problem-solving and decision-making skills. However, most of these programs gave "little attention to the development of skills required to *find problems* that need to be solved, to *plan* for the attainment of desired results, or to *carry out* operating plans once they are made.

The SBI at the University of Illinois was primarily conducted for community college instructors who taught courses or topics pertaining to small business ownership and management. Twenty instructors, representing twelve community colleges in Illinois, were enrolled in the institute. Classes were conducted periodically throughout the sixteen-week semester course. Meetings were held on Saturday to allow instructors from as far away as Rockford, Illinois (182 miles from the university) an opportunity to attend and participate in the institute.

The Small Business Institute at the University of Illinois is unique because it is the only SBI programme in the United States which is conducted in a College of Education rather than in a College of Business Administration. The primary objective of the institute is to provide in-service education to business instructors who teach at the community college and post-secondary levels.

The SBI programme at the University of Illinois concentrates its emphasis on instructors who teach, or are interested in teaching, subjects and topics relating to small business ownership and management. Courses relating to small business are especially appropriate for implementation at the community college level. Many of the community college programmes are vocationally oriented. Specific vocational skills, which are needed by businesses in the local community, are taught in the community colleges. However, the skills are taught with the expectation that the students will be working *for* some other person or business.

The SBI programme may be appropriate for all vocational education instructors at the community college level who teach career preparation courses. The career education model for the State of Illinois classifies all occupations in the "world of work" into the following five cluster areas:

(i)   Agriculture and biological sciences

(ii)   Business, marketing and management

(iii) Health

(iv)   Industry and technology

(v)   Personal and public services

By enrolling in the SBI programme, vocational instructors of subjects relating to the above career education clusters will have a better understanding of applications of what they teach to work situations. More importantly, instructors will be better prepared to teach topics that contain information relating to self-employment opportunities. For example, community college students majoring in agri-marketing, construction technology, electronics technology, food distribution or recreation leadership should be aware of career opportunities for self-employment.

At one time or another, most people have had serious thoughts of owning their own business. By integrating concepts relating to small business ownership and management into all community college courses relating to career preparation, students will be aware of the opportunities as well as the pitfalls of owning and operating their own business.

Most career preparation programmes at the high school, community college, college, adult and continuing education levels do not emphasize self-employment as a career option. Lack of information, knowledge and experience concerning small business may be a primary reason why many instructors at all educational levels do not teach concepts relating to owning and operating a small business.

Benefits of SBI programme.

The SBI programme at the University of Illinois has many benefits for instructors who are involved in career preparation programmes at the community college level. These benefits include the following:

(i)   Practical knowledge and "real-life" experiences gained from consulting with a small business can be related to classroom instruction.

(ii)   When instructors are able to relate business theory to specific problems and practices relating to small business ownership and management, students will have a better understanding of basic business concepts.

(iii)   Administrators perceive consulting as a public service provided by the community college to the local business community and are quite interested in having faculty members involved in this type of activity.

(iv)   By having instructors serve as consultants to local businessmen, good relationships will be developed between the community college faculty and the local business community.

(v)   The final consulting reports are the results of action research projects. These documents can be a part of an instructor's yearly evaluation for promotion and/or tenure purposes. These consulting reports are also an excellent source of information for writing case studies for use in the classroom.

(vi)   The SBI participants will learn specific consulting skills such as: problem identification, sources available to assist in developing alternative solutions to business problems, appropriate questioning techniques to assist in identifying potential problems, and communication skills to help consultants and businessmen develop good working relationships.

Results of the SBI programme

Because all of the community college instructors in the SBI program were either teaching or were interested in teaching topics relating to small business ownership and management, there was a high degree of participation at the class meetings. Throughout the course the participants critiqued each other's cases and provided their opinions, sources of information and suggestions for solving specific business problems.

The SBI programme provided community college institutions an opportunity to exchange ideas, personal experiences and techniques for teaching topics relating to small business ownership and management. These instructors also discussed current issues and problems confronting community colleges in the State of Illinois.

One of the most significant outcomes of the SBI programme was the impact on the participants' actions regarding the teaching of small business ownership and management. One community college initiated a two-year curriculum to prepare students to own and operate their own businesses. Three other community colleges initiated specific courses in small business administration. Various instructors have conducted short-term workshops and one-day conferences during the past six months.

These "spin-offs" of the Small Business Institute at the University of Illinois will greatly facilitate the goals of the Small Business Administration to provide management assistance services to small businesses. In Illinois, students will become more aware of career opportunities in small business ownership and management. An increase in all types of educational programmes pertaining to small business ownership and management will help people become more informed about the qualities, characteristics and knowledge necessary for success as a small businesman.

PART V

REGIONAL SCENARIOS

AFRICA

Philip A. Neck[1]

19

The African region should be viewed in the context of its particular settings, development models which have been used and the
policies, structures and programmes which have arisen.

19.1 THE SETTING IN AFRICA

Economic and social overview

The regional picture is one of hardship interspersed with
opportunities. Africa has 16 of the world's 25 least developed
countries and 13 of the 18 land-locked, low income countries. Nine
countries had a gross national product (GNP) capita of only $100,
or less, in 1973; while seven countries (Equatorial Guinea, Chad,
Niger, Senegal, Sudan, Upper Volta and Zambia) achieved an annual
growth rate of only 1 per cent, or less, for the period 1965-1973.

The Gross Domestic Product (GDP) for the whole region grew at
only 4.6 per cent per year compared to the International Development
Strategy target rate of 6 per cent. The GDP rate per capita also
fell since the population grew by 2.6 per cent rather than the 2.5
per cent a year forecast for this period[2].

Given that GNP per capita may not necessarily indicate the true
development level of a country, particularly where subsistence agriculture predominates, we can use other measures which also confirm
the relatively low development profile of countries in the region.
For instance, whereas life expectancy at birth exceeds 50 years for
most North African countries, in West and Central Africa it barely

---

[1] *Management Development Branch, International Labour Office,
Geneva. Particular thanks are offered to Mr. Desmond Fitzpatrick of
the Irish Development Authority and Mr. Aodh O'Cannain of the Irish
Management Institute for their contributions to the Irish Government/
International Labour Office Joint Study Series: Small Enterprise
Development in Africa, 1976.*

[2] *ECA, Survey of Economic and Social Conditions in Africa
(1974; Part I); p. 1-31.*

reaches 40 years, with East African countries somewhere in between.
Angola does not even reach one-half of the life expectancy of most
industrialised countries[1].

Urban congestion is another problem in Africa. Commencing as
the least urbanised region in the world (only 22 per cent in 1970),
it has since experienced an urban growth rate of 5 per cent per year,
the highest in the world. Migration from rural areas makes up more
than one-half of this growth and contributes to the growing social
and economic problems.

On the more positive side, considerable progress has been made
in education. However, it can also be argued that most educational
inputs have been directed towards the urban and modern sector minority groups. Furthermore, educational systems have generally expanded faster than the economic growth rate, particularly in the industrial sector, giving rise to problems of the educated unemployed,
and initiating rural to urban population drift[2].

Workers migrating to foreign countries is another feature of the
African scene. Apart from workers moving from Northern Africa to
Europe and the Middle East, and from the bordering and enclave countries into the South African Republic, other regional countries
absorb part of the labour force. Libya took in more than 100,000
workers in 1975. In the Ivory Coast, immigrants from Upper Volta,
Mali and Niger accounted for 21.3 per cent of the total resident
African population, exceeding the national population in urban localities in the savannah region in 1970[3]; only 25 per cent of small
industrial enterprises are thought to be Ivorien.

The slow growth of African economies is blamed largely on problems and failures in the agricultural sector. The disappointing
results can be attributed, on the one hand, to natural causes such
as droughts and other unusual climatic conditions; and, on the other
hand, to the lack of such man-made contributions as appropriate infrastructure, technology, skills and economic incentives. Since more
than 80 per cent of African populations live in rural areas, agricul-
tural-based problems affect large proportions of the population.

The manufacturing sector has generally shown greater improvement
than the agricultural sector. Eighteen countries exceeded their
Industrial Development Strategy targets for growth rate in manufacturing output between 1970 and 1973. (Examples are Algeria, Botswana,
Gabon and Mauritius growing at an average of 15 to 30 per cent
annually.) However, 21 countries did not reach the over-all target
growth rate of 8 per cent. For the period 1970-74 African manufacturing is estimated to have grown at an average annual rate of only

---

[1] *UN: Demographic Yearbook (1974).*

[2] *P. Bairoch: Urban unemployment in developing countries,*
(ILO, Geneva, 1973), p. 37-39.

[3] *H. Joshi, H. Lubell, J. Mouly: Abidjan, urban development*
and employment in the Ivory Coast, (ILO, Geneva, 1976), p. 3.

7 per cent compared with an 8.7 per cent rate during the 1960's decade[1].

Decline in the manufacturing sector may be accounted for, partly, by the poor performance of the agricultural sector and consequent shortfall in supply of raw materials for agro-industrial production and, partly, to a decline in demand for industrial products. Nationalisation and Africanisation of industries, plus the rapid growth of the public sector, may have absorbed much of the entrepreneurial skills and resources required by the manufacturing sector.

The small enterprise sector in Africa

In Africa enterprises employing less than 10 employees are not usually enumerated. Additionally, small enterprise studies are confined mainly to small-scale industries. As a result, there is little quantitative economic and social data on small enterprises operating in the trading, services, maintenance and repair, transport and construction sectors.

Small industrial enterprise studies usually deal with firms employing less than 50 persons and omit artisan or craft enterprises considered to consist of a craftsman working alone or only with a few helpers or apprentices. Moreover, enumerative studies generally exclude part-time small-scale industrialists undertaking a mix of activities or seasonal work only.

Although there does not appear to be a common definition of a small enterprise for the region, it seems that the "owner-managed" enterprise is common. For example, in Nigeria, Aluko[2] reports that 99 per cent of small industrial enterprises were owned and managed by a sole proprietor, there being few partnerships, co-operatives and registered companies. However, for most purposes, it seems as though a definition based on the numbers of persons employed would be acceptable on the African scene.

Size of small enterprises

A striking feature of small enterprises in Africa is that they are very numerous and very, very small. In a detailed study of Sierra Leone[3] the average for small-scale industrial employment was found to be only 1.9 workers per unit rising to 3.5 workers per unit in the capital, Freetown. These figures are supported by studies in

---

[1] ECA: *Survey of economic and social conditions in Africa,* (1974, Part I).

[2] Aluko S.A.: *Industry in the rural setting, in Rural Development in Nigeria (Proceedings of the 1972 Conference of Nigerian Economic Society, Ibadan University Press, 1973).*

[3] E. Chuta and C. Liedholm: *The role of small-scale industry in employment generation and rural development: initial research results from Sierra Leone (African Rural Employment Research Network, Department of Agricultural Economics, Michigan State University, East Lansing, Michigan, USA, 1975).*

rural Western Nigeria[1] in 1973 where the average number of workers
per industrial unit was three, which is consistent with ILO findings
in the same area in 1970 of 2.6 workers per industrial enterprise.
In Eastern Nigeria[2] Kilby reported an average of 2.7 workers in 1962
while Callaway[3] in 1967 estimated 2.8 workers per industrial enterprise.

An ILO Report on Kenya[4] suggested that a typical rural small-
scale industrial enterprise employed, on average, three workers.

Studies in Senegal have shown that only 15 to 20 per cent of
enterprises employed more than six persons and, in Ghana, 60 per cent
of all enterprises were individual artisans accounting for 34 per cent
of total employment.

Scope and types of small enterprises

The Sierra Leone study indicated that small enterprises could
be graded from purely traditional activities in rural areas to such
advanced activities as motor vehicle repairs in urban areas. When
moving from rural hamlets to the cities there was an increase in
size and sophistication of machines accompanied by an upwards shift
in technology. Callaway[5] also points out that enterprises using more
advanced techniques were also more likely to undertake multiple
involvements. For example, 40 per cent of bakers also engaged in
retail selling.

African entrepreneurs

Few large-scale tracer studies have been carried out to provide
a comprehensive coverage of African entrepreneurs in biographic or
psychological terms. Most reports contain descriptions of "cases"
which may, or may not, be representative of this particular sector.

It is generally thought that entrepreneurial development occurs
on a non-formal basis, simply because few formal institutions exist
to carry out entrepreneurial training and development.

Entrepreneurs succeed in spite of many problems. For instance,
in Nigeria, Aluko[6] reported that 44.2 per cent of rural small-scale
industrial entrepreneurs were virtually illiterate, and 88.8 per cent
had less than full primary schooling. The lack of success suggests
that a case can be made for developing entrepreneurs' numeracy and

---

[1] *Aluko S.A., op. cit.*

[2] *P. Kilby: The development of small industry in Eastern
Nigeria (USAID/Ministry of Commerce, Lagos, 1962).*

[3] *A. Callaway: Education for self-employment: Africa's indigenous apprentice training and its modern adaptations (ILO, unpublished manuscript, Geneva, 1977).*

[4] *ILO: Employment, incomes and equality - A strategy for
increasing productive employment in Kenya (Geneva, 1972).*

[5] *A. Callaway, op. cit.*

[6] *Aluko S.A., op. cit.*

literacy skills. Studies from Kenya[1] and Nigeria[2] respectively suggest a zero and a negative correlation exist between formal schooling and successful entrepreneurship in the footwear manufacturing business. Kilby[3] found there was no correlation for bakers in this respect in Nigeria. Harris (reported in de Wilde[4]) found there was a positive correlation between technical education inputs and success in technical-type enterprises such as printing; no correlation for those engaged in baking; and a negative correlation for rubber processors.

The general picture is that the more complex and technological the enterprise, the more important education inputs become if entrepreneurs are to be successful.

At the enterprise level the lack of successful entrepreneurs is blamed on several possible causes. One explanation is that the financial and social attractions of paid employment in the public and large-scale private sector have attracted a large part of the available supply. Workers in recorded wage employment, who are the core of the labour force in the formal sector, are the relatively well-off on the African scene. For instance, in Kenya, hourly wages in the unionised private and public sectors were between 30 and 16 per cent higher than the non-unionised sector, while the earnings of the self-employed in urban Kenya were 52 per cent less[5].

In Africa there is a limited source from which entrepreneurs might emerge. Either they seem to grow out of the informal sector, or to emerge as the extra-curricula activities of established civil servants or salaried persons. Few entrepreneurs appear to develop directly from technical and vocational training institutions.

Other possibilities to explain the absence of entrepreneurship are suggested by Charlesworth[6] who contends that role-strain problems

---

[1] P. Marris and A. Somerset: African Businessmen - a study of entrepreneurship and development in Kenya (Routledge and P. Kegan, London, 1971).

[2] E.W. Nafziger: The relationship between education and entrepreneurship in Nigeria, The Journal of Developing Areas, (Vol. 4, No. 3, April 1970).

[3] P. Kilby, op. cit.

[4] J.C. de Wilde: The development of African private enterprise (Vol. 1, main report; Vol. 2, Country Annexes; Report AW-31; International Bank for Reconstruction and Development, IDA, Washington D.C., December 1971).

[5] G.E. Johnson: The determination of individual hourly earnings in urban Kenya (Discussion Paper No. 115, Institute for Development Studies, University of Nairobi, September 1971), p. 23-24.

[6] H.K. Charlesworth: "Role strain" and the development of entrepreneurship among countries and regions of the emergent world, Entrepreneurship and enterprise development: A world-wide perspective (Proceedings of Project ISEED, the Centre for Venture Management, Milwaukee, 1975), p. 141-146.

affect development of an entrepreneurial outlook. He argues the case
for developing business attitudes to replace existing social value
systems. The Partnership-for-Productivity project in Kakamega,
Western Kenya reports positive results employing this approach
coupled with effective simple management practices.

In Ethiopia, De Missie[1] put this problem in a slightly different
form where, he claims, the cultural attitudes to entrepreneurs which
prevailed under the former pseudo-capitalistic type of government
were regarded as degrading for "proper" people.

Many persons, probably those possessing entrepreneurial characteristics, emigrate annually depriving their countries of origin of
this special resource. Nationalisation and localisation programmes
may even act to hasten this entrepreneurial demise.

The International Symposium on Entrepreneurship and Enterprise
Development, held in Ohio in June 1975, pointed out that successful
small enterprise development requires effective extension services.
However, an ILO studies series in Africa in 1976 revealed that in a
selection of African countries, such extension services were either
non-existent, or limited, or serving only a small number of clients.

The regional picture obtained for Africa is that while some
useful development work is being carried out, it appears to take
place in isolation and deserves perhaps to be co-ordinated with other
financial and technological inputs.

19.2   MODELS FOR DEVELOPMENT

Small enterprise development in Africa seems to be either adapted
from the more developed countries, or transferred from developing
countries like India. Little is written about small enterprise development schemes based on indigenous African economic, social and
cultural development potential, although these certainly exist.

Most African development programmes appear to depend on "availability of funds" rather than on availability of human or natural
resources, or market potential. Since development funds for this
sector are usually controlled by formally established financial institutions, development schemes tend to be cautious and conservative.

Although the sector may have received attention from a conceptual point of view, it is not readily visible but may well be served
indirectly within over-all economic models. It generally seems to
be assumed that the small enterprise sector behaves in concert with
economic development as a whole.

Small enterprise development schemes in Africa appear to be
treated on a project rather than programme basis.

---

[1] *S. De Missie: Cross-cultural entrepreneurship African and
Middle Eastern countries, Entrepreneurship and enterprise develop-
ment: a worldwide perspective (Proceedings of Project ISEED, the
Centre for Venture Management, Milwaukee, 1975), p. 132.*

19.3 POLICIES FOR SECTOR DEVELOPMENT

The medium and long-term development plans for nearly all African countries set the order of priority as (1) agriculture, (2) infrastructure, and (3) industrialisation; emphasising self-sufficiency and self-development.

Consequently, small enterprises in Africa mostly revolve around or become a downstream product of agro-industry. This places the sector in straitened circumstances should the agricultural sector fail for any reason whatsoever.

Initially, the policies of self-dependence were often interpreted to mean import-substitution. However, some countries, realising that they did not know what and how much was imported, turned to encouraging selective exports instead. This switch often hindered small enterprise development.

Long-lasting and effective small enterprise development depends on sound infrastructure. An example is provided by the United States where small enterprise development followed the wagon-trains, was expanded with the introduction of railway networks and, more recently, changed its shape and nature when highway construction and high-rise dwellings appeared. In Africa, similar developments to this form of sector growth can be seen in Nigeria which is embarking on infrastructural development programmes.

For most African countries integrated development is a post-independence phenomenon. Without representative statistical and other data, it is unfair to expect well integrated, all-encompassing developmental policies at this early stage; particularly, when the more industrialised countries also lack clearly expressed, well-conceived policies for small enterprise development.

Because industrialisation influences other sectors of the community by binding them together in certain proportions, policies for small enterprise development must take into account the leverage exercised by the industrial sector.

Although development strategies for the small enterprise sector may not be obviously seen in many African countries, people responsible for developing sector activities like handicrafts and cottage industries, rehabilitation of handicapped workers and industrial estates, have not remained idle. Many worthwhile projects exist. However, this sometimes means duplication of institutions and overlapping efforts because there is no integrated approach to sector development as a whole.

In countries like Kenya, Sudan and Uganda this problem has been realised and proposals to set up Small Enterprise Development Organisations or Corporations have been made, but not yet put into practice. On the other hand, institutions like OPEI in Ivory Coast, Centre d'Assistance aux Petites et Moyennes Entreprises in Cameroon, the Ghanaian Business Bureau and OPEV in Upper Volta already exist.

Some writers recommend selective specialisation rather than global efforts when promoting small enterprise development. How this might be done without fragmenting the total development effort is not an easy problem.

One disturbing feature about policies for the sector has been their lack of awareness amongst those people they were designed to help. In the Sudan[1] policies for the sector are said to be widely unknown by entrepreneurs. This finding is also reported in similar studies from other regions.

19.4 STRUCTURES FOR PROMOTING SMALL ENTERPRISE DEVELOPMENT

An encouraging feature of the African scene is the wide range of financial, technological, managerial and developmental institutions with the capacity, or potential, or both, for assisting small enterprise development. Although most structures are not specifically geared to assist the smaller enterprise, they can be expanded or strengthened to do so.

Financial institutions

Whereas governmental and non-governmental financial institutions exist in most countries, the major hindrances to development appear to be lack of experienced personnel and domestic and foreign funds.

Staffing problems emerge in many forms. One obvious area is the lack of qualified project officers capable of preparing, or assisting entrepreneurs to prepare, feasible proposals. Officials able to appraise proposals are also scarce. Major personal shortcomings are inexperience and lack of knowledge about such production processes as machinery utilisation and requirements.

Other deficiencies include loan officers able to assess proposals on their developmental potential rather than collateral security. It is fair comment to say that ultra-conservative funding practices exist throughout the region.

The abnormally large numbers of delinquent accounts in the small enterprise sector, in some cases close to 100 per cent, are due to a mix of causes. These include lack of adequate supervision, providing loans for reasons other than the feasibility of the proposals, the absence of appropriate extension services, and poor management. The common finding is that many of these problems could have been avoided if qualified staff were available.

Further cause for concern is shortage of foreign exchange. Not only is this a problem in itself, but it also leads to time-consuming struggles between rival promoters for these scarce funds. When allocations are not made quickly, inflation can force project costs beyond realistic breakeven levels for all projects concerned.

Other complaints include high borrowing rates, short repayment periods and similar issues. These problems, however, appear only minor compared to the problems of having no funds at all.

---

[1] *D. Fitzpatrick: Small enterprise development in Sudan (Joint Study Series; Irish Government/ILO, Geneva, 1976).*

A general conclusion for the African region is that, in spite of the many and varied financial institutions which exist, most adopt conservative philosophies and commercial practices. They seldom exhibit the developmental outlook and behaviour necessary for growth and promotion of small enterprises in the region.

The World Bank's interest in promoting small enterprise development for the region may provide the necessary stimulus to move things in the right direction.

Technological development

Institutions enhancing development and transfer of appropriate technology are probably the weakest structures assisting small enterprise development in the African region.

Because there are such large managerial and technological gaps to be overcome, it seems logical that an "only the best will do" approach should be adopted. However, our findings suggest that technological development is either poorly served or ignored altogether. One exception is the Technology Consultancy Centre, University of Science and Technology, Kumasi, Ghana.

There are many problems but underlying them all is the absence of such basic industries as iron and steel, and cheap energy. Most observers conclude that viable basic industries require regional, or sub-regional, participation. Unfortunately such proposals often clash with the feelings of nationalism generally associated with newly found political independence.

It is also difficult for developing countries to find the right technical partners. Tanzania[1] complains about difficulties met when negotiating with principals to obtain favourable terms of agreement. They suggest standardising agreements to soften the hard ride so often sustained when dealing with experienced industrialised partners. They also complain that technical partners can be unwilling to train local people as expeditiously as they might, but mention exceptions when dealing with friendly countries.

On the domestic scene it may also be difficult to overcome consumer preferences for foreign-made goods. Additionally, there are often production problems in developing or acquiring the technology necessary to convert local produce into acceptable consumer goods.

Attempts to acquire or develop technological capacity in Africa are handicapped by underqualified technical personnel, outmoded equipment, and non-availability of equipment, spare-parts and materials. Few institutions in the region can deliver adequate extention services.

---

[1] *H.M. Kalomo: Problems concerned with industrialisation in the least developed countries and their possible solutions (Paper submitted at UNIDO Intergovernmental Expert Group Meeting on the Industrialisation of the Least Developed Countries, 15-24 November 1976, Vienna, Austria).*

The general situation is grim. Something needs to be done!

Management development

That management development problems exist is clear, but where to begin tackling them is difficult to see. Some experts[1] argue, convincingly, that we should commence with techno-economic and man-power planning surveys to assess the potentialities and requirements necessary to frame policies and programmes.

Management development is a long-term exercise requiring plan-ning, programmes and evaluation to suit. In the absence of follow-up and review exercises, it is difficult to know whether "crash" pro-grammes in the region succeed or, indeed, crash!

Most people agree that foreign-based training, except in special circumstances, is expensive, often inappropriate, and may produce undesirable long-term effects such as "brain-drain". However, local management development programmes also have problems because faci-lities are generally limited, institutions employ inexperienced or under-qualified instructors, teaching equipment is difficult to obtain and repair, and teaching materials and approaches can become out of date.

Most African countries have experimented, with mixed results, in using expert-counterpart type training schemes as part of tech-nical assistance programmes to develop or upgrade management trainers. Commonly reported successes of such projects include: creating and developing viable institutions such as productivity and management development centres; conducting courses in management development, particularly in functional areas; fellowship training; developing management training materials applicable to the local scene; and surveys and needs analysis for sectoral development. However, these programmes also have had some problems such as advisers unable to adjust to the particular demands of their assignments, shortage of counterpart staff, and attempts to implement project designs that were too ambitious.

Another relevant feature is the need to accommodate industria-lised managerial practices within the ideological and philosophical framework of religious and cultural groups in the region.

Training for the small enterprise sector suffers from mismatches of demand and supply, and lack of harmonisation. For instance, following independence in the Cameroons, a large boost to vocational training resulted in a new skilled labour force with no jobs avai-lable. One considered solution was to promote self-employment which, in turn, led to demands for managerial training. However, such training was unavailable at that time.

---

[1] *N. Tandon and B. Tomé: Special problems facing least deve-loped countries in promoting industrial development: actions and special measures required to meet the needs for accelerating their industrialisation (Paper delivered to UNIDO, Intergovernmental Expert Group Meeting on the Industrialisation of the Least Developed Countries, Vienna, Austria, 15-24 November 1976).*

Developmental structures

In conducting this review of small enterprise development in the African region, the enormity of the problem really comes into focus when sectoral developmental aspects are taken into account.

Africa, being the youngest continent and the most recent to undertake development, has had a slower start than other regions. Unlike many industrialised countries with a well-established private sector, recent political independence has thrown the greater emphasis of development on to governments. Consequently, African countries are faced with the task of managing a newly formed civil service enmeshed with industrial sector management and its accompanying responsibilities. On top of this, emergent nationalism almost precludes opportunities for promoting regional growth during the formative stages of nation building.

Although small enterprise development structures or corporations may exist, they do not appear to accept either the responsibility, or to command the authority required to do the job expected of them. These structures should not be expected to undertake all development activities, but they should see that they are carried out and appropriate assistance provided.

The ILO studies series conducted in Africa identified the following elements as legitimate functions of developmental structures for the sector:

Legislation and resources allocation

Obtaining resources for sector development requires some form of legislation. Human resources need to be allocated as either management or labour; financial resources need to be provided as appropriate equity and loans; and material resources such as access to equipment, supplies and the necessary raw materials should be made available.

A small enterprise development organisation could conduct the necessary research, initiate legislation, provide impetus to obtain government consent, and organise beneficiaries to exert the proper pressure to ensure that they receive fair treatment.

Markets

Almost universally, the market system serving small enterprise development in Africa is severely limited because adequate communication and distribution networks are not available. The few available studies show these to be outmoded in the extreme and may, qualitatively at least, be assessed as the single biggest hindrance to progress[1].

An unusual feature of this particular problem is that distribution systems can often be improved for relatively little capital cost. This, however, calls for a departure from traditional ways

---

[1] F. Meissner: *Marketing as a tool of development, Development Digest, (Vol. XII, No. 4, October 1974)*.

and innovative practices have to be introduced. For instance, in some areas it could mean enhancing, rather than abolishing, the often misunderstood "middleman".

A major problem is caused by the lack of impact in foreign markets of small-scale industrial goods. Poor quality control seems to be the bugbear, although the sophisticated merchandising techniques used by large-scale enterprises may have something to do with the difficulties experienced by the smaller producers. These marketing and related problems could be looked after by a developmental structure set up to protect the interests of small enterprises.

Infrastructure

The lack of "hardware" infrastructure, such as roads, handicaps small enterprises engaged, for example, in mining. Because such projects do not obviously demonstrate an immediate and direct impact on economic development, funds for such infrastructural necessities are often difficult to obtain.

Additionally, high illiteracy rates such as the 95 per cent of the workforce in Ethiopia[1], can deplete the "software" component of developmental infrastructure. Again, it is usually difficult to obtain the funds to overcome these types of problems.

Developmental "packages" can be expensive, or inappropriate, or both, if designed in a donor country only. It may not necessarily be a question of open-bias by the designers, but local preferences may subconsciously come into play when, for example, choosing equipment. This happens simply because project designers usually understand and prefer familiar equipment.

In Africa, there is not much backward integration incorporating industrial production functions within foreign-owned companies. Most foreign-based parent companies are more concerned with the primary production or the end-marketing aspects, than in promoting industrialisation within developing countries. Consequently, opportunities for sub-contract work for small enterprises providing speciality services, such as repair and maintenance, do not readily emerge.

Many reasons, real and imaginary, are offered to explain why foreign companies are reluctant to set up production units in Africa. These include fears of nationalisation and loss by take-over, with or without compensation; difficulties in obtaining special materials such as sheet metal and spare parts; lack of a skilled and disciplined labour force; and political turbulence and unpredictability. The small enterprise sector in Africa will, most likely, continue to suffer until these developmental inputs are put in order, and are seen to be put in order. This could mean that well conducted public relations campaigns are needed to highlight investment opportunities when these problems no longer exist.

---

[1] *S. De Missie, op. cit.*

There is also the need to introduce into government circles, persons equipped with the right sort of experience and interest to foster and promote development of small enterprises. This is especially so in those sensitive areas where development funds are allocated and approved.

Some countries attempt to undertake too many projects at one tome. One solution offered is that it might be better to adopt selective rather than all-fronts growth strategies.

A responsible developmental structure or institution is usually required to look after these pertinent environmental and unfrastructural problems if the sector is to receive its fair share of attention and assistance.

19.5 PROGRAMMES FOR DEVELOPING SMALL ENTERPRISES

The main structures provide assistance to the sector by carrying out individual and related programmes.

Programmes for two types of structure are reviewed in Charts 19.1 and 19.2 which illustrate the range of institutions and agencies involved, their location, timing and method of operation.

CHART 19.1:   FINANCIAL PROGRAMMES: AFRICA

Location	Type	Agencies/Institutions	Timing	Execution
International	*Grants*	*Bilateral Aid e.g.* *SIDA, NORAD*	*No repay-* *ment*	*With tech-* *nical as-* *sistance*
		Development Funds *e.g. FED*	*"*	*As part of* *loan* *package*
	Loans	*Banks e.g. IBRD*	*Long term*	*Wide* *spread of* *interest* *rate ½% to* *10%*
		Bilateral Funds *e.g. Fed. Rep.* *of Germany*	*Medium to* *long term*	*"*
		Development Funds *AESDF*	*"*	*"*
Regional	*Loans*	*Banks e.g. ADB*	*Medium to* *long term*	*Medium to* *high int.* *rates*
National	*Grants*	*Government* *Departments*	*No repay-* *ment*	*Special* *conditions*
	Subsidies	*"*	*"*	*Preferen-* *tial pur-* *chasing*
	Loans	*Government* *Dev. Banks*	*Medium to* *long term*	*Medium to* *high rates*
		Non-Government *Commercial banks* *Credit Unions* *Leasing* *Hire Purchase* *Curb Markets*	*Short to* *medium* *"* *"* *Short*	*High rates* *" "* *" "* *" "* *" "*

CHART 19.2: TECHNOLOGICAL PROGRAMMES: AFRICA

Location	Type	Agencies/Institutions	Timing	Execution
International	*Basic Research*	*UNDP specialised agencies, e.g. FAO, ILO, UNIDO. Governments e.g. Foundations e.g. Food*	*Continu- ous*	*Commissioned Studies University Grants*
	Appli- cation	*I.D.T.G. Ltd*	*On request*	*Papers*
	Training	*UNDP specialised agencies*	*"*	*Seminars*
		Governments	*"*	*Fellowships*
Regional	*Basic Research*			
	Appli- cation	*UNDP specialised agencies bila- teral*	*On request*	*Field projects*
	Training	*" "*	*"*	*Courses*
National	*Basic Research*	*Universities*	*Continu- ous*	*Degree programme*
		Institutes for Development	*"*	
	Appli- cation	*Government (Prod. Centres)*	*"*	*Extension Services Publications*
		Equipment Suppliers	*"*	*Sales and adaptation*
		Professional Associations	*"*	*Professional Journals*
	Training	*Government e.g. Productivity Centres Voc. Training Institut.*	*" "*	*Seminar Courses Courses*
		Professional Associa- tions		*Meetings*
		Equipment Suppliers	*"*	*Demonstra- tions*

19.6 SUMMARY OF FINDINGS

This summary is based partly on literature reviews and field
studies, and partly on conclusions drawn by participants at the ILO's
Symposium on small enterprise development schemes in Africa held in
Abidjan in March 1977.

Some generalisations

The small enterprise development scenario within the present
economic and social environment in Africa, is a contrast of challenges
and problems. Challenges emerge because although the continent has
had a relatively late start in development, there is an expressed
enthusiasm by all concerned to accelerate the development process.
The identified problems are similar to those facing the sector in
other regions but, at times, appear to be even greater.

Little information is available about the sector which ranges
from informal artisans to formal modern enterprises.

African entrepreneurs tend to be self-developed rather than
products of organised development schemes.

Little literature is readily available about small enterprise
development schemes based on indigenous socio-cultural systems.

Policies for the sector are often unclear, fragmented or absent.
Where policies do exist, entrepreneurs may be unaware of them, or do
not know how to make best use of them. Because political independence is relatively recent, most African governments are expected to
provide the developmental initiatives for small enterprises traditionally left to the private sector.

Well established financial, managerial and developmental structures exist to serve the sector. In many cases they need reorien-
ting, or strengthening, or both. Technological development structures
are generally weak.

Wide-ranging assistance programmes are available. However, they
appear to need to be integrated to promote more effective growth.

Specific findings

During the ILO Symposium in Africa 1977 the following issues
were highlighted.

Policy matters

A major common problem faced at policy level is that of co-ordination at two levels: the sectoral level and the geographical or
regional level. One country (the Ivory Coast) intends to solve this
problem by setting up an interministerial co-ordinating committee
for the purpose.

Owing to their relatively recent accession to economic independence, the accelerated development of many African countries has
tended to favour the choice of large units and projects. Whenever

this is the case, there should be a policy of subcontracting complementary products and services to smaller enterprises.

Existing legislation in several countries is not particularly
favourable to the survival and growth of small undertakings. A
revision of the legal framework is an important ingredient of policies aimed at stimulating smaller enterprises.

While certain African countries lack policies specifically
directed to the small enterprise sector, other countries have set up
a varying range of strategies whereby, for example:

(i)   nationals are encouraged to become entrepreneurs by
       providing a sufficiently motivating infrastructure
       of training, financial and extension services
       (e.g. Togo);

(ii)   the government itself takes a primary initiative in
       setting up small and medium undertakings (e.g. Algeria);

(iii) potential national entrepreneurs are encouraged to buy
       viable small enterprises from expatriates (e.g. Ivory
       Coast).

Operational structures

To implement a policy to promote small enterprises could be
furthered by establishing a framework of institutions to provide the
necessary support and draw up specific programmes for that sector.
Such institutions would cover training and extension, financial
questions and development needs.

With regard to financing, only a fraction of loans to development banks have reached small enterprises as those banks tended to
consider loans to small undertakings to be risky and costly. New
intermediaries and channels are needed to reach that sector and
development bank and loan officers needed to be trained in project
assessment and evaluation.

At the country level, some countries (e.g. Sudan) report that
entrepreneurs have to rely almost entirely on commercial banks for
financing, which cover only up to 10 per cent of the cost of the
venture. Most commercial banks ask for extensive collaterals and
guarantees. Other countries (e.g., Ivory Coast) indicate that they
have set up special guarantee funds with state participation to
finance up to 80 per cent of the cost of forming or expanding a small
undertaking. The availability of necessary credit at the right time
is the most crucial financial factor for the entrepreneur, rather
than the interest rate charged.

Development institutions necessary for support purposes include
industrial estates subsiding essential services to small enterprises
as well as institutes conducting technical and economical feasibility
studies and exploring market potential in relation to local resources.
In some cases (e.g. Swaziland) such services are grouped in one institution which also provides training services.

There is a pressing need in most African countries for a service to be provided to small entrepreneurs in the choice and adaptation of technology.

Some countries (e.g. Kenya and Ivory Coast) are experimenting with the establishment of small entrepreneurs' associations which could play a useful role in pressing for the reform of existing small enterprise development schemes in their countries. Such reform could touch on policy issues or deal with simplifying the procedures to be followed in establishing and strengthening small enterprises.

African programmes

In most African countries it is urgently necessary to allocate sufficient resources to building and strengthening support institutions. In the case of one country (Upper Volta) it is estimated that the training and extension services institute is able to provide facilities for no more than 1 per cent of small enterprises in the country - a ratio not uncommon in many African countries. A related issue is the cost of technical assistance provided by such institutions. In certain countries (Togo and Zaire) it is provided free of charge, while in others (Kenya) a nominal fee is charged. No institutions are financially self-supporting.

Contrary to experience in other countries, such as India, there do not appear to be any cases where the selection of eligible potential entrepreneurs for training or financial assistance is based on tests aimed at assessing the individual's desire for achievement and his ability to rationalise operations entailing risk. Some benefit might be drawn from the experience of others in this respect.

With regard to training, the lack of managerial competence is the single most important factor leading to the failure of small enterprises. In essence, any training effort should aim at imparting knowledge, developing skills and changing attitudes, the last of which is often neglected in African institutions. In some Asian countries experiments are being carried out to introduce elements of entrepreneurial skills in the final years of secondary education. Similar experiments have been designed to find short-cuts to skill formation by selecting potential entrepreneurs among persons already possessing technical or commercial skills. The need to develop both technical and managerial skills is very acute.

Training methods more suitable for small entrepreneurs should be developed.

In many cases African countries often restrict their schemes for developing small enterprises to manufacturing concerns. These schemes should also cover other activities as well, such as trading, transport, construction and service undertakings. Similarly, policies in this field should at times, consider regional and community needs irrespective of whether or not the proposed ventures are financially attractive.

The conditions of work in small enterprises in many African countries leave much to be desired. The ILO, in co-operation with the countries concerned, might make a valuable contribution in this area.

By and large there is no doubt that the African region is set for tremendous activity in the field of small enterprise development. The task is formidable but challenging, the prospects exciting but frightening for, if development efforts fail, social and economic development will be seriously retarded.

THE EUROPEAN COMMUNITY

Peter J. Lennon[1]

20

This chapter serves to outline the general policies and specific measures for small and medium-sized enterprises (S.M.E.) in the European Community.

Given:

(i)   the size of the Community - 9 Member States (Federal Republic of Germany (F.R.G.), Belgium, Denmark, France, Ireland, Italy, Grand Duchy of Luxembourg (G.D.L.), Netherlands, United Kingdom (U.K.) and a population of 260,000,000 people approximately,

(ii)   the complex nature of the subject matter,

(iii) the considerable variations which exist in this area within the Community,

the policies and measures can only be sketched in a very general manner.

The author is responsible for the contents of the paper, which may not necessary reflect the position of the institutions of either the European Community or the Member States.

20.1   THE CONCEPT OF S.M.E. IN THE COMMUNITY

No Member State has a legal definition of what constitutes S.M.E.. Usually, they are defined by the various states on the basis of quantitative criteria for purposes such as statistics, taxation, finance, the right of establishment, technical or management assistance. The quantitative criteria used may vary from one policy or programme to another.

---

1 *Head, Small and Medium-Sized Enterprises, Artisanat Division, Commission of the European Communities, Brussels, Belgium. This chapter was specifically prepared for this publication in April 1977 and does not take into account changes made since that date.*

Considerable diversity exists between Member States in the general concept of S.M.E., such as the widely accepted upper limits terms of *number of employees* for small and medium-sized *industrial enterprises* varies as follows:

- Belgium   50 or 100
- Denmark   75
- Ireland   100
- United Kingdom   200

France   )
Fed. Republic of Germany) 500
Italy   )

The Federal Republic of Germany (F.R.G.), France, Italy, Belgium and the Grand Duchy of Luxembourg (G.D.L.) have official definitions of the artisanat. With the exception of the Federal Republic of Germany and the Grand Duchy of Luxembourg where the criterion is based on the possession of a certificate of competence, the general criterion is the number of persons employed (usually 5 or 10 people in addition to members of the family).

The European Community has no official definition of either S.M.E. or the artisanat. However, as in the Member States, exemptions in Community directives or regulations are provided for in certain cases and for certain enterprises on the basis of their size.

The Commission's Small and Medium-sized Enterprises, Artisanat Division, which is responsible for examining the problems of these sectors and for their general promotion at Community level, considers, in practice, that industrial enterprises which are legally and financially independent and with no more than 500 employees form part of these sectors.

In the commerce, distribution and service sectors the number of employees would obviously be much less.

20.2   THE EVOLUTION OF S.M.E. IN THE COMMUNITY

The European Community was, amongst other reasons, established so that industrial, commercial and service enterprises - both public and private - could benefit from the opportunity and the stimulus provided by a continental scale market. Many people feared that in such a large scale market S.M.E., would have a bleak future. However, contrary to the worst fears they appear to have maintained their position in the Community.

An analysis of national statistics carried out internally a couple of years ago indicated that, during the 1960s, *industrial S.M.E.,* in general, maintained their relative position both in terms of the number of enterprises and the number of people employed. The analysis indicated that industrial enterprises employing less than 500 people accounted for approximately *95 percent of individual enterprises* and for over *50 percent of the people employed* in industry - at both the beginning and the end of the decade.

The relative importance of S.M.E., in the economy as a whole, i.e., industry plus commerce, distribution and services, is even greater. For example, the government of the Federal Republic of Germany estimates that S.M.E. account for approximately *two-thirds of all employment* outside agriculture and public administration.

Sectoral and national variations in these percentages exist.

20.3 GENERAL POLICIES

All national governments and Community institutions are conscious of the characteristics and special problems of S.M.E, and have taken steps to help them. Even though the accent varies from one country to another all countries do give some assistance to S.M.E. by means of *exemptions* from certain general requirements, e.g., responsibility for value added tax below a certain level of turnover or by *positive measures* such as credit guarantees, vocational and owner/manager training programmes, technical assistance.

It is not always clear, however, to what extent these exemptions or positive measures form part of an explicit homogeneous national policy towards S.M.E, in each country or are heterogeneous actions taken to deal with immediate problems.

Some Member States have announced explicit S.M.E, policies. For example, the government of the Federal Republic of Germany published, in 1970, a basic policy document entitled "Guidelines for a structural policy for S.M.E." and the French government announced in March 1976 a programme of actions in favour of small and medium-sized industrial enterprises.

The objective of the Federal Republic of Germany's policy is to help S.M.E. to improve their efficiency and competitivity, to help them to adapt to structural changes. The policy is based on the principle of helping those who help themselves. It is not designed to subsidize and preserve outdated structures.

The objectives of the French policy are to encourage the creation of S.M.E., to promote the development of existing S.M.E., and to help them adapt to changing conditions.

In contrast, "the policy of the United Kingdom government towards small firms is one of non-discrimination. The Government does not normally give special advantages to firms because they are small but it tries to make sure that they are not put at a disadvantage."

Although, on the surface, these would appear to be a considerable difference between the approaches of the Federal Republic of Germany and of France, on the one hand, and of the United Kingdom, on the other, it is difficult to evaluate the extent of the difference as the overall effect of the various measures which are taken in these countries may, in practice, be relatively equivalent.

The policy of the European Community as such is to allow enterprises, of all sizes, to benefit from the advantages which an enlarged market offers them whilst at the same time submitting *all* enterprises to the free play of competition in the open market. This involves, among other things, the elimination of obstacles - such as customs duties, quotas, technical barriers to trade, restrictive public purchasing policies - and the harmonization of the fiscal and legal framework within which enterprises operate.

The elimination of such non-tariff barriers is probably of greater benefit to S.M.E., than to large enterprises, for the latter can bypass national barriers to trade without great difficulty by establishing themselves in individual Member States of the Community whilst S.M.E. cannot in practice do so.

20.4 SPECIFIC MEASURES

S.M.E. are found in practically every sector of economic activity and can be affected in one way or another by a wide range of national and Community policies and programmes. For that reason all national governments and Community institutions try to ensure that every policy or programme which can have an influence on them is examined from their point of view to ensure that the proposed policy or programme will not unconsciously affect them adversely. Some typical examples of the concrete results of such surveillance are as follows:

Federal Republic of Germany: the tax on industrial and commercial activities was raised, on January 1st, 1975, from DM 7,200 to DM 15,000 thereby freeing around 50 percent of all enterprises from it;

Belgium: although the law of July 17th, 1975, concerning bookkeeping and annual accounts is applicable to all enterprises the data required from S.M.E., have been reduced to the minimum.

United Kingdom: the provision of a "low profits" rate of corporation tax which, although based on the amount of profits earned and not on the size of the enterprise as such, is obviously of benefit principally to small rather than large companies.

This "watchdog" role of public administrations is of fundamental importance.

In addition, a wide variety of specific measures have been taken in each of the Member States and at Community level to help S.M.E. overcome the problems which are peculiar to them because of their limited size. Some examples of such measures in the Member States are:

(i) Creation of new enterprises

France
The installation of special offices in the Chambers of Industry and Commerce to help potential entrepreneurs to set up in business; the development of special training courses for such enterprises.

Ireland
The proposed introduction of an Enterprise Development Programme designed to encourage highly trained people such as engineers, accountants, scientists and business-schools graduates to undertake new manufacturing projects.

(ii)   Financing

Denmark
A 1975 Act allocated an annual budget to the Ministry of
Trade and Industry to allow it to grant loans for moderni-
zation and rationalisation to enterprises with up to 75
employees; another 1975 Act allows the State, within certain
budgetary limits, to guarantee up to 50 percent of short
term bank loans to artisanal and small industrial enterprises
which have undertaken an extensive reconversion to new
productions techniques or to new markets.

Italy
In recent years a number of laws have been introduced which
allow enterprises wishing to restructure or to convert their
production lines to obtain finance on preferential terms.

Netherlands
Provision has been made for the self-employed to build up
a fiscal reserve for their retirement and this reserve can
be reinvested in the enterprise.

(iii)   Consultancy services

Grand Duchy of Luxembourg
The O.L.A.P. (Luxembourg Office for Productivity Growth),
which is almost exclusively used by S.M.E., carries out
surveys and provides technical assistance for rationalization
schemes.

United Kingdom
The Government announced, in April 1976, a pilot counselling
scheme using retired executives to help owner-managers of
small businesses to diagnose and solve their problems
and when necessary to help them select appropriate sources
of more detailed advice.

(iv)   Cooperation

Federal Republic of Germany
The Federal Ministry of Economic Affairs has published a
Guide to Cooperation ("Kooperations-fibel") which contains
guidelines concerning competition law in relation to
cooperation; it has also published a list of forbidden
practices.

United Kingdom
In April 1976 the Government announced a scheme by which
it would meet 50 percent of the costs (up to a maximum of
£5,000 in individual cases) incurred in carrying out
feasibility studies, by groups of four or more small
businesses, into the possibility of establishing inter-firm
collaborative arrangements.

There are, of course, in every Member State many other
specific measures for S.M.E.

At Community level, measures which have been taken in a
number of fields, e.g., in relation to competition, fiscal
and social policy, vocational training, the right of
establishment, the setting-up of a Business Cooperation
Centre and various Community sources of finance such as

the Regional Development Fund, the Agricultural Fund
(Guidance Section), the Social Fund, the financial aids
of the Coal and Steel Community and the global loan scheme
of the European Investment Bank can play a positive role
in the development of S.M.E.

The way in which the Community's competition policy and the
European Investment Bank's global loan scheme can stimulate
the growth and development of S.M.E. is of interest.

(v)   The Community's competition policy

The European Commission considers that national aids which
are given to S.M.E. must be designed in such a way as to
enable S.M.E. to compete effectively, but without involving
artificial protection which would place them outside the
normal play of competition. Operating aids of a purely
preservative nature would turn them into "permanent beneficiaries", keeping them from making the necessary adaptations
and from exploiting their full potential. Such aids would
be contrary not only to the general social and economic
interest since they would tie up factors of production in
uneconomic uses, but also against the S.M.E.'s own interests.

On the other hand, the Commission gives favourable consideration to State aids which assist S.M.E. to overcome their
specific handicaps and face up to competition. The Commission
has also striven to promote - with due respect for the rules
of competition - the conclusion of cooperation agreements
which strengthen the competitive capacity of S.M.E.

(vi)   The global loan scheme of the European Investment
Bank (E.I.B.)

During its early years, the E.I.B. granted an appreciable
number of direct loans of relatively low individual amounts
for small and medium-scale industrial projects. However,
the number of these operations soon grew to the point where
it would have been difficult for the Bank to cope with any
further increase under its normal appraisal and financing
procedures. To overcome the problem the E.I.B. introduced,
in 1968, the "global loans" scheme, through which it can,
with the collaboration of financing institutions in the
various Member countries, help to finance a larger number
of small and medium-sized ventures. These global loans are
granted to banks or financing institutions which, subject
to the E.I.B.'s approval in each case, on-lend the proceeds
in sub-loans of varying amounts.

20.5 THE FUTURE

The above picture of S.M.E. in the European Community appears
reasonably positive. But it is positive in the sense that people's
fears have not been confirmed, that S.M.E. are still in business,
that they have not been eliminated by large national or multinational
enterprises.

There are, however, a number of important weaknesses in the
present situation. To facilitate the future development of S.M.E.

it will be necessary:

- to present clearly and explicitly the rational case for encouraging their creation and development;
- to reorientate policies and programmes so that S.M.E. are regarded as the norm rather than the exception;
- to improve the effectiveness of their representative organizations;
- to create an environment in which personal initiative and enterprise are encouraged.

(i) The presentation of the case for S.M.E.

There is at present a tendency - both on the part of S.M.E. themselves and on the part of those concerned with their interests - to act generally from a defensive position, almost to adopt a "siege mentality".

S.M.E. are often presented - either implicitly or explicitly - as being an end in themselves, as being in one way or another a repository of traditional cultural values, as being good, as being beautiful. They may indeed be good, they may even be beautiful. But they have not an exclusive monopoly on all the virtues nor a total exemption from all the vices.

It is, therefore, essential to present, clearly and explicitly, the *rational* case for encouraging their creation and development. A very strong case can, in fact, be made. But it should be based on S.M.E. *not as an end* in themselves but as a means to one or more ends, such as the more efficient utilisation of scarce resources (an economic end), the diffusion of economic power (a political end), a better working environment (a social end).

(ii) The reorientation of policies and programmes for S.M.E.

Although their special characteristics and problems are usually taken into account when policies and programmes are being framed, in considering their needs S.M.E. tend to be regarded as the exception to the rule, as something abnormal for which special provisions should be made.

It can be argued, on the contrary, that S.M.E. should be regarded as the norm and that large and multinational enterprises, for example, should be treated as the exception to the rule, as a category requiring special attention.

Given the fact that S.M.E. taken as a whole, play a major role in the Community - not least of all as a major source of innovations and as a means of continually renewing existing structures - it would seem reasonable that policies and programmes should be reorientated so that S.M.E. are regarded as the norm rather than the exception, that they should be framed so as to facilitate and encourage the creation and development of enterprises and to ensure that the people and material resources employed in enterprises which go out of business, because they failed to respond to changes in the market, are effectively redeployed elsewhere.

(iii)   The effectiveness of representative organisations

The fact that S.M.E. are found everywhere is one of their
strengths. It is, however, also one of their great weaknesses.

Their interests may be represented by sectoral, inter-sectoral
and/or specialist organisations. An individual enterprise may, in
fact, often be represented by two or more such organisations. On
the other hand, many S.M.E. do not belong to any representative organisation. Where they do belong to sectoral or inter-sectoral organisations many of the smaller enterprises believe that their point
of view is only taken into account where it does not conflict with
the interests of the larger members. As a result, many people consider that their voice is diffused and their real economic weight
is not represented adequately at national or international level.

It would appear to be essential, therefore, that S.M.E. improve
the effectiveness of their representative organisations and where
necessary, coordinate their efforts better. If they do not take the
necessary steps to protect their interests, nobody else is likely to
do so - or if other people do they will not do so with the same
knowledge, conviction and determination.

(iv)   Creation of a suitable environment

In addition to these three factors there is another factor which
will have a profound effect on the future of S.M.E. This factor,
which is more amorphous and yet possibly of greater importance than
any single one of the other factors, is the significant change which
has taken place in social values and attitudes.

The excesses of some enterprises have given private enterprise
a bad press. As a result of these excesses and the regular or irre-
gular crises which Western economies have experienced - e.g. inflation, unemployment, balance of payments difficulties - there has been
an increased tendency to expect national governments and semi-state
agencies to intervene directly in the economy, especially in industrial production. In addition it is claimed that high levels of
company and personal taxation have reduced the incentive to undertake
new initiatives. It is evident that such an atmosphere is not encouraging for S.M.E. There are signs that attitudes are changing and
that there is less than complete satisfaction with the results of an
increased degree of centralised direction and control, that the
strengths of private enterprise are more widely appreciated. However,
it is equally evident that the creation of an environment in which
personal initiative and enterprise are encouraged will depend to a
considerable degree on the extent to which the weaknesses of the
private enterprise system are eliminated.

In conclusion, given the considerable, and growing, degree of
support for S.M.E. which already exists in the Community it is reasonable to expect that these weakenesses can be overcome.

It can be predicted with confidence, therefore, that S.M.E. have a future in the Community. However, even with the assistance given by Member States and the Community, the future is not guaranteed for S.M.E. in general nor will it be easy for individual S.M.E. if they do not make a continual effort to adapt themselves.

The future of S.M.E. will depend, therefore, on the spirit of enterprise and the dynamism which they manifest. These are qualities which have not been lacking in the past. Everything must be done to ensure that they will not be lacking in the future.

Postcript   (October 1977)

The individual institutions of the European Community have shown a particular interest in the problems of small and medium-sized enterprises and the artisanat. For example, both the Economic and Social Committee and the European Parliament have recently carried out special studies in this area. The responsible services of the Commission itself are currently drafting a major document, the object of which is to identify as clearly as possible the specific actions which should be taken at Community level to help such enterprises overcome the problems with which they are faced and to benefit from the opportunities which exist both inside and outside the European Community.

STRUCTURES PROVIDING ASSISTANCE

A wide range of financial, technological, managerial and deve-lopmental structures are available to assist small enterprises. They are commonly classified as:

1. Financial structures

2. Technological structures

3. Structures providing managerial assistance

4. Developmental structures

1. FINANCIAL STRUCTURES

Financial structures may assume widely different institutional forms of ownership, management and operational procedures. Their general characteristics include:

Institutional forms

- government development/industrial banks;
- government development finance companies;
- commercial or trading banks;
- credit unions;
- savings and loan institutions;
- investment and promotion institutions;
- workers' banks;
- co-operatives;
- pawnbrokers/moneylenders/curb markets.

Objectives

These structures exist essentially to provide: fixed capital (long-term finance); working capital; equity money; hire purchase; leasing; discounting and factoring.

Types of assistance

Financial assistance for developing small enterprises include:

(i) direct grants and loans from government funds for capital investment;

(ii) participation loans with government guarantees to cover lending by financial institutions;

(iii) subsidised loans for expanding or developing small enterprises borrowed from specific institutions;

(iv) disaster loans for rehabilitation, to cover cost of repairs or replacements, or to provide relief when business is interrupted because of major construction activities such as building bridges and highways;

(v) providing special loans for working capital;

(vi) hire purchase schemes, or leasing, to provide fixed capital for service and manufacturing enterprises;

(vii) rediscounting facilities, where central banks rediscount commercial bank loans and eventually build up a "roll-over" fund;

(viii) specialised, or sectoral, banks to assist the whole range of small enterprises by opening special "windows" in development banks. These usually require concessionary sources of finance to accommodate the high costs of servicing small loans;

(ix) credit guarantees where specialised development agencies or funds provide guarantees to suppliers against invoices and delivery notes, after approval by a certified official;

(x) industrial banks to finance industrial estates able to offer rental, or "for purchase" factories together with common service facilities; bulk purchasing of raw materials and, in some instances, managerial and technical assistance;

(xi) curb markets, moneylenders and pawnbrokers who often finance small enterprise development at interest rates ranging from reasonable to high. Most operate on a very short time basis for loans and usually depend on refinancing arrangements, and are thus more suitable for providing working rather than fixed capital requirements;

(xii) commercial banks who advance credit against collateral securities, mortgages or debenture notes;

(xiii) schemes operate in several countries whereby suppliers guarantee purchases by borrowers, or trade membership groups guarantee individual members.

Problem areas

The major problems usually reported in operating these types of financial assistance structures are:

- relatively high administrative cost in servicing loans; preparing and evaluating projects; disbursing and collecting loans and monitoring delinquent accounts. The lack of enthusiasm for the small enterprise sector amongst most financial institutions, particularly in developing countries, means that little collective experience has been accumulated. Consequently, high formative costs usually have to be borne by subscribers. However, as experience grows and a range of examples is worked through, this relatively high expense should eventually decrease;

- the "conservative-banker-syndrome" where disproportionate importance is paid to collateral as the basis for securing loans might be modified, or at least complemented to a larger extent than at present, by making return on investment and ability of the borrower to repay the major criteria for investment;

- the high-risk nature of financial loans to small enterprises is omnipresent and should not be overlooked. Severe problems in repossessing equipment financed on hire purchase agreements can arise;

- a major problem of many small enterprises is in gaining access to funds. When access to funds is possible, many small enterprises can pay high interest rates and survive;

- leasing arrangements can lead to over-mechanisation and build-up of over-capacity; considerable caution is required in undertaking these agreements;

- loan officers often have only limited experience in small enterprise development. Because of their relative inexperience, and faced with a career dependent upon their showing "good judgement", trainee loan officers often look too readily for security as the basis for granting credit and fail to pay sufficient attention to potential return on investment as a major criterion for loan approval. Consequently, poor projects having collateral may receive approval but good projects short on security never take off;

- growth funds for expanding successful small enterprises can become difficult to acquire since further equity can mean reduced control by the original management; further difficulties can arise in trying to understand and accommodate a new management structure. This is particularly the case in such countries as France, where venture capital is moving from a passive role dealing with physical and financial assessment to a more active role of continual monitoring and involvement in the venture.

2. TECHNOLOGICAL STRUCTURES

Technical assistance to the small enterprise emanates from several formal and informal sources. These include:

Institutional forms

- management development and productivity centres;

- technical institutes and colleges;

- vocational training institutions;

- university research and development units;

- professional and tradesmen's associations;

- machinery suppliers and distributors;

- consultants;

- common service facility units.

Objectives

Technological institutions serve the sector by providing advice, facilities, testing, research and general technological information.

Types of assistance

These technical structures provide a wide range of services including:

(i)   advice on using materials, machinery and auxiliary equipment, requirements for new machines, plant layout, techniques and methods of production, production planning and control, quality control for raw materials, work in progress and finished goods, maintenance schedules, repairs, inventory controls, purchasing procedures, cost reduction, recording and control of machine performance, general housekeeping, working conditions dealing with lighting, heating and safety;

(ii)   common service facilities of which the most usual are: toolrooms for maintenance and repair and manufacture of tools and auxiliary equipment, jigs, dies, fixtures, forging, moulding, pressing; - testing and quality control of raw materials, finished and semi-finished goods;

(iii)   special workshops for heat treatment, galvanising, electro-plating, die-casting, foundries, pattern making and sand testing for ferrous and non-ferrous materials, wood-working shops, textile-testing facilities and tool sharpening;

(iv)   leasing and renting of specialised machinery for one-off jobs;

(v)   upgrading of design, quality and standards to increase export potential and productivity and adapting designs to suit new machines and methods; studies to accommodate special customer requirements;

(vi)   conducting industrial research for testing raw materials and new products; quality control tests;

(vii) providing information collection and dissemination services to cater specifically for small enterprises;

(viii) provision of general maintenance and repair facilities.

Problem areas

Major problems in providing technical assistance are shortages of adequately trained personnel and appropriate demonstration and teaching facilities, particularly equipment and supplies. A further complication is caused by the lack of adequately trained people interested and capable of being developed to manage their own enterprises. Regrettably, many potential clients feel that their vocations lie in larger enterprises, including government service. A case can be made for introducing into educational systems encouragement of self-employment attitudes and practices among the newly emerging labour force.

Those responsible for instigating technological transfer by means of entrepreneurship development complain that they are often overwhelmed by technological details and short of practical guidelines.

Concerning technological development and adaptation there is a lot to be said for examining facilities and developments in nearby countries and those having a similar technological background. In this way the choice of technological approaches is more likely to be appropriate. For instance, compare the choice of a tractor unit produced in India with the custom-made air-conditioned, 8-track stereophonic hi-fi, power-steering-on-four-wheels models produced for a specific North American market.

3.   STRUCTURES PROVIDING MANAGERIAL ASSISTANCE

A wide range of institutions and related structures exist to provide assistance in developing managerial functions and entrepreneurial skills.

Institutional forms

Structures capable of delivering managerial assistance to the sector are recognised as:

- management development and productivity centres;

- university departments and business schools;

- institutes and colleges of technology;

- professional consulting[1] and training organisations;

---

[1] Readers may wish to refer to the following:

ILO: Management consulting: a guide to the profession (Geneva, 1976), Ch. 22, and

ILO: Management and productivity: an international directory of institutions and information sources (Geneva, 1976), p. 233.

- government advisory units;

- chambers of commerce and industry;

- employers' federations;

- professional and trade associations.

Objectives

These institutions provide counsel and assistance in planning, organising, directing, controlling and taking corrective action in the major functional areas of management.

Types of assistance

The types of assistance which can be offered include:

(i)   management development and functional training for workers;

(ii)   general management assistance including diagnosis of operational and financial positions; organisational structure; delegation of authority; and management succession;

(iii) personnel management advice on recruitment, selection and appointment of personnel: industrial relations, labour legislation; wage and salary administration; social welfare and legal responsibilities;

(iv)   financial management and control including information on sources of finance, assistance in preparing credit applications, book-keeping, cost accounting, budgeting, cash flows, information on taxes, tariffs, and similar areas;

(v)   marketing assistance to cover local and export market studies and research; development of distribution and sales channels; preparation of conditions of sale; establishing dealer contacts; information on legislation and procedures; packaging; advertising; sales promotion; pricing and sales procedures; facilitating government ordering and tendering procedures; co-operative marketing schemes; forming trade organisation and protection schemes; and selection and training of salesmen;

(vi)   production management to cover the planning, organisation and control of the production function; plant layout and plant maintenance; productivity studies; purchasing; control of inventory, work in progress and finished goods; quality control and product development.

Problem areas

The problems of these institutions are similar to those of the technical assistance structures. In many countries it is difficult to recruit and retain staff who have appropriate experience and the necessary qualifications. This is particularly the case for management accounting and production management.

The curricúla of institutions dealing with small enterprises do not appear to match observed needs. Many business schools appear to prepare students for middle-management positions in larger-sized enterprises on the theory that, after a few years of working in rather departmentalised enterprises, they will be qualified to start highly centralised enterprises of their own. At the same time, many institutions attempt to take the "risk" out of management by proposing ever-changing systems rather than teaching students how to reduce risks by dealing correctly with the "people", in business namely supplier people, customer people, banking people, government people, tax people, and workers.

Not all small enterprise managers require detailed analytical skills; they usually operate on a short-time frame where changes are relatively small and immediate. A case can be made for teaching "intuitive" managerial practices, employing ready-made management tools in place of current "analytical" systems involving understanding fundamental concepts.

Managerial skills have internal (such as preparing books of account) and external (such as dealing with customers) aspects requiring very different training methods. In many instances, trainers are unable to provide the necessary inputs, one example is judging a new season's "fads" which requires considerable expertise and knowledge not commonly found amongst persons outside the trade. Consequently, appropriate training approaches such as self-development techniques are required.

The specialised nature of most small enterprises means that managerial practices relate quite closely to the nature of the enterprise. For instance, the budgeting procedures in running a laundry are quite different from those used in manufacturing furniture, or in running a taxi business. Managerial practices need to be included in vocational and technical training programmes and not left to become a post-experience phenomenon usually supplied on a generalised catch-all basis entitled "accounting for small business" as is often the case.

4.   DEVELOPMENTAL STRUCTURES

Governmental and non-governmental structures are available to help the sector by providing a range of assistance "packages".

Institutional forms

These structures take the form of:

- small enterprise development corporations;

- industrial estates;

- industrial and commercial promotion services;

- merchant banks;

- general development corporations.

Objectives

Using counsellors and consultants these institutions offer packages of services, subscribe to development costs and maintain an active interest in the ventures undertaken.

Types of assistance

The types of assistance rendered include:

(i)   conducting pre-investment studies or general economic studies to identify sectoral possibilities which are further refined by feasibility studies, market research and industry profiles or enterprise fact-sheets;

(ii)   selecting prospective owners and managers, which involves identifying screening, selecting, training and developing managers;

(iii)   preparing project proposals and submitting feasibility studies; advising on methods of incorporation, organisational procedures, selection of location, building, layout, plant and machinery, licensing, import requirements, foreign exchange requests; applications for fiscal and tariff concessions; using available facilities and benefits such as industrial estates, hire-purchase agreements, government purchase schemes, extension officers, co-operative schemes, government officials and financial institutions;

(iv)   providing specific finance to cover infrastructure costs to be repaid by rental or service charges;

(v)   book-keeping, general accounting and managerial services such as diagnosing the operational and financial position of the enterprise provided on a fee-for-service basis;

(vi)   soliciting principals and partners for joint participation and sub-contract; investigating, franchising and licensing possibilities both nationally and internationally.

Problem areas

Most recorded complaints mention difficulty finding "good projects" and "good management". It is somewhat surprising to learn that financial or physical constraints are generally considered more as facts of life to be overcome than as major problems.

.As with any reasonably sized developmental programme devising and formulating the activity should be carefully carried out. Poor planning in market research, labour prospects, types of firms, access to materials, changing legislation and similar issues has proven extremely costly in past projects; especially in constructing industrial estates[1].

---

[1] *Report on the Industrial Estate Programme in Six Countries, UNIDO and SIDA, Restricted Report UNIDO/OID 16, Vienna, March 1976.*

Regional development schemes meet problems when attempting to relocate established enterprises in new areas. Most evidence points show that entrepreneurs who create new enterprises become relatively immobile and, once settled, are difficult to relocate. A possible solution is to provide appropriate infrastructure in the region to be developed to attract the very new entrepreneurs before they become established elsewhere. Entrepreneurs might be considered proactive rather than reactive.

Would-be entrepreneurs often have difficulty preparing submissions for developmental authorities. Assistance by extension officers could help. However, extension officers with the necessary technical and economic background are difficult to recruit and, even if selected and developed, they are often hard to keep.

Long delays between project submission and final approval often mean that inflation causes costs to escalate and the original feasibility studies are no longer valid. Means of reducing the leeway need to be found.

Publications of the International Labour Office

Career planning and development

Malaise at work, and the accompanying tension, conflict and high labour turnover, has been on the increase in recent years, particularly among young people. This volume first identifies some of the causes of these problems, then goes on to propose ways in which career development systems at the individual, organisational and sectoral levels can help to reconcile satisfaction at work with the requirements of higher productivity, evolving social values and changing technology.

The papers contained in this book are based on the experience of a number of organisations in Europe and in the USA. They include, among others, an analysis of theoretical and practical issues of career development for organisations, by E. H. Schein, a substantial contribution on career development issues in socialist enterprises, by Dr. László Horváth, and J. A. Miller's demonstration exercise in individual career planning.

Management Development Series No. 12
ii+140 pages   ISBN 92-2-101447-9

Management and productivity: an international directory of institutions and information sources

An indispensable reference to institutions, libraries, consultants, enterprises and individuals involved in management development or looking for sources of information on the practice and theory of management.
Over 1,600 institutions and 800 information sources in the management development and productivity fields.
World-wide coverage, including most developing nations, North America, Eastern and Western Europe.

Part I   **Institutions**
Management development institutes, centres and university faculties, management and training associations, productivity and small enterprise development centres, public administration institutes, management consultants' associations, computer training centres, co-operative management training institutes and other international bodies interested in management development.

Part II   **Information sources**
National and international directories and catalogues of training programmes and institutions in various special fields, management bibliographies, abstracts, dictionaries, encyclopaedias, handbooks, selected periodicals, publishers, documentation services and sources of information on the production, acquisition and use of audio-visual aids.

1976. Management Development Series No. 13
Trilingual (Engl., Fr., Sp.) 243 pages (limp cover)   ISBN 92-2-001606-0

Available from booksellers, ILO offices in many countries or direct from ILO Publications, International Labour Office, CH-1211 Geneva 22, Switzerland.